"Even though people r̶ [...] they rarely consider h̶o̶ [...] skills. A good place to ̶s̶t̶a̶r̶t̶ ̶i̶s̶ ̶t̶o̶ ̶r̶e̶a̶d̶ ̶R̶a̶l̶p̶h̶ ̶K̶e̶e̶n̶e̶y̶'̶s̶ ̶n̶e̶w̶ book, which is chock-full of wisdom, stories, and highly practical advice. By the time you finish it, you will have the author whispering in your ear the next time you face a big decision."

Richard H. Thaler, Professor of Economics and Behavioral Science, University of Chicago, co-author of Nudge, *and winner of the 2017 Nobel Prize in Economic Sciences*

"Please 'give yourself a nudge' to read this book. If you are not yet sure how, you soon will be. Decision-making really is a learnable skill and Ralph Keeney is a master teacher with compelling examples, exercises, concepts, and steps to share."

Daniel Goroff, Vice President and Program Director, Alfred P. Sloan Foundation

"Read this book to build your wealth or bolster your health. Using practical advice wrapped in accessible language, distinguished decision-making expert Ralph Keeney explains how to identify and analyze critical decisions in your life, how to enrich your set of alternative choices, and how to value possible outcomes. It is precisely the primer you need to foster better choices in your professional or personal life."

Richard Zeckhauser, Frank P. Ramsey Professor of Political Economy, Harvard University

"Ralph Keeney introduces an innovative perspective: don't try to select the best option when facing a choice, but create better choices. Be your own choice architect! The book provides plenty of evidence and convincing arguments for this claim and is a must-read for anyone who wants to improve their decision-making skills."

Ortwin Renn, Scientific Director, Institute for Advanced Sustainability Studies, Potsdam, Germany

"This book details innovative, yet practical, gems to nudge you toward making better choices that will undoubtedly enhance the quality of your life. Without grasping such life-enhancing opportunities, you will be at the mercy of life 'as it happens.'"

James M. Tien, Distinguished Professor and Dean Emeritus of the College of Engineering, University of Miami, and Foreign Secretary, National Academy of Engineering

"In this exceptionally readable and interesting book, Ralph Keeney highlights ways that we all can use to improve our decision-making process by using our values and objectives to create and compare different alternatives. You will be rewarded personally by following the guidelines from this book."

Howard Kunreuther, Co-Director of the Wharton Risk Management and Decision Processes Center and James G. Dinan Professor Emeritus of Decision Sciences and Public Policy, University of Pennsylvania

"Ralph Keeney's new book is an inspiring nudge to us all; he coaches us to keep giving ourselves nudges to make better decisions. The book is packed with ideas for designing better alternatives based on what matters to you."

L. Robin Keller, Professor of Operations and Decision Technologies, University of California, Irvine

"When we can't have one of the world's leading decision analysts at our side when making the choices vital to our lives, the next best thing is to heed Ralph Keeney's advice about what really matters in defining the decision we face, specifying our objectives, and creating better alternatives to consider."

Paul Slovic, President of Decision Research and Professor of Psychology, University of Oregon

"Ralph Keeney has distilled a distinguished career's insights into a practical guide to decision-making that produces creative, rich results. This essential book encourages us to 'nudge' ourselves towards embracing decision opportunities and expanding the range of alternatives to consider."

Ken Peterson, Board Chair, BC Hydro

Give Yourself a Nudge

The best way to improve your quality of life is through the decisions you make. This book teaches several fundamental decision-making skills, provides numerous applications and examples, and ultimately nudges you toward smarter decisions. These nudges frame more desirable decisions for you to face by identifying the objectives for your decisions and generating superior alternatives to those initially considered. All of the nudges are based on psychology and behavioral economics research and are accessible to all readers. The new concept of a decision opportunity is introduced, which involves creating a decision that you desire to face. Solving a decision opportunity improves your life, whereas resolving a decision problem only restores the quality of your life to that before the decision problem occurred. We all can improve our decision-making and reap the better quality of life that results. This book shows you how.

Ralph L. Keeney is Professor Emeritus at the Fuqua School of Business of Duke University, North Carolina. Throughout his career, he has been a professor and consultant on making important decisions for policy-makers, businesses, and individuals. He received his PhD from the Massachusetts Institute of Technology, is a member of the US National Academy of Engineering, and has authored or co-authored several books, including *Smart Choices*, *Value-Focused Thinking*, and *Decisions with Multiple Objectives*.

Give Yourself a Nudge

Helping Smart People Make Smarter Personal and Business Decisions

RALPH L. KEENEY
Duke University

CAMBRIDGE
UNIVERSITY PRESS

CAMBRIDGE
UNIVERSITY PRESS

University Printing House, Cambridge CB2 8BS, United Kingdom

One Liberty Plaza, 20th Floor, New York, NY 10006, USA

477 Williamstown Road, Port Melbourne, VIC 3207, Australia

314–321, 3rd Floor, Plot 3, Splendor Forum, Jasola District Centre,
New Delhi – 110025, India

79 Anson Road, #06–04/06, Singapore 079906

Cambridge University Press is part of the University of Cambridge.

It furthers the University's mission by disseminating knowledge in the pursuit of
education, learning, and research at the highest international levels of excellence.

www.cambridge.org
Information on this title: www.cambridge.org/9781108715621
DOI: 10.1017/9781108776707

First published 2020

Printed in the United Kingdom by TJ International Ltd. Padstow Cornwall

A catalogue record for this publication is available from the British Library.

Library of Congress Cataloging-in-Publication Data
Names: Keeney, Ralph L., 1944– author.
Title: Give yourself a nudge : new ways to make better personal and business
decisions / Ralph L. Keeney.
Description: Cambridge, United Kingdom ; New York, NY : Cambridge University
Press, 2020. | Includes bibliographical references and index.
Identifiers: LCCN 2019042292 (print) | LCCN 2019042293 (ebook) | ISBN
9781108715621 (paperback) | ISBN 9781108776707 (ebook)
Subjects: LCSH: Decision making.
Classification: LCC HD30.23 .K3539 2020 (print) | LCC HD30.23 (ebook) | DDC
153.8/3–dc23
LC record available at https://lccn.loc.gov/2019042292
LC ebook record available at https://lccn.loc.gov/2019042293

ISBN 978-1-108-71562-1 Paperback

To Danny Kahneman, Amos Tversky, Richard Thaler, Howard Raiffa, and Dan Ariely, who have had key roles in influencing millions of people to recognize the importance of making better decisions and enhancing their desire and determination to do so.

CONTENTS

PREFACE

You can become a better decision-maker regardless of how good you are now at making decisions. Improving your decision-making skills is worth a bit of your time, because the only way that you can purposefully influence anything in your life is by your decisions. The rest of your life just happens. This book provides practical concepts and useful procedures that guide you to improve your decision-making. Even if you have the fantastic skills necessary to manage a company, raise a family, play a musical instrument, play a sport, cook, invest funds, write, or do anything else, neither you nor nobody else benefits from your abilities until you make some decisions. You might greatly enjoy activities such as special family gatherings, travel, participating in organizations or clubs with friends, or contributing your time and effort to a non-profit helping others, but, if you don't make any decisions about pursuing these activities, nothing happens. So you must make decisions, and the better the decisions you make, the more you will enjoy your life and work, and the more you will contribute to the lives of others.

I have spent years helping individuals and organizations make better decisions. In my professional career I have been a professor at three universities, a vice president at an engineering firm leading the decision and risk analysis group, and a private consultant for national and international companies and governments. When I am teaching at universities and offering programs to organizations, my goal is to provide practical procedures to make better decisions and help participants apply them to personal decisions and the organizational decisions they face. When I am consulting, for businesses or government agencies, I help groups use these same procedures for their major decisions.

Of course, I do not make any of these decisions, nor does any analysis ever make a decision. In all cases, working with individuals or organizations, my intent is to develop information that provides a better understanding of and insights into the decision under consideration. That new information is a nudge that guides the decision-maker to make that decision better. This book is about practical procedures that you can use to nudge yourself to make better decisions.

It is now well known that decision-makers (you and me, businesses, governmental agencies, other organizations) often do not make decisions in our own or an organizations' best interests. Psychologists, led by Daniel Kahneman and Amos Tversky, have identified a wide range of biases that are the cause of many decision-making shortcomings. Over the last decades numerous researchers and practitioners in the field of behavioral economics have demonstrated that these shortcomings are relevant to almost all decisions. Essentially, a decision-maker's choice of an alternative strongly depends on how the decision is described and how the alternatives are presented and perceived, rather than on the potential impacts of the various alternatives. We can and should make better decisions—much better.

Thaler and Sunstein, in their 2008 book *Nudge*,[1] present numerous decisions where individuals, using their natural decision processes, routinely select inferior alternatives that have major negative impacts on their lives. They also introduce the term "nudge" and demonstrate that using the concept significantly influences individuals to make better decisions. A nudge involves designing the presentation of alternatives for a decision to the decision-maker that is intended to push that decision-maker toward choosing the alternative that best achieves his or her interests. In their book, they focus on decisions where an authority (e.g., government agency, organization, or the person in charge) has the responsibility to present the alternatives from which other decision-makers must choose. This concept is based on two principles, referred to as choice architecture and libertarian paternalism. Choice architecture refers to selecting the way to present the alternatives to the decision-maker. Libertarian paternalism refers to nudging decision-makers to make better choices that improve their circumstances as they define them, while maintaining the decision-makers' right to choose.

Thaler and Sunstein's nudge concept has been widely implemented by numerous authorities throughout the world over the last decade.[2] Collectively, this has had a positive impact on millions of individuals in many countries. Nudges have led to improved nutrition, increased savings for retirement, fewer traffic accidents, less pollution, and more high school graduates entering colleges.

To date, the concept of nudging has not been applicable to decisions where there is no authority to identify the decision that should be faced or present alternatives to the decision-makers. This

includes all of the specific decisions faced by individuals, businesses, or governments. For these important decisions, the framing
of the decision and the presentation of the alternatives must be
done by the decision-makers themselves.

This book indicates how to use the concept of a nudge on your
own decisions. It describes and illustrates several different types of
personal nudges that can help you make better decisions. These
nudges are based on clearly defining the decision that you face,
thoroughly articulating what you want to achieve by making that
decision, creating better alternatives to consider, and deliberately
identifying more desirable decisions to face. Personal nudges are
applicable to all of your decisions.

Near the end of their book, Thaler and Sunstein state: "One of our
main hopes is that an understanding of choice architecture, and the
powers of nudges, will lead others to think of creative ways to
improve human lives in other domains."[3] I believe the ideas in
this book are consistent with this desire.

Whether to nudge yourself on a specific decision is a small decision itself, as creating a nudge requires some time for focused
thought. The issue is whether the use of this time is rewarded by
the improved consequences of the decision being made. Is it worth
30 minutes to select a better airline itinerary that likely will result
in a more enjoyable and less stressful two-week vacation or business trip? Is it worth a few days to understand the implications of
three distinct medical treatments for a malady that may reduce
your mobility for years? Is it worth a three-month effort to select
a high-quality downtown office for your firm of 100 employees?
These are decisions that I think are worthy of focused thought. We
all face a large number of such decisions. This book describes what
to think about when facing decisions that are worthy of thought
and how to do it clearly in order to give yourself powerful nudges to
make better decisions.

Practice is important. The first decision on which you try to
nudge yourself should not be the most complex decision you face
but, rather, one where five to 15 minutes constitute an appropriate
investment of time. You will be doing specific practical tasks for the
first time that require some skill. As you pursue these tasks, you will
have some useful thoughts about your decision, but may not be
sure whether they were valuable enough to justify your effort. But
remember: it is your first use of ideas and procedures that are new.
Practice is necessary to develop any skill. Each time that you nudge

yourself should have positive impacts on your decision and it will provide practice to improve your skill at creating your nudges. With practice you will get much better and more efficient, and the nudges for each of the decisions you face should clearly be worthwhile.

ACKNOWLEDGMENTS

Decisions have had a very significant influence on all aspects of my life. I have thought about and talked about decisions and decision-making with numerous friends, teachers, colleagues, and family members—and learned from each of them. I have consulted for numerous organizations on business and governmental decisions—and, inevitably, learned from my coworkers and my clients. All of these individuals, to whom I owe many sincere thanks, have contributed to the ideas, concepts, and procedures in this book.

When I was growing up in Lewistown, Montana, a small town of some 7,000 people, my mom, Anne Keeney, gave me tremendous freedom to make my own decisions, and experience the consequences of those decisions. So, from an early age, I realized that making decisions empowers you to do what you want, as long as you don't get into trouble or bother others, and I worked on learning how to do this well. It was clear to me that good decision-making was a key to an enjoyable and worthwhile life.

In college, I majored in engineering because it required balancing knowledge about technology and about the applications and decisions to make it work. In graduate school, I began formally studying decision-making at the Massachusetts Institute of Technology (MIT) with Al Drake, who was my master's thesis advisor. Soon afterwards I met Howard Raiffa of Harvard University, who became my dissertation advisor on the topic of decisions with multiple objectives. I had the privilege to work with Howard and continue to learn, and I enjoyed our special friendship until 2016, when he passed away. I have also greatly benefited from long-time combined personal and professional relationships with Detlof von Winterfeldt, David Bell, Robin Gregory, Tim McDaniels, Craig Kirkwood, Robert Winkler, Paul Slovic, John Hammond, Richard John, and Johannes Siebert.

Numerous individuals have had a major impact on raising our collective knowledge about how people descriptively do make decisions and how they prescriptively can make better decisions. A short, and surely incomplete, list of some who have made substantial contributions includes those already mentioned above plus Ward Edwards, Herbert Simon, Amos Tversky, Daniel Kahneman,

Ronald Howard, Larry Phillips, Richard Thaler, Cass Sunstein, Dan Ariely, and Carl Spetzler.

Some of my colleagues accepted the onerous task to read earlier drafts of this book and offer detailed comments. Several suggestions of Johannes Siebert, Richard John, Robin Gregory, Detlof von Winterfeldt, and Larry Neal certainly improved the content. Keith Pfeffer offered useful advice throughout the process of finding an appropriate publisher.

My wife, Janet Beach, herself an author and marketing consultant, read many drafts of the book and had excellent suggestions, not only to improve what was written but to include important missing topics and ideas. Soon after graduating from college our son, Greg Keeney, once jokingly commented on his difficult life growing up, saying "You can't believe how many times I had to hear 'What are your objectives?' and 'Why don't you create some better alternatives?,'" but now he routinely uses these personal nudges in his decision-making. Janet and Greg both contribute to the quality of my life in numerous ways. One way is that each of them sometimes uses ideas in this book to guide me to nudge myself on some decision that I am facing. What could be better than that?

1 NUDGE YOURSELF TO MAKE BETTER DECISIONS

Your decisions offer you the only way to purposefully influence anything in your life. Everything else just happens beyond your control. Thus, the only way that you can improve your life or anything else that you care about is to make better decisions.

The rationale for this book is based on three facts.

1. A large collection of practical studies and research has identified numerous shortcomings in both the intuitive and conscious thought processes that we each use to make decisions.
2. A complementary body of studies and research has developed a logically sound approach to making thoughtful decisions. Using this approach to make decisions requires specific knowledge and skills, takes time and effort, and may be costly. As a result, this approach is used to guide only a very few individual and business decisions.
3. Almost all decisions, including most important decisions, are made by our flawed intuitive and conscious thought decision processes.

A balanced approach is needed to get many of the benefits of a thoughtful appraisal of alternatives, one that is not complicated, time-consuming, or expensive. This book presents the concepts and procedures of such a practical approach, which reduces the frequency and severity of the numerous shortcomings that occur in our natural decision processes and guides you to make better decisions.

Our Understanding of Decision-Making

The fields that study decision-making began to flourish in the middle of the last century and have rapidly grown since then. Research and practical studies focus on two distinct things: *describing* how people *do* make decisions; and *prescribing* how they *should* make better decisions.

The descriptive research, led by psychologists, discovered numerous shortcomings in people's decision-making habits. The prescriptive research, led by academics in management and policy areas, developed techniques and procedures to evaluate and select alternatives consistent with the interests and available information of the decision-maker. These two paths of study are intertwined and complementary. How decisions should be made sets a basis for identifying shortcomings and understanding their implications, and shortcomings indicate aspects of decision-making where prescriptive techniques and procedures would be most useful.

In 1954 Ward Edwards wrote a seminal article that stimulated research into how decisions are actually made.[1] The next year Herbert Simon's work on bounded rationality convincingly explained that individuals usually do not try to optimize the choice of an alternative in their decisions.[2] Rather, they try to select alternatives that are good enough, given the time and difficulty identifying, acquiring, and processing additional useful information.

Beginning in the 1970s Daniel Kahneman and Amos Tversky published several articles focusing on important intuitive procedures that many individuals tend to use to simplify their decision-making.[3] Their research influenced many other psychologists and economists and led them to question the reliance of much of the previous economic research based on the supposed rationality of the historically called "economic man theory." Consequently, the amount of research and number of experiments on decision-making and interest in the results have grown substantially.[4] The specific name for this type of research has evolved from decision research and behavioral science to behavioral economics.

By now we have learned a great deal about the weaknesses that individuals demonstrate when making decisions. Whether decisions are made using either intuition or a conscious thought process, numerous common shortcomings of our decision-making habits have been identified and categorized into specific biases, which are called decision traps, and these often lead us to make inferior decisions.

Over the past two decades Dan Ariely has been a leader in studying and communicating the fact that these biases have notice-able effects on almost everything we do.[5] He has demonstrated that understanding the reasons for our repeated irrational behavior on small decisions provides insights into dealing with important deci-sions that we personally and collectively face. He also indicates how these insights can guide our behavior to reduce such irrational influences on important aspects of our lives.

The prescriptive work on decision-making led by Howard Raiffa in the early 1960s developed a set of steps to address the various aspects of a decision in a logical and systematic manner.[6] Gathering the information needed for each step provided the founda-tion for evaluating the relative desirability of the alternatives. These steps were to state the decision being faced, specify the objectives to be achieved, identify the alternatives, describe the consequences of each alternative (i.e., the possible levels of their achievement, includ-ing the chances of those levels), weigh the pros and cons of each alternative, and calculate the overall desirability of each.[7]

You naturally want to make the best decision you can, as long as the decision process is not too complicated, too time-consuming, or too costly. Unfortunately, for essentially all of your personal decisions, following the prescriptive advice to guide your decision is too time-consuming and too complicated, and most indi-viduals do not have the background to carry out a thorough evalua-tion of alternatives. Thus, almost all personal decisions are made intuitively or using a self-developed thought process, rather than a systematic prescriptive evaluation. For some important business and government decisions, one can hire trained decision consultants, but that is usually expensive and time-consuming. The implication is that the vast majority of business decisions are also made without the benefit of a systematic prescriptive evaluation of the alternatives.

The Importance and Uses of Nudges

With a better understanding of how individuals make decisions and recognition of the many routine shortcomings of decision-making processes, the field of behavioral economics came into existence, led by Richard Thaler. His work with Cass Sunstein developed and popularized the concept of nudging individuals to make better decisions, which today is used by numerous organizations throughout the world.[8] An example application is useful.

Some years ago I accepted a faculty position at a large university. Each new employee was given the decision of whether or not to enroll in the university's retirement plan. The plan required that 5 percent of my annual salary would automatically go into my personal retirement account, and the university would add twice that amount each year. To establish my retirement plan, I had to fill out a few forms; otherwise, the default alternative of not being in the plan required doing nothing. It seemed obvious to me that I should join the plan, which I did. Sometime later I was astounded to learn that only 55 percent of new employees had signed up for the retirement plan. The university administrators were dismayed and concerned about the 45 percent of employees who did not choose the retirement plan, which seemed to them to be a much better alternative for the majority of employees.

Psychological research and studies indicate that the way in which alternatives are described and/or presented to decision-makers strongly affects their choice of an alternative.[9] Given this knowledge, the university decided to nudge new employees toward entering the retirement program, and also to let those who thoughtfully chose not to be in the program to also have their preferred choice. The university changed its procedures, so that the default alternative was that a new employee would automatically be included in the retirement program, unless he or she filled out the new forms necessary to not be in the program. The result was that approximately 90 percent of new employees joined the retirement plan, from which they greatly benefited.

A nudge is a presentation of the available alternatives to a decision-maker designed to improve the chances that the decision-maker selects the alternative that best achieves his or her interests. The use of nudges to date has focused on policy decisions, where some organization (e.g., governmental or a private company) has the responsibility to provide alternatives to individuals who are each facing a similar decision. That organization has the decision of how to present the alternatives, and can nudge decision-makers by the way it presents these alternatives. Since the available alternatives remain the same, with no modification of their substance or consequences, nudges do not limit the decision-makers' autonomy. The decision about joining the retirement plan is one of thousands of applications that have helped millions of people make better specific decisions.[10]

For your personal and business decisions, no organization has the responsibility to present the alternatives to you or the opportunity to nudge you to make better decisions. For all of these decisions, which include your most important decisions, you have the responsibility and opportunity to present these decisions to yourself as well as to create the decisions that you want to face.

Nudging Yourself to Make Better Decisions

A personal nudge is a modification of the choice architecture for your decision that may influence the alternative that you eventually choose. This modification essentially improves and clarifies an aspect of your decision that nudges you to make a better choice. Being better informed about the substance of your decision facilitates the selection of an alternative that is more consistent with your interests.

To illustrate this concept of a nudge, imagine that a potential client for your services visits your city, and requested to have dinner with you to discuss a new project. Selecting the restaurant was important; you decided that it should have excellent food and a trendy clientele, and be convenient to your guest's hotel. The restaurant met these interests well, but it was noisy and difficult to talk. As a result, the evening was a failure, and you ended up not being involved in the new project. If you had more carefully considered what you wanted to achieve by selecting the restaurant, you might also have identified the desirability of having a quiet location to facilitate having a conversation. Knowing this additional consideration would likely have nudged you not to select the restaurant that you chose and select a much better one considering all of your interests.

This book expands the applicability of the nudge concept from those decisions where an authority has the opportunity to nudge you to all other decisions that you face. It presents ideas and procedures for you to nudge yourself to make better choices. Many of these nudges are based on clearly and thoroughly doing one or more of the following three tasks: defining the decision that you face; specifying what you want to achieve by making that decision; and creating better alternatives to consider. If you thoughtfully pursue these three tasks for any decision that you face, you will usually have a more comprehensive basis for choosing alternatives, better alternatives among which to choose, and a better understanding of how to appraise the pros and cons of each alternative. These will provide you with powerful nudges to choose better alternatives for your decisions. If you routinely develop such nudges for your decisions, the collective consequences of these better decisions will significantly contribute to the quality of your life. Moreover, since you are totally in control of nudging yourself, such nudges do not affect your autonomy as a decision-maker.

Personal nudges reduce the negative implications of the biases that occur in the natural decision processes that we use to make our decisions. In addition, they eliminate two serious flaws in our intuitive individual decision processes.

The first flaw is that our natural way of making decisions is backwards. Once we recognize a decision that we face, we naturally want to solve it, so our initial effort is often to identify alternatives that may solve it. Usually this occurs before we understand all that we want to achieve by making that decision. Alternatives are relevant only because they are the means to provide what we want to achieve by making the decision. How can you create high-quality alternatives for a decision before you thoroughly understand what you want to achieve by making it?

The second flaw is that most of the decisions that we end up facing are decision problems that occur beyond our control. They occur due to the decisions of others or happenstance. Examples include when we have a serious medical problem or consequences from an accident, or our manager informs us of changes at work that will negatively affect us, or our company products are not selling as well as they did last year. Obviously, we do not purposefully cause these situations, and yet we must react by making decisions to deal with them. Our intent with such decisions is usually to restore our circumstances to what they were before the problem occurred.

Why just wait for problems to occur? Rather than wait for decision problems to occur, you could make your life better tomorrow by proactively creating and pursuing what I refer to as *decision opportunities*. Creating a decision opportunity is a significant nudge toward making better decisions, as decision opportunities that you face directly improve your circumstances and/or avoid or lessen the occurrence of unwanted future decision problems.

Even though you have the power and authority to nudge yourself, you need to develop specific skills to do this effectively. This book presents practical ideas and procedures for addressing the fundamental aspects of decisions in a thoughtful manner that will nudge you to make better choices. Specifically, it focuses on:

- defining the decision that you want to face;
- clarifying why you care about a decision by identifying your values, which are the basis for describing what you want to achieve by addressing it;
- creating innovative alternatives better than those that initially come to mind;
- identifying your own decisions—meaning decision opportunities—to raise your quality of life above where it currently is;
- obtaining the authorization of others, when they control whether alternatives that you desire can be implemented; and
- providing a consistent guide for all of your decisions by describing how to identify, organize, and use your strategic life values.

Learning the practical ideas and mastering the procedures to address any of these fundamental aspects of decisions constitute a nudge for improving your decision-making skills, which allows you to routinely create better nudges for specific decisions. Therefore, these ideas and procedures can be considered nudges to nudge yourself in your decision-making. Practice applying the procedures to nudge yourself on specific decisions is both a nudge for that decision and a nudge to further improve your decision-making skills.

None of the concepts or procedures useful for personal nudges are quantitative, nor do they neglect your feelings and emotions. They are grounded on your beliefs, what you care about and how you feel regarding the decision, and common sense. Hence, the ideas and procedures for how to use them in your decision-making will be natural for you to use and have a significant positive impact.

This book focuses on the front end of decision-making: defining the decision you should address, specifying what you want to achieve by addressing it, and creating good alternatives for consideration. Most other books on decision-making and most decision-making methods focus on the back end, which involves gathering information to describe the potential consequences of the alternatives and their risks, balancing the pros and cons of each alternative, and selecting the best. The quality of any decision depends much more on the quality of the front-end clarification and presentation of that decision than on the back-end evaluation of alternatives. You cannot make a good decision by choosing the best alternative from a narrow range of alternatives using an inferior set of objectives to evaluate those alternatives. This important point is succinctly made in a quote that is attributed to Albert Einstein: "If I were given one hour to save the planet, I would spend 55 minutes defining the problem and five minutes resolving it."[11]

Decision-Making Is a Skill

Numerous behavioral experiments about decision-making, and my consulting experience, clearly indicate that it is very difficult to develop a quality front end for an important decision. Most decision-makers have not developed the decision-making skills required to routinely do this task well. As a result, they often end up addressing an inappropriately stated decision that omits key factors of the decision they really face.

To become proficient with any skill, you need to first learn how to perform the necessary activities of that skill, and then you must practice using them. Few people have had training in decision-making, and fewer have thought about the notion of practicing to improve their decision-making skills. This book not only describes what you need to do to thoroughly understand the decision you face, but it provides detailed procedures for how to effectively implement them and illustrates them with numerous real examples.

For developing your decision-making skills, you will not get enough practice (i.e., experience) if you use them only on your very important decisions. There simply are not enough of these decisions. In addition, important decisions routinely include many intertwining complexities, so it is very difficult to learn the basic skills. Fortunately, we each face numerous less significant decisions that are worthy of thought. The concepts and procedures that you need to improve your decision-making skills can be developed by applying them to these decisions. In Chapter 9, many examples of common decisions worthy of thought that each of us regularly face are described. These can be used for this training process.

Numerous real applications in this book indicate how you can conveniently introduce your new decision-making skills into your life. Initially, applying these skills may require a bit more of your time, but you will soon be making better decisions more quickly and with more confidence. The ultimate benefit will be a noticeable improvement in your decision-making, and subsequently in your personal and professional life.

Everything in this book is relevant to decisions in organizations, including businesses, institutions, governments, non-profits, and groups of any nature. It is the decision contexts and expertise that are different for individual and organizational decisions, not the ideas and procedures to address them. As all thinking occurs in the minds of individuals and we each have similar experiences with the decisions in our lives, the most effective way to introduce the ideas and procedures necessary for high-quality decision-making is in the context of individual decisions. The last section of each chapter clarifies how the ideas and procedures are relevant and applicable to organizational decisions.

2 YOUR DECISIONS AND YOUR LIFE

Your decisions are critical in pursuing the life that you desire. To understand this, consider the metaphor of your life where you are walking down your life path, on which there are forks at various locations. Each fork represents a decision that you must make, and the different paths originating from the fork correspond to the alternatives for that decision. The life that you experience depends on your decisions about which path to take at each fork.

Now imagine that your life has no decisions, so there are no forks. Starting now, you enthusiastically begin walking down the path that begins the rest of your life. Initially, you do not arrive at any forks. Maintaining high hopes, you walk further—and still no forks. All you can do is keep walking at the pace of time. Now disillusioned, you walk on, but there are no forks on your path. At some time in the future, your path ends.

I imagine that this description of your life with no decisions is very unappealing. Fortunately, we each make many decisions every day. The rest of your life will include a very large number of decisions that offer you the opportunity to make it enjoyable and rewarding. Some of your future decisions will be life-changing; numerous others will be well worth your thought. Collectively, they will create the rest of the life that you choose to pursue. There are numerous possibilities for the life that you create with your decisions. Recognize that some of the life-changing decisions that you face, or have faced, concern your education, your choice of friends, your lifestyle choices, what jobs you hold and where they are located, whether you marry and to whom, whether you have children and how many, how you try to avoid and address serious health and medical issues, and retirement. If there are just ten life-changing decisions with only five alternatives for each of these, there would be close to 10 million distinct possible lives represented. You can imagine that the quality of your "better lives" and your "worse lives" would be very different.

Your decisions empower you to enhance the quality of your life and the lives of your family and friends and to make contributions at work in businesses, organizations, and government. The other influences on your quality of life occur beyond your control, from the decisions and actions of other individuals and organizations, happenstance (e.g., weather, accidents), and the consequences of the actions you take without thinking.

> **The only way for you to purposefully influence anything in your life is by your decisions. So, your decision-making is your only tool to enhance the quality of your life.**

How We Learned to Make Decisions

Some of us are better decision-makers than others. Regardless of these differences, we all are vulnerable to the numerous cognitive biases that misguide our decisions.[1] Each of us can identify decisions that we wish we had made differently and/or better. Nevertheless, and most importantly, we all can improve our decision-making.

We all learned to make decisions the same way: by trial and error. Very few of us have had any training to learn how to make decisions well. Rather, we developed habits over time for dealing with various decision situations. Aside from the "I wish I had…" or "I wish I had not…" reflections about previous decisions, there is little appraisal of the decision-making process used for past choices. Hence, little is learned that may be helpful for making better future decisions.

It is interesting to consider some general experiences in our early lives that likely contributed to our own decision-making style. As a baby, you probably did not have any sophisticated innate decision-making abilities. Your main decision problems concerned basic needs that occurred when you were hungry or wet. Without language skills, you hollered. And what happened? Usually a loving mother or father quickly solved your problem. After this tactic worked thousands of times, you understood it well and probably recognized it as life decision lesson #1: "Hollering solves decision problems." There is perhaps a corollary that hollering louder solves problems more quickly.

A few years later you were a toddler and developing some opinions about what you wanted: a cookie, not going to bed now, or to watch television. You made decisions to get what you wanted, but the process often turned out to be negative. In some cases, a parent took over your decision and provided what you wanted, or not. In other cases, you may have been scolded or punished for doing something your parents did not want you to do. From this, you learned life decision lesson #2: "I have little effect on what occurs, as someone else frequently takes over my decision"; and life decision lesson #3: "When I try to make decisions, I often get into trouble."

As a result, when you became a teenager you certainly wanted to make your own decisions and not inform your parents or teachers about them. Now you made some choices in school, after school, and with friends. You tried not to involve your parents in these decisions unless necessary, because they would reverse some and influence others, which would limit doing what you wanted to do. Oversimplifying (which I am of course doing here), the consequences of the collective decisions of most teenagers during high school might be categorized into two groups. For many teenagers, the consequences are generally perceived as good (translation: the teenager does well in school, has nice friends, and does not get into too much trouble). These teenagers do not appear to their parents or teachers as individuals requiring additional guidance on decision-making; they are "good kids."

For other teenagers, the consequences of some of their decisions are bad. Parents will find out about these decisions. Parents will soon be informed of your poor performance in school, they will learn if you have even a minor accident when driving a car, and there is a good chance they will become aware of any participation in disruptive or illegal activities. From experiences such as these, you may have learned that the consequences of some choices can be bad. But, unfortunately, you may have thought they are bad only because others found out about them, not because you made some poor decisions that had bad consequences.

Oddly enough, teenagers categorized into both "consequence groups" may perceive the same life decision lesson #4: "I am a pretty good decision-maker." For those who mainly had good consequences, they incorrectly assume that having few bad consequences indicates that they are a good decision-maker. For those with several bad consequences, they can reason that many decisions that they made had reasonably good consequences. For the fewer other decisions with the bad consequences, there are always excuses, such as "It was someone else's fault," "I had no other choice than to do what I did," and "It was just bad luck that led to the bad consequences."

By the time we finish high school, most of us have developed ingrained habits for making decisions that do not provide a foundation for good decision-making. Very few people begin to think about and reflect on making decisions before college age, and too few even after that. It is important to understand that decision-making is a skill that can be improved with knowledge and practice. There are principles, ideas, and techniques that anyone can learn to guide them to make their decisions better. Unaware of this, most individuals tend to be stuck with the same decision-making habits that they developed early in life. Moreover, the misperception about one's decision-making ability persists past the teenage years, as many adults overrate their decision-making skills.[2]

> **We each developed our decision-making style by trial and error, rather than learning fundamental skills of decision-making. Thus, we can all learn to make much better decisions.**

Using our ingrained decision-making habits, whenever something occurs that presents a decision problem, we react. Our initial thinking is to think about alternatives that would solve the problem, and we typically choose the first acceptable alternative that we identify. This general procedure works reasonably well, because most of the decisions we face are not too important nor particularly complex, and any acceptable alternatives for most decisions are roughly equivalent.

Nudges and Value-Focused Decisions

For the decisions worthy of thought that you face today as an adult, your crucial first step should be to identify your values, meaning what you want to achieve by facing that decision. These values should guide all of your effort to solve it. If you know and understand your values for a decision, it significantly nudges you to make a better choice. How can you possibly create good alternatives if you don't know what you want those alternatives to achieve? How can you reasonably evaluate the relative effectiveness of alternatives without that knowledge? Guided by your values, your resulting decisions will be what I refer to as *value-focused decisions*.

> **Your crucial first step for any decision that you face is to identify what you want to achieve by facing that decision. Pursuing what it is that you want should guide all of your subsequent effort to make a good decision.**

For making a decision, the idiom "Keep your eye on the ball" means "Keep your focus on the values of that decision." To focus on values requires that you spend time at the beginning of your decision-making process to identify and understand them. For important decisions, there are invariably competing values that are relevant. Identifying your values for most decisions is not easy. Several concepts and procedures to facilitate this task will be described that improve your ability to articulate your values for the decisions that you face. Guided by your values, you will be able to

1. convert some unappealing decisions into appealing decisions;
2. create better alternatives than those readily apparent for your decisions;
3. stimulate thoughts to create more desirable decisions to face; and
4. compare alternatives more consistently and better.

Each of these will nudge you to make better decisions. They will enhance the quality of your decision-making and contribute to your life.

To illustrate the importance of being value-focused in your decision-making, consider the following case.

▶ Finding a Job

After graduating from college, Kate worked eight years in her job as a human resources (HR) manager for an international company in its headquarters near Seattle. Then, in a move to reduce expenses, the company announced that its human resources division would be moving to Albuquerque, New Mexico, in three months' time. Because of family connections to the greater Seattle area, she chose not to move with the company. She now had to look for a new job, something that she had never really done previously in her life.

After a relaxing vacation, Kate returned and began looking for a new HR-related job by checking various job boards for positions for which she felt qualified. There were 12 positions that she liked that were listed. She applied online for all of these, and was invited for an interview by only one company, which did not result in a job offer.

A colleague familiar with the ideas in this book had known Kate for years and offered to help. She first asked Kate about her values, describing what she wanted in a job. She initially stated her values as "a nice place to work," "with a decent salary." My colleague helped Kate articulate several other values that were clearly important to her, including: "work that is interesting," "contributing to others' careers," "improving her communication skills," "friendly and competent colleagues," "a financially sound company that is growing," "a company with a long-term interest in Seattle," "not a government organization," and "a reasonable commute time."

These values started Kate on a search, using numerous sources, for all of the companies in the greater Seattle area that would hire someone like her into HR and potentially meet the values she had identified. After compiling a list of target companies, Kate's new decision opportunity was "to pursue working with some of these companies." She used her network of friends and family connections to identify anyone they knew who worked for any of these companies. She asked her connections to help arrange informational interviews with these individuals. These interviews were either a discussion over coffee or a telephone call to find out an insider's view concerning the hiring process of the company and how Kate might get introductions to people who could facilitate an interview and/or send an internal referral recommending Kate for an open position. This entire process required Kate's time and persistent effort. It resulted in three job offers, two of which Kate recognized were clearly better than her previous job.

After weighing the pros and cons of these two offers in terms of her values, she selected one. ◄

A few observations about Kate's process are worth noting. When Kate began her job search, she was alternative-focused, the opposite of value-focused, in that her decision process focused on finding an alternative (i.e., a job) for which she was qualified and accepting it. She was also reactive, as she responded online only to posted openings for which she felt qualified. Fortunately, Kate received no offers, since the job she eventually chose was much better for her life and career.

When my colleague began to help Kate, she helped her become value-focused by identifying her values, which provided Kate with a lot of insight about what she really wanted from a job and guided her subsequent decision process. The decision Kate ended up facing changed from finding an acceptable job for which she was qualified to finding the best job in terms of her values. In creating this different decision, Kate also recognized and addressed two other important related decisions, concerning how to obtain the information on all of the companies of interest in the Seattle region and on how to identify and communicate with contacts for each of these companies.

Skills of a Value-Focused Decision-Maker

The key concepts of value-focused decision-making provide the foundation for creating important nudges to help you make better decisions. Learning to use these concepts will help you develop new decision-making skills so that you can

- identify and understand your values for making any decision;
- create better alternatives;
- identify decision opportunities to improve something you care about; and
- influence others' decisions that can have an influence on your life.

These key concepts are described below. Procedures to implement them and several applications to various decisions follow.

Identify and Understand Your Values. Why bother to make decisions? Why put in all the time and effort, and perhaps suffer anxiety, regret, and disappointment in the process? The answer is that your decision provides a way to make something that you care about better. It is impossible to make a sound decision to achieve your purpose if you do not thoroughly understand the values characterizing what you want to achieve.

Identifying your values, which define what you want to achieve by making that decision, requires thought and skill. Once you have identified and understood your values, you have the basis for allocating your time and effort to the decision, including that dedicated to creating desirable alternatives and then evaluating and selecting the best of them.

Create Alternatives. You can never choose an alternative that you have not thought of. And your chosen alternative can be no better than the best alternative among those that you are considering. In addition, it is rarely the case that important decisions are simply solved or not. Rather, the degree to which alternatives achieve your purpose can vary significantly. Thus, only in rare circumstances should you choose the first alternative that comes to mind before you have identified at least a few good alternatives. Some dedicated thinking will frequently generate alternatives that you consider to be much better than the first one you identified.

Identify Decision Opportunities. Ask yourself: who should be making your decisions? That is easy; you should, of course. So now ask yourself: who should be in control of selecting the decisions that you end up facing? This question usually causes a bit of introspection. Quite likely, you should exercise more control over selecting your decisions than you currently do. By creating some of your own decisions, rather than simply accepting decisions that are problems, you can face decisions that you want to face where the alternatives can make a positive improvement to your life.

Identifying a decision opportunity begins by recognizing something, tangible or intangible, that you would like to occur and then defining your decision as how to make it happen. Decision opportunities created and successfully pursued can also reduce the chances of particular undesirable decision problems occurring in the future that would otherwise have occurred. For example, if you create a decision opportunity to learn an additional skill so you can contribute more at work and you use that skill, not only might you increase your interest in the work you are doing and perhaps increase your pay, you may also have averted a subsequent decision problem resulting from losing your job during a future economic downturn.

Influence Decisions of Others that Influence Your Life. For many important decisions in your life, you can think of great alternatives that you would like to have implemented. However, someone else has control over whether that alternative will be implemented. Examples include a promotion within your organization, when you want the seller of a home to accept the offer that you are now developing, a six-week leave of absence to deal with a personal matter, or going on a lengthy international trip with a particular friend.

How can you influence the other party to authorize the decision that you want? The general idea is to embellish the alternative that provides what you want by including features that also render it more desirable for the other party than the current situation. Then propose that better alternative, and he or she should willingly choose it. You will have achieved what you want, and the other party is also better off. The foundation for creating such an alternative is to understand the values of the other party.

Learning and using the value-focused decision-making concepts and procedures will nudge you to improve your decisions. This claim is based on extensive experience using these ideas in helping many friends and colleagues think clearly through their decisions and in consulting with numerous businesses and governmental organizations to structure significant decisions and choose logically sound and justifiable alternatives.

I practice what I preach, and have routinely used the ideas in this book on my own decisions. Using value-focused concepts guides me to make better decisions. The following personal decision illustrates its usefulness. Although this decision occurred years ago, the topic is more relevant today, as many more people are consciously interested in balancing aspects of their personal and professional lives.

► A Working Leave of Absence

I accepted a job working for a geotechnical-environmental consulting firm in San Francisco. Half a year later I met Janet, an interesting young woman with a wonderful mind and a beautiful smile, who lived in New York City. After several months in an enjoyable long-distance relationship, Janet and I agreed that it would be nice to spend a longer period of time together. The idea was for me to move to New York City for three or four months, but continue working for my firm. For this, I would need the authorization of Kesh Nair, my manager at the consulting firm.

During my first day at work I had said to Kesh: "I assume that my overall responsibilities are to contribute financially and professionally to the firm, and, subject to that, there are essentially no other requirements. Is that correct?" Kesh reflected and said, "That is correct." So, to obtain Kesh's authorization for my proposed absence, I wanted to create an alternative that would increase my contribution to the firm while working in New York.

I created an alternative that would increase my contribution to both the financial and professional objectives of my company. Financially, I would bill clients for 40 hours per week, whereas my average weekly billing was about 32 hours in San Francisco. I would be able to do this by accepting a request from a client for some additional work. Professionally, I would write a draft of a book about an important part of our firm's consulting services concerning the application and usefulness of decision analysis for evaluating sites for power plants and other major energy facilities. Also, if the need arose for me to be in San Francisco for any specific reason, I would arrange to be there.

I suggested this "better" alternative to Kesh, and my proposal was accepted. Janet and I enjoyed New York together and I met the work commitments that I had made for those four months. Later, I had another proposal accepted; Janet and I have now been married for 35 years. ◄

This decision was definitely a decision opportunity, created by the decision-maker (i.e., me) because of its potential to enhance not just my life but Janet's as well. This case also illustrates how to create an alternative that has the features that you want and, at the same time, is better for another individual who has the power to authorize the decision. You will be able to identify numerous desirable decision opportunities with this characteristic in your life. Of course, you first need to know what you want: your values. In this case, I definitely wanted to live in New York for a few months. This would require being absent from the offices of my firm in San Francisco, which would have some negative effects on the firm, both because I would not be as readily available and because it would set a precedent for potential similar requests by others. My boss had the authority to authorize my remote work and also the responsibility to manage the firm's interests.

To obtain authorization for my desired alternative, I needed to create an alternative that contributed more to achieving the values of the individual with the power to authorize it. In this decision, those values were clearly specified in my initial discussion when I accepted my job position. The added modifications to bill more time to clients and write a book on a service that our company provided represented a major increase relative to my current acceptable contribution. I felt that it was an offer Kesh could not refuse, and, when proposed, it took him no time to accept it. My suggesting this acceptable alternative to Kesh was, essentially, a nudge to make the alternative that I desired a viable alternative for him to choose.

With such arrangements, it is critical that you fulfill your commitments. This is essential to build and maintain trust, which itself provides more opportunities in the future. I did bill 40 hours per week with satisfied clients and completed the original draft of a book on siting energy facilities.[3]

Improving Your Decision-Making Skills

Making decisions is a critical life skill. Regardless of how good you currently are at making decisions, you can improve your decision-making with knowledge and practice.

*The **value proposition** of this book is that you can expand your decision-making skills so that you will naturally nudge yourself to improve the quality of your decisions and become a more effective decision-maker.*

There are concepts and procedures that you can learn and use to nudge yourself to make better decisions. Unaware of this, most of us tend to be stuck with experience-based incremental improvements to our current decision-making habits that we developed earlier in life. The concepts and procedures I am referring to are based on the foundation for making value-focused decisions. The learning and the application of these concepts will be interesting, useful, and enjoyable. You will be able to apply the individual concepts to your decisions as you learn them. In addition,

> **Making decisions is a critical life skill. Learning and using fundamental concepts and procedures that underpin thoughtful decision-making will nudge you to make better decisions.**

you will notice the progress that you are making with each concept and procedure learned and recognize the improvement in your decision-making.

The best way to learn the concepts and practice the necessary procedures to improve your decision-making skills is to use them on your own personal and professional decisions. Although this is obvious for improving an individual's decision-making, it may seem counterintuitive for improving decision-making in businesses, governments, and other organizations. However, the reasoning that supports this claim is compelling.

The key elements of all decisions, namely values that indicate what you want to achieve and alternatives that provide ways to achieve them, are the same for personal, business, organizational, and governmental decisions. The general purpose of each decision is also the same, namely to select the best alternative in terms of the stated values. Thus, the concepts and procedures that you should master to improve your decision-making skills are the same. It is only the decision contexts and subject matter substance that are different for individual and organizational decisions.

> **The ideas in this book are applicable to all business and organizational decisions. Original thinking occurs in the minds of individuals, which can then be shared with colleagues in making any decision.**

To enhance your understanding of the concepts and develop skill with the procedures necessary to use them requires practice in applying them to real decisions. You must understand the decision context and the factual and emotional substance relevant to each of these decisions. This is essential in order to learn how to develop values relevant to a decision, create good alternatives, and identify decision opportunities worth pursuing. You cannot learn any practical decision-making skills without understanding the substance of the decisions used in the applications.

Individuals in one business field rarely would have a sound knowledge of the decision contexts and substance relevant to other business fields. As a result, business decisions in one field are not particularly useful for professionals in other fields to use for improving their fundamental decision-making skills. Fortunately, each of us has numerous common experiences and many similar decisions that we personally face at home, at work, and for enjoyment. All of these decisions are real and realistic for each of us.

The use of the concepts and procedures described here relies on common sense and qualitative thinking; no quantitative analysis is required. In fact, for the great majority of personal and business decisions, there will be no subsequent systematic analysis needed to evaluate alternatives. In these cases, the relevant values and alternatives created for the decision being faced provide the basis for fruitful discussion and thoughtful appraisal about which alternatives are better than others, how much better, and why. Such clarity will certainly nudge you to improve your decisions.

3 MAKING VALUE-FOCUSED DECISIONS

The intent of making any decision is to achieve something that you desire. If you do not know what you want to achieve by making a decision, you cannot usefully think about how you might achieve it. Thus, once you recognize any decision that you face, your initial thoughts should be to focus on what you want to achieve by making that decision. But we rarely address our decisions in this way.

Our Intuitive Decision-Making Process

Most of us make our decisions on the basis of decision-making habits developed over time. Once we recognize a decision that we need to face, our initial thoughts are usually about alternatives to solve the decision problem. This is alternative-focused decision-making. Sometimes the first alternative that comes to mind seems good enough, so we implement that alternative and hope that it works. Decision made! Problem solved!

For other decisions, we may identify a few alternatives. One may obviously seem to be the best, so we choose it. But other situations are more difficult, when it is not clear which alternative is best. In these cases, we may identify a few criteria, some of which may relate to our unspecified values, to compare the alternatives. Then we use our general knowledge and any relevant information to consider how well the alternatives meet the criteria. Finally, we intuitively compare the pros and cons of each alternative to select what we perceive to be the best choice.

For the important and complex decisions that we face today, our ingrained decision-making habits have three serious inadequacies.

1. We do not consciously know all that we want to achieve by making the decision being faced. If we want to achieve something, which is clearly the case when making any decision, we have a much better chance of achieving it if we thoroughly understand what it is that we want to achieve.

2. We are not particularly skilled at, nor do we focus time on, trying to create additional alternatives better than the first acceptable one. As the effectiveness of potential alternatives can greatly vary, selecting the first identified acceptable alternative is a poor procedure for important decisions.

3. We seldom deliberately conceive of desirable decisions to face that would likely enhance our lives if we did. Since we are each an expert on what we want in our life, it would be beneficial to become skilled at creating the decisions to make such desires come true.

These three inadequacies all concern what I refer to as the neglected front end of decision-making, namely defining and structuring the decisions that you want to face. Solving the wrong decision or a poorly or incompletely stated decision has little chance of providing what you want to achieve by facing any decision.

The Foundation for Your Decisions

The foundation for any decision is your *values*, which I define as *what you want to achieve by making the specific decision that you face*. The fundamental role of values in decision-making is beautifully illustrated in Lewis Carroll's *Alice's Adventures in Wonderland*. After falling into a rabbit hole, Alice begins walking down a path. Arriving at a point where two paths continue in different directions, she is not sure which path to follow. Fortunately, she notices a very intelligent-looking cat in a nearby tree, and

> **Your values for a decision are what you want to achieve by making that decision. These values should guide all subsequent effort in the decision-making process. I refer to this process as value-focused decision-making.**

inquires for advice. "Cheshire Puss – would you tell me please which way I ought to go from here?" "That depends a good deal on where you want to get to," said the cat. "I don't much care where," said Alice. "Then it doesn't matter which way you go," said the cat.

If you do not care where you are going, any choice is equivalent. So—why bother to make a decision about it? Make decisions about something else that you *do* care about. Suppose that you care where you are going, but what you are not sure about is where it is. Then it is essential to figure it out. Clearly, you have a much better chance of getting to where you want to be if you know where it is that you want to be.

Suppose that you are bored with your current job and are planning to secure additional education next year, but have not yet given much thought to what you specifically want to achieve by obtaining this education. In this situation, your initial effort should be to identify all of your values relevant to your decision. For example, in selecting what specific education to obtain, important values may be to learn specific material, prepare for a particular interesting job, improve your social skills, meet lifelong friends, become self-sufficient, have fun, live in a certain region of the country, and minimize costs.

Once you understand your values for a decision, all of the subsequent effort of the decision-making process is to figure out how to best achieve these values. I refer to this process as *value-focused decision-making*. When your values are made explicit, they nudge you to make a better decision by providing a basis for creating alternatives, identifying the possible consequences of each of these alternatives, and appraising the competing alternatives so as to choose the best one.

A Value-Focused Decision-Making Process

Since values are the foundation for your decisions, values should also be the foundation for your decision-making process in order to guide your choices for those decisions. The value-focused decision-making process is designed to develop insightful personal nudges to improve your decision-making. It is composed of a series of steps, listed in Table 3.1, based on logic and common sense that address the key components of any decision-making process. The procedures for addressing these components produce nudges for you to more clearly understand all of the aspects of the decision you face,

Table 3.1 The Steps of a Value-Focused Decision-Making Process

---

Front end: define and structure the decision that you face

1. State the decision problem or decision opportunity that you face
2. Identify your values, and state them as objectives, to clarify what you want to achieve
3. Create alternatives that contribute to achieving your objectives

Back end: evaluate your alternatives and make your decision

4. Describe the possible consequences of each alternative to indicate how well it achieves your objectives
5. Identify the pros and cons of each alternative and weigh their importance
6. Select an alternative using information and insight from your evaluation

---

modify some of the decisions you are addressing to make them more appealing, and identify more appealing decisions to address, which will almost surely improve your life. All this is done in the first three steps of the value-focused decision-making process. These three steps are the front end of the process, which provides the basis to define and thoroughly describe the decision that you eventually face. The three back-end steps help you evaluate the desirability of those competing alternatives.

A high-quality front end for a decision has a much greater influence on making a better decision than a high-quality back end. After having produced a quality front end, this claim is supported by five fundamental reasons.

1. You will have identified the decision that you want to face, so you won't spend time and effort solving the wrong decision.
2. You will have a much better understanding of what you want to achieve by making your decision, so you enhance your chances of achieving it.

3. You will often identify better alternatives for your decision than any of the alternatives that you previously recognized.
4. You will create more appealing decisions to face, including important decision opportunities and not just decision problems.
5. The quality of the back-end evaluation is completely dependent on the quality of the front-end sets of values and alternatives.

Unfortunately, most of the books and literature about decision-making focus on the back end. In doing so, they explicitly or implicitly assume that your decision is well understood, meaning that the three front-end steps are explicitly considered and completed well. The first line of these books could be "Given a specific decision with the following sets of values and alternatives, here is how you can solve it." In this rush to solve the decision problem as it was first perceived, the front end is often not carefully or thoroughly considered. As a result, the insights provided from appraising the alternatives for a poorly or incompletely stated decision are greatly degraded, as explained by the "Garbage in, garbage out" principle.

The value-focused decision-making process is different from others on decision-making. This book concentrates on the three front-end steps, so as to define your decision well. It does not just state that values and alternatives must be identified but describes in detail several procedures useful to do these two critical tasks well and illustrates them with several case studies and examples. The book also includes the creation of decision opportunities, addressing your decisions that are influenced by others, and the key role played by your collective decisions in your life.

> **Very few personal and business decisions are informed by a systematic evaluation of the alternatives. Fortunately, a thoughtful structuring provides a sound understanding of your decision that nudges you to select alternatives that better achieve your interests.**

Once a high-quality front-end decision structure is developed, organized thinking supported by some information and data, rather than detailed back-end analysis, will resolve most of your decisions worthy of thought.[1] For complex decisions typically faced by businesses and organizations, a complete evaluation of alternatives using a mathematical model will provide additional useful insight.[2] For any decision, its decision structure also provides a sound logical basis to guide meaningful discussions about all relevant aspects of the decision. This reality further stresses the importance of doing the front end of the decision process well.

Although the back-end steps for evaluating the alternatives of a well-stated decision are not a main topic of this book, a concise description of these steps and their relationship to the front-end steps of a value-focused decision-making process is provided in the Appendix.

Defining the Decision that You Face

The roles of the three front-end steps of a value-focused decision-making process are interrelated. Because of this, you should usually revisit each step more than once to provide a good foundation for your decision. An overview of the three steps and their relationships is presented below. The three following chapters provide details about how to conduct each of the steps and become skilled and at ease in using them.

The first front-end step is to create an initial decision statement of the decision problem or decision opportunity to be addressed. The decision statement should be clear and concise and begin with the word "decide." A personal decision statement is "decide which new passenger car to buy," and a corporate example is "decide on our strategy to introduce new stores in the Republic of Korea." Your decision statement provides the initial information to guide your effort to create the sets of values and alternatives in the other two front-end steps. Guidelines for how to create a useful decision statement are presented in Chapter 4.

Specifying your values for a decision results in a complete list of relevant values. Each value suggests something that you care about in that decision. Most of these values concern or suggest something that you want to achieve by making your decision. Expressing each value as an objective clarifies what it is that you want to achieve. In a decision about the choice of a job, your objectives may be to learn about the business rapidly, make a clear contribution, enjoy the work, have a reasonable commute, make friends and contacts, and be paid well. Chapter 5 describes in detail how to identify your values and express them as objectives.

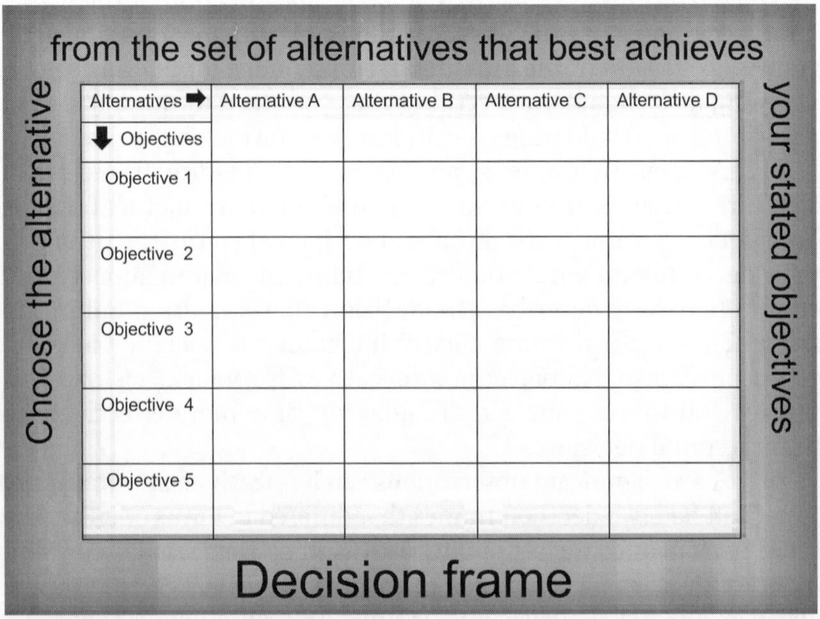

Alternatives ➡	Alternative A	Alternative B	Alternative C	Alternative D
⬇ Objectives				
Objective 1				
Objective 2				
Objective 3				
Objective 4				
Objective 5				

Choose the alternative from the set of alternatives that best achieves your stated objectives

Decision frame

Figure 3.1 Your Decision Frame

The alternatives that you should be interested in are those that will contribute to better achieving at least one of your objectives. The set of your objectives allows you to clearly differentiate between alternatives that are good enough to warrant careful consideration for your decision and those that are not. Procedures to stimulate your thoughts to create better alternatives are discussed in Chapter 6.

Your objectives and the set of alternatives for your decision statement provide the basis for a precise description of your decision, referred to as a *decision frame*. As illustrated in Figure 3.1, given your objectives and alternatives, the decision frame is "choose the alternative from the set of alternatives that best achieves your stated objectives." This decision frame for your decision replaces the initial decision statement for guiding the description and evaluation of alternatives and making a sound decision.

Each component created for your decision frame helps you better understand the decision you are facing. Thus, your identified values,

Your decision frame thoroughly describes the decision you plan to make. It includes everything that you should consider in order to make a sound decision.

their descriptions as objectives, and the specification of the viable alternatives are all nudges toward making a better decision. The resulting decision frame provides a strong nudge for making a good decision, as it includes everything that you need to think about in describing and evaluating the alternatives for making a choice.

A decision frame is analogous to a picture frame, with a picture inside the frame and everything not in the picture outside. Your decision frame is specific about both what you are including in your decision and what you are excluding. It unambiguously and comprehensively describes the decision that you are planning to make. The decision frame clearly indicates the specific back-end effort needed to evaluate the alternatives for your decision. This nudges you to use your decision-making time more effectively to make a sound decision.

A few significant observations can be clearly seen from Figure 3.1. If you had two decision frames that differed in terms of either the set of objectives or the set of alternatives, then they would represent different decisions. Even if only one objective or one alternative was added or subtracted, they would be similar but different decisions. For example, if you and your family do not spell out rest and relaxation or family time as values for selecting a vacation, you may find yourselves considering only the vacations that have you spending every day in museums and cultural sites, with no downtime.

One direct way to make a decision more appealing is to create a new alternative that is better than any in the current frame. One indirect way to make a decision more appealing is to identify a previously unrecognized objective that is relevant to the decision. Because of the greater contribution toward achieving this objective of some alternatives, the desirability of those alternatives will become more appealing and you will be nudged toward choosing them. In addition, the recognition of this objective may stimulate your thoughts to create a new alternative that is better than any in the original decision frame.

The Distinction between a Good Decision and a Good Outcome

The purpose of this book is to help you develop specific skills to make better decisions, so it is useful to pause and define the concept of a good decision. A good decision is one made consistent with your values for that decision and using all the information about that decision provided in steps 1 through 5 of the value-focused decision-making process, described in Table 3.1. In simpler terms, a good decision is one that chooses the alternative that you think best achieves your objectives using all of the relevant information that you have at the time of the decision.

When you begin thinking of a decision, there are uncertainties about each of these five steps. All of the uncertainties in the front-end steps are due to you not being clear or complete about defining the decision to be addressed, stating all of the values for that decision, and identifying all of the reasonable alternatives to consider. When these steps are thoughtfully and thoroughly done, there will be fewer uncertainties about your decision. The better they are done, the less likely it is that you will proceed with a poorly defined decision, omit key values for that decision, or not identify potential alternatives that could be very desirable. For step 4, you may recognize uncertainties about the possible consequences of each alternative, which indicate how well that alternative measures up in terms of your values. Finally, in step 5, you may be unsure about how you want to weigh the pros and cons of the alternatives.

You can make better decisions more easily when there are fewer uncertainties concerning your description of the decision you face. Fortunately, you have total control over reducing uncertainties in steps 1 through 3 and 5. By carefully framing your decision by following steps 1 through 3, you substantially reduce the uncertainties about the decision that you are addressing. Details on how to do this are provided in the following three chapters. You can also reduce your uncertainties about how to appropriately weigh the various pros and cons in step 5. This issue is discussed in the Appendix.

You have less control to reduce the uncertainties about the possible consequences of each alternative in step 4. You can do your best to describe the possible consequences of each alternative and the likelihoods that they might occur, as described in the Appendix. Also, you may be able to create alternatives that have fewer uncertainties with respect to the consequences. However, it is usually not possible to eliminate all of this uncertainty, as circumstances over which you have no control can influence those consequences. Hence, you must make a decision such that these uncertainties about the consequences that might occur are described and accounted for in the decision. This situation renders it important to clarify a crucial concept necessary to understand the definition of a good decision.

Each decision has possible consequences, and these indicate how well or poorly the chosen alternative measures up in terms of your values. The consequences that occur after choosing an alternative are referred to as the *outcome* of that decision. To understand the meaning of a good decision, it is essential to distinguish between the concepts of a good decision and a good outcome of a decision.

Important decisions usually have uncertainties about the eventual consequences of each of the alternatives. To make a good decision, you should recognize the chances of the possible consequences that may occur. After you have made your decision, you have no additional control over which consequences will occur. The general distinction between the outcomes of good and poor decisions is that the outcomes of good decisions will, on average, be better than those of poor decisions, in two ways. From good decisions, you will experience more good outcomes; and, on average, these good outcomes will be better and the bad outcomes will not be as bad.

The following examples illustrate these ideas. You are the founder of a new startup company. Significant progress has been made since its founding two years ago, and you are planning a two-day retreat for 60 professional employees at a well-known conference center about 100 miles from your office location. The purpose of the meeting is to make sure that everyone has a thorough understanding of accomplishments to date and the key necessary steps for the company to take in the near future. A highlight of the retreat, which will be held on the first evening, will be a speech by a well-liked and respected individual in the field, followed by plenty of discussion time.

Before the meeting the company elicited suggestions for potential speakers from all of the employees who would be attending the retreat. Several candidates were considered, and one individual was strongly preferred. He agreed to participate in the retreat, and the specific date was chosen. The purposes of his talk were to communicate some key aspects of the history of the field to employees, to stimulate productive thinking about ways to improve the products of the company, and to energize and inspire attendees. Everyone was looking forward to this aspect of the retreat.

On the first day of the retreat, the company learned that the speaker had been involved in a serious traffic accident and was now in the hospital. Fortunately, he would completely recover, but he certainly could not attend the retreat, nor was he in any condition to speak remotely to those at the meeting. Plan B had to be developed quickly during the morning of the retreat. Four important company issues were identified, and groups were formed to discuss them during the evening that had been planned for the key speech.

The decision to have the legend as the key speaker at the retreat was a good decision based on all of the information available when the decision was made. However, due to circumstances beyond the control of the company and information that could not have been known when planning the meeting, the outcome of the retreat was much less desirable than expected, namely a less successful and less inspiring event and much wasted effort. This bad outcome does not mean that the decision was poor. Uncertainties beyond your control can influence the consequences of your decision. In all situations, a good decision is made using the best information available at the time with regard to those uncertainties.

You can also make a poor decision and yet a good outcome may result. Suppose that you drive to a house party 20 miles from your home. While you are there you end up drinking alcohol, and more than you think you should. You are invited to stay overnight at the house of the party, but choose to drive home that evening. Fortunately, no problems occur on the drive: you are not in an accident, you cause no accidents of others, and you are not stopped by any law enforcement officers. Even though the outcome was the one that you desired, this decision was obviously poor.

Additional Thoughts for Decisions in Organizations

Just as with individual decisions, the values of an organization provide the foundation for clear thinking and any data collection or analysis to make a high-quality decision. The organization's values should be the basis for any time and effort allocated to the activities for making a decision, as described in Table 3.1.

There are often multiple individuals and groups concerned with organizational decisions. They may all have strong opinions about what choice should be made and may not be reluctant to publicly express opinions about what they consider to be poor choices, even if they are not informed about many of the relevant issues that should be considered in making the decision. Obvious examples are government at all levels, where members of the public have legitimate concerns, and decisions of public companies, where shareholders, customers, and employees are directly affected.

Such a decision-making environment puts pressure on the decision-makers to have a decision-making process that is transparent and a choice that is justifiable to others. The way to enhance transparency is sometimes mistakenly thought to mean that the process should be objective and data-based, rather than understandable, logical, and value-based. As a result, sometimes the decision-maker will even state that the first thing that needs to be done is to collect all the available data. But this can lead to high costs over a long time just to collect a lot of irrelevant data. It may also distort a clear understanding of the decision, as the data typically pertains to the more easily quantifiable concerns, such as cost, and it neglects the "soft" but perhaps more relevant concerns such as health and safety, environmental, and social implications, as well as public and stakeholder responses. Data—and, more broadly, information—that does not help provide a meaningful and insightful appraisal of alternatives in terms of the organization's values is not worth the time or cost of collection.

When stakeholders are going to be significantly impacted by an organization's decisions, it is often important to give them meaningful involvement in the decision-making process and incorporate their concerns in thinking about the decision. It is also important to include them early in the decision-making process, especially prior to making any decision. A highly appropriate way to include them is to explicitly identify their values that are relevant to the decision and include these values in the appraisal of alternatives. One benefit is that you can then honestly communicate to all stakeholders how and where their values were addressed in the decision-making process, and, depending on the decision, what aspects of the chosen alternative were included to explicitly address their values.

Many decisions do not need to be explained or communicated to others. But, sometimes, you may wish to communicate the reasons for your choice to check your reasoning before acting, or to have stakeholders understand how their concerns were legitimately considered. The basis for explaining your decision in a meaningful manner is to describe the various pros and cons of the alternatives in terms of the stated values and explain how you considered those pros and cons in making the decisions.

4 DEFINING YOUR DECISION

The trigger for any decision is the event that caused your first conscious thought that eventually led you to conclude that you must or should make a decision. That event could be external, such as an important business meeting being canceled, or an internal thought, such as realizing that you miss being a member of a sports or singing group.

For many decision problems, the time between the trigger and recognition is very short. Suppose that you return to your parked car to drive to an important meeting and notice that you have a flat tire. Almost instantaneously, you realize that a decision is necessary. You may begin to make decisions to solve your problem without even thinking about what your immediate decision is. If you have a spare tire in the vehicle, you may begin to use it to replace your flat tire. If you don't have a spare tire, you may take the flat tire to a garage, where it can be fixed or a new tire purchased and installed on your wheel. In either situation, you may do the work yourself or call a service to help you. For all of these situations, you will have pursued an alternative-focused decision procedure to solve the unstated decision statement of "decide how to fix my flat tire" or "decide how to get my car in operating condition as soon as possible." But do these decision statements address the decision that you should now face?

Before acting to solve some recognized decision problem, it is important to think, at least briefly, about which immediate decision you should face. If you have a critical business meeting scheduled to begin in an hour, the statement of your immediate decision might be "decide how to get to my meeting on time and prepared." The alternatives may be to take a taxi or Uber, call a colleague for a ride, take a bus or subway if available, or walk. After the meeting is over you can focus on the decision to address the flat tire. Selecting which decisions you should face is a key element of good decision-making.

For decision opportunities, the time between the trigger and the recognition that a decision should be made can vary greatly. You may have recently moved to a new city because of your job. Your work is going very well, and now you hope that your personal life will improve. You may think that it will just take some time until your life is more interesting. After a few more months you may realize that not much has improved, and your life is still not that interesting. You may react by going to organized events more frequently. This may help, but a reaction is not a decision. A decision requires that you consciously consider at least two alternatives and have some understanding of what you hope to achieve by making the decision.

Life goes on but doesn't get much better. Then one day you think: "Something in my life is not as good as I would like and I am ready to take action to improve it." You think about what is wrong and conclude that the main reason is that you don't have a great friend to be with, as you did in your previous location. You formulate your thoughts as a decision opportunity about how to meet potential friends and begin creating alternatives to do that. This is good news, as you are likely to have a more enjoyable life sooner.

This simple story indicates bad news as well. Five months elapsed between the trigger—your conscious awareness of a situation that you would prefer to be better—and your declaring a decision to identify and pursue alternatives to improve it. The consequence was five not very enjoyable months. If you had been more proactive regarding decision opportunities, you could have begun your pursuit of alternatives to improve circumstances five months earlier.

Creating Your Decision Statement

Once you recognize a decision, you want to develop a clear and concise statement of this decision. Your decision statement is the starting point to nudge your thinking about sets of appropriate values and alternatives to create the decision frame for your decision. Your decision frame includes both the values that characterize what it is that you want to achieve by making the decision and the set of alternatives that you feel are appropriate to consider in order to achieve those values.

> A decision statement concisely defines the decision that you face. It guides your thoughts about the values you want to achieve by making that decision and the alternatives to consider.

Sometimes creating a decision statement appears to be straightforward, but initial thoughts can be misleading. Suppose that you have been looking for a job and have received three job offers. You may state your decision as "select one of my three offers." But are there, or should there be, just three alternatives? Is negotiating with an organization to encourage it to enhance its offer among your thoughts? If so, your current decision is not which offer to select. If there is a potential fourth offer that may come soon that you think you may prefer, your current decision may be how to keep the current alternatives open for another week or more. You may also define it as deciding how to enhance your chances of receiving an offer from the fourth company and how you might shorten the time until you get a response from that company.

To state the decision that you intend to face, a simple rule is helpful. Begin any decision statement with the word "decide," typically followed by "which," "what," "when," "whether," "how," or "if." Your decision statement should then clarify what it is that you want to decide. The "what it is" characterizes either the overall value you want to achieve or the category of alternatives you want to consider. Respective examples are "decide how I can have more enjoyable evenings" and "decide which pair of new skis I should buy." Seemingly similar statements, such as "decide to have more enjoyable evenings" or "decide to purchase a pair of skis," are not clear decision statements but, rather, assertions of intent that will require decisions to accomplish.

Do not just accept a decision statement as you initially perceive it. You have a choice—actually, a decision itself—about the decision statement for the decision that you want to face. It is often useful to develop a few potential decision statements for your decision. Thoughtfully consider whether your initial decision statement would be better if it were stated more broadly or narrowly. You may also consider whether you can express an unappealing decision statement in a more appealing way that provides better suggestions for appropriate values or innovative alternatives. Your examination of the decision statement may even result in changing the entire decision to be addressed, as happened in the case above: to get to the meeting on time rather than fix the flat tire.

Your decision cannot be stated as an objective, such as "make money," "enjoy my vacation," or "meet interesting people," though it can be created from an objective. Corresponding to these objectives, respective decision statements could be "decide how to increase my salary," "decide where to go on vacation," and "decide what I should do to increase my chances of meeting more interesting people." Your decision statement should also not be an alternative for a decision, such as "I am going camping next weekend." Related decision statements are "decide whether to go camping next weekend," "decide where to go camping next weekend," or "decide when to go camping."

Before accepting any decision statement posed for you by someone else, you should carefully consider whether you want to address that decision. Many such decision statements are presented as choices of alternatives, with only one explicit alternative and an implied default alternative of *not* selecting that explicitly stated alternative. An example is a specific offer to purchase a house or not. You should perhaps consider changing aspects of the decision by creating other additional alternatives, such as identifying other potential houses to purchase.

You want to avoid the tendency to narrow the decision statement by stating just a part of the decision. This would limit the subsequent decision frame and therefore degrade all of your decision-making effort. If being in your house gives you the feeling that there is too much clutter, you might state your decision as "decide how to arrange my garage so it can be used to store more material." However, this statement de facto omits alternatives, including any disposal of numerous unwanted items.

You also do not want to limit your description of why you want something. Suppose that you were chosen as the top salesperson last year in your company, and the company offered to buy you the automobile of your choice. You might initially state your decision as "decide which automobile is best for my work." With further consideration, you may recognize that you would use your new automobile for many personal reasons in addition to your work, so the decision statement might be better as "decide which automobile is best for me." A good automobile for your work might be very different from a good automobile for all of your vehicle uses.

In general, you want any mention of values in your decision statement to be broad, and any mention of alternatives to be broad too. But how broad? The answer in both cases is: sufficiently broad that it does not limit your subsequent thinking as you construct your decision frame. The reason is that your decision statement provides the basis for stimulating your thoughts about specific values and specific alternatives appropriate for your decision frame. It is easier to delete stated values and alternatives that are recognized subsequently as irrelevant to your more carefully constructed decision frame than to have to generate values and alternatives later that were not evoked by an inappropriately narrow initial decision statement.

Decision Statements that Lack Clarity

The initial stimulus for a decision is sometimes quite vague: "My job is not very interesting," "I don't feel like myself," or "We are moving to Montréal for my husband's work for two years and I'm not sure what to do." Such feelings or thoughts definitely suggest that decisions are needed, but more specification is necessary in order to make any useful improvement. For "My job is not very interesting," is it that you are not learning anything new at work, your colleagues are uninteresting, or that work is not at all enjoyable? Are the implications that you are thinking of a new job, a new field, a transfer within the company, developing additional skills, or what? Is not feeling like yourself a physical issue, an emotional issue, a psychological issue, or some combination? Regarding your husband's transfer, is your concern to go or not, how to maintain your current job during these two years, what to do personally when you are living in Montréal, how to get a good job there, the type of job you want to find, or something else? With some serious thought about what really concerns you, you will be able to construct a clear decision statement for each of perhaps several decisions that you recognize should be made.

The individual with the uninteresting job may know that he wants to be with his company for the long term and to progress to higher-level positions in the future. He would like to learn more about how the entire company works but his learning has leveled off in his current position. His decision statement may be "decide where and how to transfer to a more challenging position within the company." Likewise, the woman whose husband is going to Canada may be enthusiastic. She may know that her decision statement is "decide how to actively integrate into Montréal life and experience and contribute as much as I can." She may also recognize a separate decision statement, namely "decide how to find an interesting part-time employment position."

Stating a decision as a situation to do something or not is often ambiguous. Suppose that a couple state their decision as "decide whether to take this year's vacation to Chile and Peru." The reason this is not adequate is that there is no indication of what the default alternative, "decide to not visit Chile and Peru," entails.[1] Without this, it is impossible to consider the relative desirability of the alternative to Chile and Peru. If they don't go on this trip, do they stay home, and, if so, what do they do? Or might they go to either China or Australia instead? Obviously, knowing what the other alternatives might be is necessary to appraise the relative desirability of the Chile/Peru trip. It is useful to have the decision statement include information about this.

Retirement decisions are among the most important decisions that you will make. The decision about when to retire is certainly a life-changing decision. Retirement offers numerous opportunities for the rest of your life, but it requires your thought, effort, and energy to pursue the life you would like to live. All of a sudden, the only rules of life that pertain to you are those that you wish to accept. This freedom and responsibility can intimidate the timid and worry the adult children of retirees.

► Your Retirement Decision

Too frequently the decision statement of a prospective retiree is inadequate. Whether explicitly stated or implicitly considered, the decision statement is something like "decide whether to retire at the end of this year or not." If retirement is not chosen this year, the same decision statement is considered next year, and possibly in future years. This decision statement can be reversed to be "decide whether to remain employed next year or not," which highlights the major shortcoming of not knowing much about the "default" alternative, as discussed above.

An important benefit of retirement that is desired is to have a high quality of life. Hence, before retiring, it is critically important to think about what you want your life to be in retirement and begin implementing steps to make it a reality. Otherwise, you will have to figure out what future life you desire after having retired. And, once you figure that out, you may realize that it would have been much better if you had not retired when you did. Therefore, your retirement decision should consider more than simply when to retire, as it also involves what to do for at least the next few years, or perhaps the rest of your life. For some individuals, it may also include how to retire, as it is often possible to reduce the amount of work time over several years.

A more appropriate decision statement for some prospective retirees might be "decide when to retire, how to retire, and what to do with the rest of my life when I am fully retired." The key elements are to seriously consider the best balance of time between work and leisure and develop sound ideas of at least some meaningful activities you will pursue in your retirement life. ◄

For some decisions, it may be very difficult to spell out specific alternatives for the decision that you face. If you are in a serious relationship, you may face decisions concerning whether to propose to or whether to accept a proposal from your partner. In these cases, reasonable decision statements are, say, "decide whether to propose to Jennifer" or "decide whether to accept a proposal from Philip." For both of these decision statements, there are a lot of uncertainties related to the "no" alternative. For each decision, it may be helpful to consider related issues, such as whether this is the right time in your life to marry, whether there will be good alternatives later, and when these might occur. But, of course, many uncertainties will remain, since you cannot know many things that will happen regarding these issues in the future. In addition, it should be recognized that the "yes" alternative also has significant uncertainties regarding the future. Being as clear as possible about life-changing decisions such as these is obviously important.

Decision Statements that Are Too Narrow

Often you will face a series of related decisions concerning a specific purpose. In essence, you make several narrower decisions that collectively establish the chosen alternative for the broader decision that you did not explicitly recognize. Sometimes the seemingly better alternatives for the narrower decisions result in a poor choice for the broad decision. The implication is that your appropriate decision statement should address the broad decision. This is illustrated in the following example.

► Visiting Your Grandmother

Your grandmother is in her 80s and you have not seen her for two years. You would very much like to visit her, but the problem is that you do not seem to have the time, as she lives a long airplane ride away. However, there is a three-day weekend coming up, and you think maybe you can go then. You state your decision as "decide whether to visit my grandmother during the next three-day week-end." You think a lot about the decision, and decide that you just cannot go this weekend as too much is happening. This decision statement is poor, partly because the alternatives that you might pursue if you do not visit your grandmother this weekend are not explicitly considered. In addition, there is a well-known bias toward selecting the default "do nothing" alternative.

But, more relevant for this case, you definitely want to visit your grandmother reasonably soon, so choose a decision statement that will make it happen. Suppose that you decide that you want to go within the next six months. Now your decision statement can be "decide when to visit my grandmother in the next six months." Reviewing your calendar suggests there are about nine possible weekend alternatives, and each involves visiting your grandmother, which is your purpose. Choose the best of these and make a commitment to your grandmother and yourself.

The original decision statement was inappropriately narrow. If you consider separate decisions for each of the possible weeks when you could either visit or not visit, you might conclude in each case that it was better not to go. However, collectively, the overall consequence of this—not visiting your grandmother—is poor. With the new decision statement, there is no default alternative. You are really examining which combination of staying home for eight weekends and visiting your grandmother on the other weekend is best. This alternative—and maybe several of the eight other alternatives—is better than not visiting on any of the nine weekends. Having each alternative include a visit to grandmother meant that this decision statement clearly nudged the decision-maker to make that desired visit. ◄

This same type of difficulty—making a decision at the wrong level—can occur when you should be making what I refer to as a *personal policy decision* about how to manage repeated similar decisions rather than considering each decision separately. Suppose that you want to increase or maintain your fitness by regular exercise. Each evening, after work, you could decide whether to exercise that evening. Too often there may be reasons not to exercise when decided day by day, and these naturally hinder your pursuit to regularly exercise. To clarify your commitment to this, perhaps your decision statement should be "decide how to maintain regular exercise," where you may understand "regular exercise" to mean about an hour at least five times per week. To fulfill your personal commitment, your basic plan may be to exercise Monday through Thursday evenings after work and either Saturday or Sunday. If you cannot exercise one day because of a special occasion that conflicts, you can plan to exercise on one morning prior to work or on both weekend days.

Decision Statements for the Wrong Decision

Sometimes the initial decision statement for a decision is not for the decision that you should be facing. The result is that you make little headway on your real decision, since you are, essentially, starting in the wrong place.

▶ Resigning from the Massachusetts Institute of Technology

Early in my career I was an associate professor in the MIT Sloan School of Management and affiliated with the Operations Research Center. Professionally, it was an exciting place to be, and I enjoyed my colleagues and the university community.

A new international institute, called the International Institute for Applied Systems Analysis (IIASA), had just recently been created by the national academies of science of 13 nations. Members included the academies of the United States and the Soviet Union, and its facilities were in a former Habsburg palace in a suburb of Vienna. Its purpose was to work on problems common to industrialized societies, such as those concerning energy, water resources, and the environment. I was offered a position to work there for two years beginning in June, which I planned to accept. As a result, I faced the immediate decision of "decide whether to resign from MIT or request a leave of absence."

I first conceptually thought about this as a year-to-year decision: "decide to stay at MIT or resign." Each year it seemed better to stay, as I could always resign next year if I stayed this year. However, it was clear that the same choice could repeat annually, and a decision about how to live my life—essentially, which life to live—would be made by following inertia without explicitly thinking about that life-changing decision. Also, if I requested and was granted a leave of absence, I realized that MIT would expect me to return after two years and I would have an obligation to do so. Not returning or resigning within a few years after returning would certainly be inappropriate treatment by me of MIT and my colleagues there.

I changed my decision statement to "decide whether to pursue a career at MIT or in the western part of the United States." Now I considered whether I should remain at MIT for my career, assuming that I would have that option. In addition, playing a devil's advocate, I assumed that, if I stayed at MIT, I would have a professional career equivalent to that of the faculty at MIT and elsewhere whom I most respected. Even if such a great career came to be, I knew that I would not be satisfied with my life. Hence, it seemed obvious to me, using this frame, that I should leave MIT. The reasons included the fact that, relative to 20 and 30 years earlier, the professional opportunities available to someone such as me were much more widely distributed geographically. Because of better and cheaper communication and transportation alternatives, it was practical to remain connected with colleagues not in your geographical area. In addition, the weather in the western part of the United States was more dependable and suitable for recreational activities of interest.

Having made the decision that I should not stay at MIT forever, I considered when I should leave. This was now relatively easy. It would be better to leave sooner rather than later, both for MIT and for me. With the understanding outlined above, I felt comfortable resigning. ◄

It is often useful to consider and use different decision statements to examine aspects of a significant decision. For this decision, I first used an annual decision frame looking forward, and subsequently used a lifetime career frame looking backward from near the end of my career. Using different frames can lead to different insights, nudging you to develop an appropriate decision frame. For any decision with the potential to be life-changing, it is useful to view it from a lifetime frame. You should consider the potential impacts on all of your life objectives in appraising your alternatives. Any narrower perspective, such as using your professional objectives only, could neglect any implications of your alter-

> An important decision that you routinely make is deciding what specific decision to face when solving a decision problem or pursuing a decision opportunity.

natives that might change your judgments about what alternative you should choose.

A third category where you may create a decision statement for the wrong decision arises when you already have made that decision, but you feel great anxiety, difficulty, or pain associated for announcing and implementing the decision. An example might concern divorce. Suppose that circumstances lead you to decide whether to seek a divorce from your spouse. You spend a great deal of time thinking about the different future lives for you and your spouse and the children, if there are any, for both alternatives. Your conclusion is that you should seek a divorce. However, because you feel the divorce proceedings would be terrible, you keep misleading yourself to believe that you are still deciding whether to get divorced.

Additional Thoughts for Decisions in Organizations

The decision statement for any decision faced by an organization requires careful articulation. This is important, because it provides the foundation for identifying the set of values and the relevant alternatives for that decision.

In businesses and organizations, it is useful to include input from a range of professionals with different information and viewpoints when developing the decision statement for a significant decision. Then, before beginning to solve that decision, it is important to get agreement on the decision statement from the relevant individuals who will be involved in the process to solve the decision. This is important for several reasons. First, it is inclusive and allows all relevant individuals to have their say and, presumably, some influence when their thoughts have merit. Second, it is the first step in building the team that will work together on the decision. Third, it sets the stage for all else in the decision process, which will progress more smoothly when everybody agrees on the decision to be addressed.

If you do not have an explicit agreement on the decision statement, some key individuals for the decision may feel that all is going well until the decision process is about finished. Becoming aware at such a late stage that some individuals feel that an incorrect or incomplete decision was addressed is obviously unfortunate for all concerned individuals. It may also result in the choice of an inferior alternative or major delays in making an important decision. Nobody in an organization wishes to be in such situations. The message is clear: involve key individuals in defining any important organizational decision, get agreement on the decision statement, and ensure that all concerned understand the meaning and implications of that statement.

▶ Managing a Consumer Product

Some years ago a major cereal company introduced a new granola-type cereal that was tastier and more nutritious. The cereal included natural ingredients, which made it more expensive than most other cereals. The company entered the market with a solid advertising campaign that explained the additional benefits and convincingly conveyed the message that these benefits were well worth the higher cost. This campaign lasted three years and resulted in a respected and profitable product. In an effort to increase profits, the company then reduced its advertising; sales continued to increase, albeit at a slower pace.

A few years later a recession in the national economy occurred and consumers became more cost-conscious. Sales of the cereal fell, and within two years had dropped to a point that the product was no longer profitable. The division manager had a marketing study carried out, and the conclusion was that consumers who had quit purchasing the cereal did so because of its relatively high price. As a result, the manager had a meeting with his product and production teams. He announced the reason for the significant decline in sales and stated that what the company needed to do was this: "decide how to reduce the cost of our product."

His teams accepted this decision statement and tested various ways to cut product costs, choosing the one they thought was best. Sales did not drop any further for the next few months; but then they began to fall again. Subsequently, new market research indicated that some loyal customers who were not particularly cost-conscious were now no longer purchasing their product because it was less nutritious and did not taste as good as the original product.

In less than a year the cost-reduced product did not generate enough sales and was no longer available.

A post-mortem study suggested that the company and product manager team addressed the wrong decision by considering only cutting costs to regain lost customers and attract new customers. They could have defined their decision statement as "decide how to increase the profitability of our cereal product," which is clearly a broader statement than the one focused solely on cutting costs. It would include, for instance, investment in various advertising campaigns, focusing the marketing more narrowly, or other cost management options as alternatives. In retrospect, the original advertising campaign had built a successful product that was good-tasting and nutritious in a relatively short time. The core prospective customers of the campaign were not cost-conscious but, rather, taste- and quality-conscious. Naturally, some customers were, or became, cost-conscious during the recession and reduced their consumption of the product. A higher proportion of the customers remained and still liked the taste and quality of the cereal—until it was degraded by having some ingredients removed so that costs could be reduced. Perhaps an advertising campaign analogous to the original one, which had ended after the first three years, would have led to an increase in sales to additional quality-conscious consumers and kept the cereal brand from disappearing from the shelves. ◄

Without taking the time to carefully think about the appropriate decision to be faced, it is more likely that thoughts become anchored on recent and readily available information. In this case, since the market research indicated that sales had fallen because of the high cereal costs, the manager and his group latched onto the *obvious* decision statement, which was a decision about how to reduce costs. We all have the tendency to anchor our thinking to the information that is most readily available. By taking into account the thinking of a range of informed individuals, we are less likely to end up with an inappropriately narrow decision statement.

5 IDENTIFYING YOUR VALUES

Each decision that you face should have a purpose. This purpose is specified by your values for that decision, which identify all that you care about in making it. So, once you create your decision statement for a decision, your first critical thoughts need to focus on your values for that decision. Collectively, these values provide the basis for a logically sound and justifiable decision process. They nudge you to focus all of your thinking in making the decision on what you want to achieve. Using your values to stimulate thoughts about how best to achieve what you want makes good sense. How could you productively think about achieving what you want without knowing what you want?

A simple example to clarify the meaning of the term "values" as used in this book is useful. Suppose that you are trying to select a birthday present for a special person. You care about both the cost and quality of the present, as well as your desire to please that special person. Therefore, cost, quality, and pleasing the special person are your three initial values for the decision. It would be useful to define "quality" more specifically, as it would likely be different depending on whether the present is clothing, a watch, or a weekend trip.

For almost all of your decisions, more than one value is relevant, but you may not immediately recognize this. For the rather simple decision about what movie to see alone this evening, you may initially think your only value is enjoyment. You look in the newspaper and find the best one, but the theater is 30 minutes away. You don't want to travel that far, so you find a movie that is almost as enjoyable but about 10 minutes away. Your second value, unrecognized initially, concerns travel time.

Where Do Values Come From? It is *your values* that are relevant for your decisions. Your values for a decision must result from your thinking. If someone else, or a common understanding (or misunderstanding), suggests appropriate values for a specific decision that you face, you should independently decide

> **The values for your decisions must be specified by you. There are no externally determined correct values for your decisions.**

whether these values are appropriate for your decision.

Here is an example. Many financial advisors act as if the only appropriate values for investing are financial, such as to provide a high return, to avoid losses, to provide income, and to minimize volatility. If you accept this assumption, knowingly or blindly, you should clearly prefer a stock with a return of 8 percent annually to another stock with a return of 6 percent. Yet many individuals do not have such simple investment preferences. In addition to preferring a high return from your stock investments, your values may include investing in a product you believe in or wanting to support smaller companies, local companies, environmentally friendly companies, or companies that treat employees well.

► **A Stock Investment**
Suppose that you have just the following two values: provide a higher financial return and avoid supporting a company whose products harm people. With these values, you may prefer a 6 percent return from an investment in an organic food products company to an 8 percent return from a cigarette manufacturer. This investment would be inconsistent with the advice of financial advisors concerned only with financial returns. However, based on your values, such a preference makes sense, and is certainly consistent with my concept of a logical decision. Whatever your values are, it is reasonable, rational, and important to use them to guide your decisions. ◄

It is crucial to understand your values for your decisions. Knowing your values for a decision naturally nudges you to choose an alternative more consistent with your interests. Inappropriate or incomplete values can lead you to identify and pursue greatly inferior alternatives.

> **Knowing your values for a decision strongly nudges you to choose an alternative more consistent with your interests.**

Suppose that you are looking for a job and have interviews planned with a few companies. Do your values indicate what you want to achieve in each interview? In discussions with some job hunters, I have been told that the purpose of the interview is to decide if you want a job there or not. Big mistake! If you are even possibly interested in working for the company, your key value in any job interview should be to enhance your chances of obtaining an offer. Recognizing this key value is a strong nudge that guides you to make better decisions in your interview. You can reject an offer to work at a company, but you cannot choose to work there if you do not receive an offer.

Once you receive an offer, you face a separate decision about whether you want the job or not. If you do not understand your values for a decision, the alternatives that you think of and the one you choose (i.e., in this case, how to act in a job interview) may significantly hurt your chances of achieving what you want.

Identifying the Relevant Values for Your Decisions Is Difficult

When individuals face a decision that they believe is important, you might suspect that they know their values. All they would need to do is take a couple of minutes and make a list of their values. Yet, for important decisions worthy of thought, identifying your values for the decision is often difficult. Specifically, when individuals or organizations try to list their values for an important decision, several relevant values are often missing. Many consulting experiences and several scientific experiments document this reality.[1] One important case is illustrated in the following example.[2]

▶ Selecting an MBA Internship
A full-time MBA program usually involves classes in two academic years with an internship in the summer between those years. This internship is very important because MBA students are trying to identify what work they like to do and, possibly, where to work after graduating. At a large and respected university, I was asked to

present a lecture on decision-making to the first-year MBA class. To make key points more relevant to the audience, I arranged to have the students provide useful information about their decision-making in an electronically administered homework assignment, which they knew would be graded mainly for effort, to be completed prior to my lecture.

There were 295 participants, almost all of them in the first-year class. One early question asked each student to list all of the values that he or she hoped to achieve during the internship. Independently, prior to the homework assignment, colleagues and friends helped me generate a master list of 32 values that an MBA student might find appropriate for his or her decision. The master list is given in Table 5.1. On the homework, after the student had listed all of the values for an internship that came to mind, they were all provided with this master list and asked to check all of the values that were appropriate for them. They were then asked to match each value that they initially generated to any value on the master list with the same meaning.

The results will likely surprise you. On average, the students listed 6.4 values on their initial lists. Yet, on average, they checked 20.1 values on the master list. Even when they were making a seriously effort, the students were initially able to list only 32 percent of their values for one of the most important decisions that an MBA student faces.

One possible explanation might be that the students originally listed their important values, and those other values subsequently checked on the master list were much less relevant. This was checked by asking the students to rate the relative importance of each value that they deemed to be personally relevant on a scale from 1, meaning very low importance, to 9, meaning very high importance. The average rating of the values originally listed by the students was 7.28 and the average rating of those values not initially identified by the students, but subsequently recognized and checked on the master list, was 7.23. Essentially, there was no difference in the importance of the self-identified and originally neglected objectives. The implication is that almost all individuals failed to recognize many of the relevant values for a decision that they deemed to be personally very important. ◄

It should be noted that the MBA students in the experiment were young professionals, with much more experience and

Table 5.1 Master List of Values Possibly Relevant to an MBA Internship

I would like to choose an internship that...

Is at a well-recognized/-respected company
Allows me to meet interesting people
Is with an organization that I am passionate about
Uses skills I have learned in my first year of business school
Improves my attractiveness for full-time job offers
Helps me become more savvy about office politics
Allows me to experience a new geographical area
Offers experience leading team projects
Helps me improve my analytical skills
Is in a specific location (e.g., near family or friends)
Is enjoyable to do
Enhances my knowledge in a particular industry
Could lead to a full-time offer from that firm
Compensates me well
Provides information to help select a job after graduation
Enhances my resume
Helps me develop my leadership skills
Helps me improve my communication skills
Provides flexibility for personal interests during the summer
Gives me a substantial project of which I can feel ownership
Provides opportunities to interact with senior managers
Is with a company whose culture I identify with
Gives me pride from landing a prestigious internship
Provides a structured program for learning and training
Is professionally challenging
Involves working with a diverse group of people
Offers the chance to learn new skills
Helps me decide what courses and skills I need to develop
  next year
Is at a company that sponsors work visas for placement in US
  offices
Helps me make good networking contacts
Is a job that I would like to do full-time after graduation
Helps me decide whether the internship field is good for me in the
  long term

motivation than the fresh-
man psychology students
who participate in many
university experiments.
These MBA students had on
average three to four years
of work experience after

> **Identifying values for a decision is difficult. When listing values for an important decision, individuals frequently omit many relevant ones.**

their original university degree and were typically 26 to 28 years old. This highlights the fact that we all have difficulties articulating values for our decisions.

There are numerous informal experiments that I have carried out with friends and colleagues to demonstrate this fact. An individual may mention to me that he is going to take a one-week vacation somewhere next month. I ask him how he will select where to go. He may respond that he will check out a few possibilities to see what is available and then choose a trip that is relatively inexpensive and will not take too long to get there. I might follow up with: "What do you want to achieve by this vacation?" The response may be to get away from the rat race and catch up on some reading. There should be numerous possible alternatives that all achieve his four listed values—inexpensive, short travel time, avoiding the rat race, and doing some reading—so these values will not differentiate what would be good alternatives from bad alternatives.

This sounds like a decision to fill a one-week period of time. No values were mentioned that would help identify and evaluate alternatives for the week or make this trip a high-quality investment of the traveler's time, money, and effort. Such values may include seeing natural beauty and wildlife, meeting people with a different background, experiencing a culture different from that at home, pursuing outdoor activities, learning something new, eating healthy food, experiencing a different cuisine, or seeing old friends.

You will easily be able to duplicate this experience with your friends, family members, or coworkers. In the appropriate circumstance, people may mention an important decision they are considering. Such decisions include changing one's residence, buying a house, quitting the current job, finding or choosing another job, taking six months off for a grand trip, getting engaged, addressing an important medical condition, choosing a school for their child, finding appropriate care or a nursing home for a parent, or retiring. Ask them what their values are for this important decision. Then you should be able to think of some additional values that they may have omitted. Ask them if any of these values are possibly relevant, and it is likely that some are. Not only will you find out that they omitted some values, but you will help them identify those values. Once you have finished this chapter, you will be in a position to help identify more of their omitted values, as well as more of the values for your decisions.

If you are thinking something along the lines of "I understand that most other people have trouble identifying their values, but I have thought about mine and know them," you may be correct, and therefore a member of a remarkably small group of individuals. Some world-renowned individuals have recognized that identifying all of their values for a decision is extremely difficult. Benjamin Franklin said that important decisions "are difficult, chiefly because while we have them under consideration, all the reasons pro and con are not present in the mind at the same time, but sometimes some set present themselves, and at other times another, the first being out of sight."[3] Franklin's pros and cons refer to values. Friedrich Nietzsche said: "Forgetting our objectives is the most frequent stupidity in which we indulge ourselves."[4] Nietzsche used the word "objectives" to mean "values."

I am one of the individuals referred to by Franklin and Nietzsche, as I know that sometimes I do not recognize some significant values when facing an important personal decision. I have learned and relearned this from personal experiences and enjoyable interactions with friends. After I have thought about my values for a decision worthy of thought, I sometimes describe this decision to friends and ask them what they think might be important values of this decision. I ask them to view it first from my perspective, as they know me, and then from their perspective if they faced the same decision. Even though I might have given careful thought to my values for this decision, if I separately ask five friends, someone will often suggest relevant values that had not occurred to me.

If you think that Franklin's and Nietzsche's comments do not apply to you, run the same experiment. Create a list of your values for a significant decision that you currently face that is not similar to decisions you have previously faced. Examples may include decisions about negotiating a long-term lease for a business office, where to locate a new warehouse, whether and where to get an advanced degree, how to help your adult sibling who is clearly having personal difficulties, and what treatment to have for a serious medical condition. Ask five friends separately about the values they can think of that seem appropriate for you to consider in your decision. If you ask your friends to think hard and then discuss their thoughts for a couple of minutes with each, it is very likely that you will get some useful ideas to expand your initial set of relevant values.

If you are not sure that you recognize all of your values for a decision, then you should consciously focus your attention on identifying as many of your relevant values as you can. If you feel that you know all of your relevant values, your judgment is likely optimistic. In this case, you should also consciously focus your attention on identifying as many additional values relevant to your decision as you can. The following section has numerous ideas to stimulate your thinking in ways that will help you identify relevant, but previously unrecognized, values for your decisions.

A Process to Identify Your Values for a Decision

Your initial serious thinking about any decision worthy of thought should focus on values. However, decision-makers often pass over thinking about values and dive into solving their decision by identifying an acceptable alternative. It is folly to assume that one can make a high-quality decision without having a thorough understanding of the values that define the meaning of "high-quality" for that decision. Each identified value is a nudge to help you make a better decision.

Who should identify the values for your decision? When I ask this in presentations on decision-making, I usually get some "Is this a trick question?" looks. Your values represent what you care about in your decisions, so, clearly, you should identify your values. Fortunately, you always have access to the world's expert on your values. You are that expert!

> You are the world's expert on your values. To identify your values for an important decision requires deep probing of your thoughts and feelings.

Identifying values for a decision necessitates creative thought, so no guidelines are required as to how values should be initially expressed. The imposition of guidelines at this stage could restrict the creative thought process by diverting your attention to whether a particular thought is a value or not or how to appropriately state that value. The result may be a less complete set of potential values for your decision. Thus, when thinking about what you care about in making your decision, anything that comes to mind is either a value or the basis for a value relevant to that decision, and you can list these thoughts any way you want.

Identifying a complete set of all of your values for a decision requires hard, but enjoyable and energizing, thought. To address the difficulties of expressing a complete set of values for a decision, this section describes four simple-to-follow steps to help you identify your values. The first step is to produce a wish list of everything that you can think of that you care about regarding your decision. The second step provides several tactics to stimulate your thinking and expand your list. The third step is to ask others for suggestions that may lead to new values that should be on your list. The fourth step uses your values generated in the first three steps to systematically search for possible missing values.

Step 1. A Wish List. The starting point for creating a complete list of values is your wish list. The decision statement that you created will help direct your thinking, as it indicates the focus of your decision.

It is useful to do your own thinking first on your decisions, as they are *your* decisions. Asking others for suggestions about values before you have thought about them in person may anchor your thinking to what they have said and lead to serious omissions.

Begin your wish list by writing down all potential values for your decision that readily come to mind. Include anything that you care about concerning the decision. Some items that you care about may not directly be a value that you want to achieve, but they may guide your thinking to identify relevant values. Any item that comes to mind should be included on your wish list, as it can be deleted later if you decide that it is not relevant.

Once you seem to have run out of ideas for your wish list, accept the notion that you probably still have several additional values that are not currently on the list. Two approaches will help you identify those additional values. The first approach is simply to challenge yourself to do better. Tell yourself that you can double the number of relevant values on your list—and then proceed to do it. Doubling may be difficult, but, even if you only get halfway there, the additional values may well be very important, and they will give you a nudge toward a better decision.

In conjunction with this, the second approach is useful if the decision being considered does not need to be made immediately. Allow yourself some time to identify values, as you may become conscious of them over the next few days. Especially for major life decisions, such as whether to have a child now or whether to accept a new position in your company that would require a move, tentatively make your decision, but do not announce it to anyone. Imagine that the alternative has already been implemented, and you are beginning to experience the consequences. Other relevant values may become apparent from this after-the-decision perspective.

Step 2. Value Stimulation Techniques. At this stage there are several stimulation techniques, listed in Table 5.2, that may lead you to identify additional potential values.

Emotions and Feelings. Your emotions and feelings, both positive and negative, can evoke crucial reasons to care about any decision. Thus, probing your emotions will often lead to relevant values for a decision. If you are enthusiastic in connection with the decision you face, introspection as to why you are enthusiastic may suggest some of your values for that decision. If you are discouraged and considering whether to end a personal relationship or to resign

> **Your feelings and emotions are important to incorporate in your decisions. Understanding these can often guide you to identifying relevant values.**

from a job, try to understand why it is that you are considering such an action. Use this understanding to create the values that you think may be better served by changing or dissolving your relationship. Make sure to understand whether you want any of your values to remain private. You do not need to communicate them to anyone, or even write them down, but it is important to be honest with yourself about such values, because they may help you make a better decision.

Alternatives. For some decisions, you can experience aspects of how it would be if you chose each of the alternatives. Such experiences often indicate something that you like or do not like about an alternative but that you had not previously

Table 5.2 Techniques to Help Identify Your Values

Technique	Questions
Emotions and feelings	Articulate your emotions and feelings evoked by the decision situation. Ask yourself why you care about these and how your alternatives may influence them.
Alternatives	Identify a perfect alternative, a terrible alternative, some reasonable alternatives, and the status quo. What is good or bad about each?
Consequences	Think about what might occur after you make your decision. What might occur that is good or bad?
Goals and constraints	Review any goals and constraints you have. What are your reasons for setting these?
Different perspectives	Suppose that a friend or a competitor you know faced your decision. What might their values be? If you faced this decision at some time in the future, what would concern you?
Strategic values	Consider the strategic values that you have for guiding your life or your organization. Are any of these values, or aspects of them, relevant to this decision?
Disappointment and regret	After you have experienced the consequences of your decision, what might disappoint you and what might you regret?
Generic values	What values have you had in the past for the same or similar decisions that you have faced? Are these relevant now?

recognized as being important. This recognition indicates relevant values for your decision. Examples include test-driving vehicles that you may purchase, visiting homes for which you may make an offer, touring universities that you are considering attending, and temporary participation in social or athletic clubs.

In other situations, think of any alternative, hypothetical or real, and ask yourself what is good or bad about this alternative. Any response that you have likely indicates a value relevant to your decision. Imagine you are hiring a personal assistant. Consider an individual you know who you greatly respect. Even though there may be no possibility of that individual being interested in the position, ask yourself what skills he or she has that would be great in that position. Your thought may be of the ability to recognize potential difficulties that might occur in future situations and proactively take steps to reduce both the chances of their occurrence and their significance if they do occur. Recognizing potential difficulties and reducing the occurrence of such difficulties are potential values for your decision. You can also compare pairs of potential alternative candidates for the position and identify the relative advantages of each candidate. These advantages also indicate values relevant to your decision.

Consequences. Thoughts about possible consequences of the decision can stimulate the identification of values in a similar way. Suppose that you are planning a large party in your home. Explicitly consider how it could end up being a big failure. As a result, a rare possible consequence that flashes into your mind is ruining historical paintings of great personal value. This suggests two values: ensure there is no damage to the specific historical paintings; and, more generally, minimize any damage to your house or possessions.

Goals and Constraints. Goals and constraints directly suggest relevant values, but usually they should not be directly used to evaluate alternatives. Suppose that a well-to-do individual investor had the goal that each investment should produce an expected return of at least 8 percent annually and the constraint that no investment should ever lose money. These directly suggest the respective values of maximizing return and minimizing losses. Now consider two one-year investments: investment A yields 9 percent exactly and investment B will most likely, interpreted by the investor to mean a 90 percent chance, have a 16 percent return, but it also has a 10 percent chance of actually losing 2 percent. Investment A meets both the 8 percent goal and the 0 percent constraint, whereas investment B meets the goal but fails to meet the constraint. However, investment B may be much more appealing to the investor.

Goals and constraints do not account for the fact that exceeding a goal by a large amount could be more important than failing to meet a constraint by a small amount. Values created from goals and constraints do account for such circumstances.

Different Perspectives. Changing your perspective for thinking about potential values may be insightful. One different perspective is to assume that someone other than you—say a friend, a person you respect, or a competitor—faces the same decision that you now face. Imagine what his or her values might be. For each such value, consider whether it, or something like it or opposite to it, would be an appropriate value for you. Suppose that you are about to put your house up for sale. Of course, one value is to sell it at a high price, and this might be the only value that you have thought of, as it is important and hard to miss. Considering what a particular friend may value if she were selling her similar house, you may think that she would also value the convenience of living in her home while the house was for sale and the avoidance of legal hassles during the process. You may recognize that both are also your values.

We naturally tend to view our values for decisions faced today from the perspective of today. Yet some of these decisions have consequences for many years in the future. Hence, it might be useful to also view a decision being faced now from the perspective of looking back from ten years in the future. Suppose that you are considering changing your job from a technical position to one concerned with marketing and strategy in the same company. Viewed from today, you may identify values such as convenience, comfort, pride in doing high-quality work, and enjoyable colleagues. Viewed from the future, you may additionally recognize broader values, such as to enhance management skills, to have secure employment, and to understand how the entire business works.

Strategic Values. You likely have daydreamed about how you would like your life to be in the future. In doing so, you may also have thought about values relevant to all of the decisions in your life. These strategic values are broad and they may be relevant to specific decisions that you face. If one of your strategic values is to treat others fairly and with respect, this suggests specific values in numerous personal and work decisions. In managing a group of individuals at work, the resulting values may include to communicate clearly to your staff, to acknowledge significant individual contributions, and to promote employees on the basis of merit.

Many individuals have a strategic value—to spend more time with their family—so a value of spending quality time with different members for your family would be relevant to many decisions. Chapter 10 is specifically concerned with developing strategic life values and strategic organizational values.

Disappointment and Regret. After a decision has been made, you may be disappointed with the consequences and/or regret that you did not choose another alternative that perhaps had a better chance to avoid those specific consequences. You can also anticipate potential disappointments or regrets associated with different alternatives prior to choosing an alternative. Your natural desire is to avoid being disappointed or experiencing regret. For any particular decision, these desires can be accounted for by including values pertaining to the potential causes of any disappointment or regret.

Suppose that you are offered the opportunity to invest some funds in a private investment mainly with friends and acquaintances. You review all of the prospective financial information, and the expected rate of return is high. However, you realize that you would be very disappointed and would regret making the investment if you ended up losing any funds. The value of avoiding any financial losses would be more appropriate to capture your feelings than a value such as minimizing regret.

Generic Values. You frequently face decisions that have features similar to other decisions that you have often faced previously. Examples include chairing business meetings, organizing non-profit functions, scheduling airline trips, and going on weekend excursions. Over time, you can develop a generic set of values for each of these types of decisions. Each time a specific decision arises, you can check this generic list for any values relevant to the specific decision. After the chosen event occurs, you can review what you liked and disliked about it, and see if it met your expectations. This may suggest new values that should be added to your generic list. Such lists are, essentially, a list of specific nudges that may be useful for making similar decisions in the future.

Step 3. Ask Others for Suggested Values. Friends, colleagues, and advisors can offer insight into the values relevant to your decisions. For a difficult personal decision, a good friend may be a source of useful suggestions about relevant values. He or she knows you well and, because of your discussions, may be quite familiar with the substance of your decision. You might ask him or her: "What do you think I should do?" With decisions having more than two alternatives, you might ask: "Are there any alternatives that you think I should and/or should not choose?"

Given a definitive response about an alternative to choose or omit, inquire about how your friend reached that conclusion. You might ask about the pros and cons of the alternatives. If the original response was noncommittal, inquire about the values he or she would use to make the decision. For some important decisions, we have a tendency to anguish over specific details about readily identifiable values, and not recognize other important values that are not so immediate and apparent. A friend who is not deeply involved in your decision may easily see the larger picture and suggest previously missing values.

Suppose that you work in the United States for an international company that has its corporate office in Switzerland. Your vice president recently inquired about your potential interest in a two-year stint at the corporate office. Now, you and a respected colleague in another division of your company are on a business trip having dinner together. It likely would be easy to ask: "What are the main considerations that you would take into account in deciding whether you should accept such an assignment?" You may choose to focus the discussion on professional considerations and personal considerations separately. Depending on your relationship with your associate, you could use ideas in step 2 above to probe more deeply into any responses that interested you.

Professional advisors are an excellent source for values that may be relevant to you. If you have a medical or dental problem for which there are different approaches to consider, you should ask knowledgeable professionals what the pros and cons are of those approaches. The responses would likely suggest some values that you might not have generated on your own. Note that this inquiry is very different from asking what alternative he or she thinks is best for your circumstances. When you do receive such advice, it is useful to inquire about what other alternatives are available. And, sequentially, ask for the advisor's views on the relative pros and cons of each of the alternatives. These pros and cons may suggest values you had not recognized. In addition, if you have already identified some of your values for the decision, ask about how each alternative measures up on these values. The advisor's thoughts in this discussion will allow you to better appraise how well the various alternatives meet your values.

For important decisions that you are facing for the first time, it is often useful to talk to others who have faced the same or a similar decision in the past. Examples include deciding about taking a stint in the main corporate office, as discussed above; how to report suspected illegal activity in your company to management; selecting a spouse or a partner for life; dealing with an important aspect of raising a child; and planning care and help for an elderly parent or relative. For almost all decisions such as these, there are many individuals who have faced that decision before you. Their experiences of thinking about and choosing alternatives and living through the consequences of those alternatives are an excellent source to stimulate your thoughts and uncover values relevant to your decision.

Step 4. Using Previously Identified Values to Identify Additional Values. Values that you have already articulated for a decision are a useful source for identifying additional relevant values. Three simple questions applied to previously specified values can identify additional relevant values. These questions are "What do you mean by that value?," "Why is that value important?," and "How is achievement of that value influenced?."

Suppose that you are in the enviable position of having job offers from several companies at once and you need to choose one. You have identified your initial values for your job as interesting work, a good salary, and convenience. Asking yourself what you mean by "interesting work" may suggest working on particular types of substantial issues, knowing several coworkers, having enjoyable coworkers, avoiding involvement in legal and regulatory affairs, and being able to have business decisions rapidly made. Considering how your work could be more interesting might suggest values such as interacting professionally with individuals in the company and outside, the necessity of some business trips, continuous learning, and not being stuck at your desk all day.

Reviewing what you mean by "a good salary" may indicate that ownership of shares is separately relevant or that you want a company where you will immediately be vested in a retirement plan. Your introspection as to why you care about "convenience" may indicate a value of having your work close to home. This in turn may suggest that you want to avoid long commutes, which, among other things, increases available time for your personal life.

Clarifying Your Values

Once you have created the list of potential values for your decision, each value should be converted into an objective, which more clearly describes what you want to achieve with respect to that value by making the decision. Each objective is also a value, with a common format of

To clarify the meaning of each value, state it as an objective, using a verb followed by an object. An objective indicates what you want to achieve regarding that value by making that decision. Examples are "reduce costs," "minimize environmental degradation," and "use my time more effectively."

a verb and an object. This process is easily understood with an example.

Consider a daughter, who, with her father, is deciding which of several retirement communities best meets her father's needs and desires. They have collectively gone through procedures mentioned earlier in this chapter and created the potential values listed in Table 5.3. The potential values are stated in several forms, which indicate different ways that values may come to mind and be expressed by an individual facing a decision. There is no requirement for the format in which values are originally stated, because the purpose is to specify values any way they are perceived by the decision-maker. The third column in Table 5.3 converts each of the stated values into the common form of an objective.

In stating each value as an objective, it is useful to carefully think about the intended meaning of that value and ensure this meaning is made clear by the wording of the corresponding objective. Consider the first value in Table 5.3, namely woodworking. If the father is currently a novice at woodworking, the objective may be to learn woodworking. If he has some experience, the objective may be to improve his woodworking skills. If he is already an experienced woodworker, it may be that what the woodworking value meant was that the community had a woodworking shop. Or the woodworking value could suggest two objectives, such as "have access to a woodworking shop" and "create useful wooden objects."

For the value "account for respiratory condition," the objective might be either "avoid aggravating a respiratory condition" or

Table 5.3 Values Converted into a Common Format as Objectives

Potential value as originally stated	Stated as	Restated value stated as an objective
Woodworking	Activity	Have access to a woodworking shop
Account for respiratory condition	Circumstance	Avoid aggravating the respiratory condition
Not need a car	Concern	Have necessary goods and services nearby
Affordable	Criterion	Minimize living costs
Near my daughter	Desire	Minimize travel time from daughter's home
Sunshine over 70 percent of the time	Goal	Enjoy much sunshine
Want to enjoy outdoor activities	Hope	Pursue outdoor activities
Distance to major medical center	Metric	Have good access to medical care
Availability of many interesting people and activities	Multiple values	1. Make new interesting friends 2. Spend time doing interesting and enjoyable activities
Minimize daily inconveniences	Objective	Minimize daily inconveniences
The community is conveniently located	Sentence	Have good access to a thriving local community
Medical care	Service	Have close emergency care and access to high-quality medical services
The existence of facilities for hobbies and clubs	Situation	Participate in hobbies and clubs
Satisfaction	State	Enjoy living in community

Note: Example for the decision of selecting a retirement community for one's father.

"improve the respiratory condition." The value "affordable" could initially be considered to mean "minimize housing costs" only, but on further reflection it may be clear that a better objective expressing this value is "minimize living costs." The value originally stated as "availability of many interesting people and activities" is an example that indicates two separate values, which might be stated as "make interesting new friends" and "spend time doing interesting and enjoyable activities."

The originally stated value "near my daughter" immediately suggests the objective "minimize distance from daughter's home." With any objective, you should reflect on whether that objective really indicates what you want to achieve. Suppose that there were two retirement communities under consideration. One was only 30 miles away from the daughter's home, but would require taking municipal transit, and, including walking at each end, the average time would be two hours each way. The other community was 55 miles away, but in an opposite direction where the door-to-door trip would be an hour and 10 minutes. If you evaluated these alternatives on distance, the first retirement community seems roughly twice as good as the second. But evaluating them on what you later clarify as your real values, namely travel time and bringing your father to your house for visits, the second community is about twice as good as the former. The intent of your original value is better described by the objective "minimize travel time from daughter's home." The relatively easy door-to-door travel by car also makes it much easier for the father to visit his daughter at her home, which is a new value recognized only in this process of clarifying the meanings of the originally stated values.

The values for your decision, now stated as objectives, should guide all of your thinking and effort in making that decision. Each objective helps you think more clearly about your decision and recognize the full implications of the alternatives. The objectives also promote the creation of innovative alternatives, the recognition of useful information worth gathering, and thorough appraisals of the desirability of alternatives. Each of these can nudge you to make a more informed and better decision. Organizing your objectives so that you can clearly understand the relationships between them will further clarify your decision and facilitate doing each of these tasks well.

Knowing that it is useful to state all values in the format of an objective, you may wonder why the process of identifying values and then stating them as objectives is not combined into one step.

The reason is to avoid disruptions to the creative process of identifying values, as these may limit the breadth of the values identified. Once all of the values are explicitly stated, it is straightforward to restate them as objectives. After some experience creating values for decisions, you may find it convenient to initially list your values as objectives, but it is still worth reviewing them to ensure that they fully characterize your real values.

Organizing Your Objectives

Suppose that you are the head of your household and the sole source of income. You have a spouse and two children. You just got the results of a test on a tumor and it is cancerous, but the doctors "caught it early" and they do not think it has spread. The contending alternatives seem to be surgery, chemotherapy, and radiation therapy. It is not a decision that anyone wants to make, but it is obviously very important to make an informed choice.

Since you, or any member of your family, had not previously faced a similar decision, you and your spouse thought hard and used the procedures discussed earlier in this chapter to create the set of objectives listed in Table 5.4 for your decision. Organizing the objectives, which involves specifying the basic relationships among the objectives, will be useful. There are two important relationships between pairs of objectives.

Means versus Ends Objectives. A means–ends relationship refers to a situation where the degree to which one objective is achieved influences, positively or negatively, the degree to which a second objective is achieved. In this case, we refer to the first objective as a means objective and the second as an ends objective. The objective "get all the cancer" is a means objective to the objective "reduce the likelihood of serious complications," which is the ends objective in this relationship. "Reduce the likelihood of serious complications" is also a means objective to several other objectives, including "limit any pain and suffering" and "limit time in the hospital." A means objective can have more than one ends objective, and an ends objective can have more than one means. For example, "minimize medical risks of treatment" is also a means to "reduce the likelihood of serious complications."

Why is it important to reduce the likelihood of serious complications? One response is that reducing serious complications is a means to better achieving the objective "reduce the likelihood of

Table 5.4 Set of Objectives for Cancer Treatment

Get all the cancer
Avoid a recurrence of cancer
Ensure that the cancer doesn't spread
Minimize medical risks of treatment
Minimize medical risks of cancer
Reduce the likelihood of death in the near future
Reduce the likelihood of serious complications
Minimize personal costs of the entire procedure
Have insurance pay the maximum possible
Limit any pain and suffering
Minimize inconvenience to oneself
Have a comfortable hospital room
Avoid worry about treatment
Have trust in doctors
Minimize inconvenience to family
Receive good communication
Have the best physicians
Receive high-quality healthcare
Limit time in hospital
Minimize limits on activities after recuperation
Receive friendly service at the hospital

---

death in the near future." So why is reducing the likelihood of death important? Your response probably is "It obviously is important." This objective is important independent of any influence it may have on achieving any other objectives in the cancer treatment decision. Such an objective is referred to as a fundamental objective for the decision. Each fundamental objective is usually not also a means to any other objective for the decision, but it can be in specific decisions.

Distinguishing between the means objectives and the fundamental

> **Means objectives are important only for their implications for achieving fundamental objectives. Only the fundamental objectives should be used to evaluate alternatives, which avoids the double-counting of potential consequences and reduces complexity.**

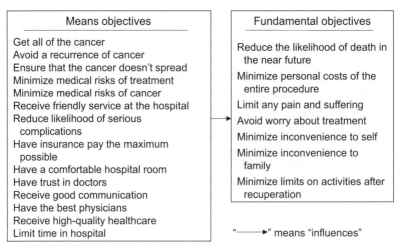

Means objectives	Fundamental objectives

Get all of the cancer
Avoid a recurrence of cancer
Ensure that the cancer doesn't spread
Minimize medical risks of treatment
Minimize medical risks of cancer
Receive friendly service at the hospital
Reduce likelihood of serious
   complications
Have insurance pay the maximum
   possible
Have a comfortable hospital room
Have trust in doctors
Receive good communication
Have the best physicians
Receive high-quality healthcare
Limit time in hospital
	Reduce the likelihood of death in
	   the near future
	Minimize personal costs of the
	   entire procedure
	Limit any pain and suffering
	Avoid worry about treatment
	Minimize inconvenience to self
	Minimize inconvenience to
	   family
	Minimize limits on activities after
	   recuperation

"———▸" means "influences"

Figure 5.1 Distinguishing between Means and Fundamental Objectives for Cancer Treatment

objectives in the decision is very useful. It reduces the complexity of the decision you are facing and focuses attention on what is crucial. Each of your means objectives is a stimulus to create alternatives or improve existing alternatives to address the corresponding decision, as discussed in Chapter 6.

Only your fundamental objectives should be used to evaluate alternatives. If your evaluation includes means objectives, which are relevant only because of their impacts on fundamental objectives, you are double-counting some of the pros and/or cons. Eliminating the consideration of means objectives in evaluating alternatives usually substantially reduces the number of objectives appropriate for that evaluation. This makes it easier to do a better evaluation, which naturally nudges you toward making a better decision. Figure 5.1 separates the means objectives and fundamental objectives for the cancer treatment decision and relates them by an arrow indicating "influences." There are only seven fundamental objectives for evaluating and comparing alternatives, whereas there are 21 total objectives for the decision.

Specifying Details of Objectives. The second basic relationship between pairs of objectives is one of specification, where one objective is a component of a second objective and specifies in more detail what is meant by that second objective. Consider, for

Table 5.5 Fundamental Objectives for Evaluating Cancer
Treatment

Minimize the likelihood of death in the near future
Minimize limits on activities after recuperation
Minimize personal costs of the entire procedure
    for the hospital
    for physicians
    for recovery
Minimize inconvenience to oneself and family
    limit any pain and suffering
    avoid worry about treatment
    limit time in hospital

---

example, what is meant by the objective "reduce the likelihood of serious complications." Part of the answer is to avoid a recurrence of cancer. Another part is to ensure that the cancer does not spread. These two latter objectives specify in more detail what is meant by the former. They answer the question "What do you mean by reducing the likelihood of serious complications?." The specification logic can sometimes be carried further when it is worthwhile to clarify the meaning of objectives. You could ask what is meant by "minimize limits on activities after recuperation." Here the response would specify the activities of concern.

The fundamental objectives for treating your cancer can be structured as shown in Table 5.5, with indentations indicating the components of the objective above them. This visualization better describes, and helps us to focus on, the main fundamental objectives of the decision.

Two additions in Table 5.5 from the previous list of fundamental objectives included in Figure 5.1 are worth mentioning. The personal costs were specified in more detail by thinking about what personal costs are of concern. This led to the recognition of recovery costs that should be included. These recovery costs refer to lost income during absence from work, as well as any implications in terms of lost income potential. The inconvenience objectives regarding oneself and family were combined, as the components of each were essentially the same.

To evaluate alternatives for cancer treatment, one should compare them using the four main fundamental objectives in Table 5.5. In such comparisons, each main objective must account for all corresponding component objectives, so personal costs include costs for the hospital, physicians, and recovery.

It is sometimes useful to specify the means–ends relationships in greater detail to further clarify which means objectives influence which ends objectives in the decision being considered. Figure 5.2 illustrates this in what is referred to as a means–ends objectives diagram. An arrow from one objective to another indicates that the former is a means to the latter ends. Note that, to avoid clutter, Figure 5.2 indicates only the object of each objective rather than the entire objective. Indentations again specify in more detail the objective above it. As many of the means objectives affect several fundamental objectives, several means–ends arrows go to the set of fundamental objectives. High-quality health care is a means to each of the fundamental objectives. Insurance coverage affects personal costs, and aspects of inconvenience, such as worry and having a private hospital room.

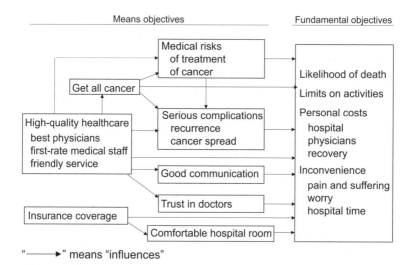

"──▶" means "influences"

Figure 5.2 A Means–Ends Diagram for Cancer Treatment

Two Values Relevant to All Decisions: Learning and Flexibility

There are two general values that should be considered as being potentially relevant to each of your decisions worthy of thought. These values are learning and flexibility. The corresponding objectives to state these values are "learn useful information for future decisions" and "have flexibility to adapt your decision in the future." Both of these are fundamental objectives of the decision that you are facing.

> **In every decision you make, there is the opportunity to learn something specific that is relevant to similar decisions in the future and something general that is relevant to your decision-making process.**

Learning. As stressed earlier, decision-making is an important personal skill. To improve your decision-making skills, you need to continually learn how to better make decisions and practice what you have learned. A useful way to promote learning is to include the value of learning in many decisions that you face. Every decision on which you use the ideas in this book to help make a better decision is an opportunity to practice what you have previously learned and to learn something to help make better future decisions.

The value of learning is most easily understood in repeated decisions. Some repeated decisions are obvious, such as commuting to work each day, subscribing annually to a journal or magazine, filing your taxes each year, and purchasing computers or automobiles over your lifetime. Other repeated decisions are not as easy to recognize. Examples are important meetings with your boss, routine group project meetings at work, discussions with your children about significant topics, dealing with important medical problems, interviewing for jobs, and organizing a party. In each of these decisions, you can learn from your decision today something that may be useful for similar decisions in the future. What you learned might be useful for hundreds of similar decisions, which collectively may result in a significant positive effect.

►**Filing Your Taxes**
In the United States, as in virtually every country, everyone who earns income in any specific year must pay annual income taxes.

The process requires filling out a tax form that has numerous questions about your income and expenses. Different sources of income and different types of expenses are treated differently for the purpose of calculating taxes owed. Decisions are made to categorize the sources of income and types of expenses. With the best of intentions, almost nobody, including many tax preparers, can file their taxes with everything done correctly given the complexity of and ambiguities in the federal tax code.

Once tax forms calculating how much you owe for your annual taxes are filed, the Internal Revenue Service (IRS) selects some of these for an audit to determine whether you reported your net income correctly and are therefore paying the correct amount of tax. Less than 1 percent of filed tax forms are randomly chosen for auditing, but this percentage increases for individuals with higher incomes and more expenses. An audit may require a lot of time from the individual being audited, could lead to financial penalties above any additional taxes owed, and can cause a good deal of stress.

The main objective for some individuals who file income taxes is to avoid an audit. Thus, their filing strategy is to give the government the benefit of any ambiguity about stating income and deducting expenses, and therefore they likely pay more than legally due. Suppose that this results in paying $2,000 more each year to presumably lower your chances of an audit. It may seem worth it if you filed taxes only once in your life. However, following that strategy for 50 years of filing taxes would cost you $100,000 that you did not owe, and you still would likely have an audit or two.

It is useful to view the filing of your taxes as a series of similar annual decisions; the usefulness of what you learn about from each annual filing and any audit is clearly relevant to all future filings. With this perspective, I have multiple objectives for my annual tax filings: to pay the appropriate amount owed, not to pay additional amounts not legally due, to avoid the inconvenience of an audit, to minimize the time required to prepare my taxes, and to learn from each filing process for future years. Therefore, the alternative that I choose is to report all of the required information as accurately as I can, realizing that this cannot be perfect.

After a few years of filing taxes, my taxes were randomly chosen for an audit. My meeting with the IRS auditor lasted about an hour with no change in my taxes. I learned something important for future tax decisions, namely that, if you have decent financial records, are not trying to cheat, and prepare for the meeting, you do not have much reason to worry and the audit is not that stressful. The most common negative finding is an inadvertent error, so I may need to pay a bit more tax to correct that error. However, if I had erroneously not paid my appropriate tax, I would not mind paying that correction and I would have learned something about the tax code that may be useful. ◄

A general insight from this example is that there are often advantages to view similar repeated decisions as a series. You can develop and compare potential policy alternatives (i.e., how to address the decision each time) that consider consequences attributed to the entire collection of decisions over time, rather than consider each year's decision separately. The repeated decision view clearly indicates the usefulness of a learning objective and its significance. What you learn need not be about a shortcoming in your decision-making; it may be about something you did very well that you can consciously use in many future decisions.

Learning is relevant not only to repeated decisions but for all future decisions worthy of thought. What you learned to improve your effectiveness in meetings with your manager may be useful in any meeting of importance to you. Suppose that you feel that you performed poorly in an important interview for new job, which subsequently was not offered to you. Upon reflecting about what you could have done differently regarding that job interview, you may recognize that a realistic "practice interview" may be a great idea for any important interview in the future. What you learned from the negative consequences of a decision that you subsequently concluded was due to incomplete thinking may be useful to ensure that you do not make the same mistake again. What you learn over time from many decisions about how you can more effectively identify your values for a specific decision will offer benefits throughout your life.

Flexibility. The benefits of flexibility pertain to the decision you are currently making, when the consequences accrue over time. For some decisions, you realize that the ultimate consequences will result from a sequence of decisions. You will learn from the consequences of your first decisions, and this knowledge is useful for future related decisions. One important decision sequence of this type concerns selecting and pursuing a major as the focus of your college degree. Many students, quite reasonably, will not be sure of what to select as a major when they enter college. Some may have all possibilities open and others may feel that there are two or three possibilities. In either case, the decisions about courses to take now should include the value of learning about what major to pursue and the value of flexibility, keeping options available in order to minimize delays in meeting requirements to graduate once you select your major.

> **Flexibility provides you with options to adapt an alternative if circumstances relevant to the decision change or if the consequences appear to be less desirable than expected.**

For other decisions, flexibility provides you with options to adapt an alternative if you realize that the consequences will not be as good as desired. Such flexibility avoids potential constraints on future decisions. Suppose that your company and a major German firm have a critical meeting in Munich two weeks from now to finalize the agreements for a joint project. The meeting is scheduled over three days, Wednesday to Friday. You must leave your office in Austin, Texas, on Tuesday, as there is another meeting in your office that you cannot miss on Monday. Since there are no direct flights from Austin to Munich, your main alternatives are to fly to either Houston, Washington, DC, or Newark and switch planes for a flight to Munich. The total travel time through Houston is an hour less than the other options, but both Houston and Washington have only one nonstop flight per day. If that flight happens to be canceled, you will miss the first day of your meeting in Munich. On the other hand, Newark has two nonstop flights each day to Munich. If you make a reservation on the earlier flight, you have a backup flight if your flight is canceled and you would still arrive on time in Munich. The flexibility of this alternative may be well worth your additional one hour of total travel time.

You can often create or modify a proposed alternative to provide greater flexibility and better consequences. Timing is frequently a key. As a simple illustration, suppose that you own a small business and are on vacation with your family. It is early in the morning and you receive an email that will require you to review and modify an important document by tomorrow evening. The review may require anywhere from one to three hours of your time. In such situations, where there is one required task (i.e., the review) and another desired event (i.e., vacationing with family), there are major benefits, arising from flexibility, from doing the required task first. By doing the required task first, you will sooner know how long the task took, which allows you to better plan and have a longer uninterrupted time for the subsequent desired event. Also, you would not be mentally distracted by the required task while enjoying the desired event with your family. If there is some information missing for you to adequately complete the required task, you will realize it sooner and there will be more time and opportunities to receive the needed information. And there will be less stress to finish the required task on time. All this means that you will likely do a better job on the required task and minimize the amount of disruption to your desired event.

You probably recognize the relevance of learning and flexibility as values in your decisions worthy of thought. But what should you do about them? How can you incorporate them into your decisions? The message is simple. Once you have essentially decided on the main elements of the alternative that you think is best, give yourself a nudge and ask yourself if there are any modifications or add-ons to that alternative that would provide useful learning or desirable flexibility. Often slight modifications that are easy to include come to mind, which subsequently leads to a revised alternative with better consequences.

Additional Thoughts for Decisions in Organizations

Values characterize the purpose of any organizational decision. Just as in personal decisions, the crucial step in the decision-making process is to articulate the relevant values explicitly. The only differences in expressing organizational values occur because there may be more than one individual involved in making the decision.

The first new issue that arises is this: who should express the values for the organization's decision? In general, the answer is that each of the individuals involved in and responsible for the decision should express the values that they think are appropriate for the organizational decision.

> When a group is making a decision, the values of each member are relevant and should initially be identified separately. Subsequently the group should consider all identified values as constituting the set of group values, which defines a common purpose.

Often the group of decision-makers is clear. For example, when the executive group of the company is making a decision, the values of each member are relevant. However, if there is ever a question about whether or not a particular individual should express values for an organizational decision, it is usually fine to include his or her suggestions of values that could be included. Except for a bit of time, there is nothing lost by welcoming this participation. It may produce some values that were not expressed by others, and yet all agree that they are relevant. If the decision-makers think that some of the expressed values are irrelevant, they have the responsibility and authority to leave these out in their subsequent thinking.

In any organizational decision, values should initially be identified separately by each individual expressing values. This enhances the chances that each individual thinks hard about what the decision should achieve and, in general, yields a broader collective list of values. The process to articulate these values is exactly that described earlier in this chapter.

Next, the values from the individuals need to be combined to create an initial list of the organization's values for the decision being considered. Any value listed by at least one individual is initially included in the organization's list of values, which is usually broader than any individual's list. In this process, any value stated by more than one individual is of course listed just once. There are judgments necessary in this process, as individuals frequently use different vocabulary to express the same value. For example, if a group of three couples is jointly considering purchasing a country vacation cabin for both winter and summer activities, all six might express a value concerning its cost and a value concerning the ease of visiting the location. The cost concerns can probably be summarized with three values: purchase cost, annual operating costs, and travel costs. The "ease of visiting" values may be stated by different individuals as "near our home," "less than three hours away by car," "easy to get to," and "convenient." A brief discussion among the members may lead to agreement that an appropriate value is "travel time from home to cabin."

Once an original list of the organization's values for the decision has been composed, the members of the decision group should state each value as an objective. This makes it easier to understand the exact meaning of each value and agree on its relevance to a decision, modify it and then agree, or conclude that some stated values require more than one objective to thoroughly express them. The process will lead to an agreement on the set of values, articulated as objectives, which characterizes the decision. Furthermore, all the members understand where their originally stated values are included and feel that they are part of a team with a common purpose.

6   CREATING ALTERNATIVES

When facing a decision, an alternative is a possible course of action that you have the authority to choose. If you have not identified at least two alternatives, then you have nothing to choose. There is no decision. Yet we have all heard someone remark that, for a specific decision they face, there is only one available alternative. What this likely means is there is only one alternative other than the status quo, sometimes referred to as the default or "do nothing" alternative, or that only one of the potential alternatives is an acceptable choice.

Alternatives, as used in this book, are defined such that only one alternative can be chosen from a set of alternatives for a specific decision. This is not a limitation, since all decisions can be stated as choosing a single alternative. Suppose that somebody makes a statement such as "We could choose alternative A, alternative B, or both A and B." However, by simply defining an alternative C to mean choosing both A and B, the decision would be to select only one of the three alternatives A, B, or C. I refer to A and B as elemental alternatives and to C as a compound alternative, when the distinction contributes to clarity of thinking.

The alternatives that you consider for a decision should be realistic, meaning that the decision-maker or someone affected by the decision thinks that it could turn out to be the best alternative. If you are making a decision about what car to purchase for your family, which includes four children, you would likely not consider a two-seat sports car to be a realistic alternative. So do not waste your time considering it.

Why You Should Create Alternatives

You want to have a set of good alternatives for any decision that you face. The reason is based on two simple facts about alternatives. First, if you have not thought of a particular alternative, you cannot choose it. Second, your chosen alternative can be no better than the best of the alternatives under consideration.

It follows from these facts that your ability to achieve what you want from any decision will sometimes depend more on the quality of the alternatives that you have identified than on the quality of your choice between those alternatives. Hence, it is important to focus some of your effort in decision-making on creating alternatives. If you create a new alternative that is subsequently evaluated as better than any of the previously recognized alternatives, you have given yourself a very strong nudge to make a better decision. However, when you are creating alternatives, it may not be immediately clear whether one alternative is better than others.

> **It is important to devote effort to creating alternatives, because**
>
> 1. **you cannot choose an alternative that you have not thought of, and**
> 2. **your chosen alternative can be no better than the best of the alternatives that you consider.**

There are some decisions for which there is no need to create alternatives. This occurs when you know all of the alternatives, which is not the same as when you think you know all of the alternatives. You are the judge of which of these, if either, is true for any specific decision that you face.

Suppose that you receive a marriage proposal from your significant other that requires thinking about. Your intuitive frame for your decision may be to accept or reject the offer, believing that your response must be "Yes" or "No." However, you may wish to consider whether other responses are realistic. You may feel that you and your significant other have not known each other long enough for a "Yes" response and respond with something such as: "If the proposal is still open in a year, I will probably say 'Yes.'" Or you might have a contingency: "We cannot get married until we both have graduated from college and have jobs." Suppose that, after thinking about possible alternatives, you believe that the only realistic choices are "Yes" or "No" and a response must be delivered soon. Then you could legitimately state that you know all the alternatives, and there is no need for any more effort to identify additional alternatives.

There are two general situations where it is useful to create realistic alternatives. One is when numerous potential alternatives can readily be identified, but most are not realistic. Suppose that you are moving to Houston and wish to purchase a home. You could obtain a list of all homes for sale, but many of these homes would likely be unrealistic for you: too large, too small, too expensive, or not in a desirable area. To identify and focus on realistic alternatives, you can efficiently eliminate the unrealistic alternatives with constraints. Suppose that it is clear to you that a house with three or more bedrooms is too large. Limit your consideration of houses to those with fewer than three bedrooms, which eliminates larger houses from consideration. If, with your savings and a mortgage, you could purchase at most a $300,000 home, all homes costing more than $300,000 can be eliminated. This process of screening out unrealistic alternatives is not particularly creative, but it saves time and helps you focus on identifying the realistic alternatives.

The other general situation requires creativity to generate alternatives, which is the main concern in this chapter. What if it seems that there are no realistic alternatives? For many decisions worthy of thought, there is nothing available such as a list of all of the potential alternatives. The situations regarding alternatives for these decisions might be characterized by one or more of the following.

- I actually have no idea what to do.
- I have no alternatives.
- I have a few alternatives, but I don't like any of them very much.
- I have thought about some alternatives, but I know there must be many others that I have not yet identified.
- I have some good alternatives, but I think I can identify at least one that is better.

For each of these cases, you can focus your thinking on creating alternatives to give yourself a nudge, which will often produce more desirable alternatives.

How Good Are Decision-Makers at Creating Alternatives?

The answer to this question is that some individuals are better than others, and there is a large variance among individuals. The more important fact is that each of us decision-makers can improve our abilities to create alternatives.

Numerous experiments have shown that individuals have difficulty creating a reasonably complete set of alternatives for a specific important decision.[1] In one set of experiments,[2] university students were presented five different personal decisions that they could easily envision facing and asked to create alternatives to solve them. One decision concerned a student who was uncomfortable with her roommate smoking marijuana in their dorm room. Different groups of participants were given different suggestions as to how to create alternatives and one group was given no advice. For the five decisions, the average number of alternatives individually created was between 5.27 and 6.47. Collectively, for the five separate decisions, the number of distinct alternatives generated ranged from 18 to 26. Individuals were identifying only a third to a fourth of the available alternatives.

Results such as these raise some important questions. Although these decisions were relevant to the study participants, they were not decisions personally faced by the participants. Would individuals do a better job generating alternatives if the decisions were actually being faced by those individuals? Are the participants generating the best of the potential alternatives and missing the less desirable ones or missing alternatives that are among the best? Siebert and I addressed these important questions in the following experiments.[3]

Most German university students whose studies include a business curriculum choose at least one internship with a business, non-profit, or government organization near the end of their studies. The intent of an internship is to learn practical knowledge about working full-time in the "real world" and enhance employment opportunities for the future. It is generally recognized as a significant experience, and students are motivated to benefit as much as possible from an internship.

Prior to conducting a study about creating alternatives, we managed a process to list all of the types of alternatives that an intern could pursue to enhance the quality of an upcoming internship. The master list ended up with 31 distinct types of alternatives, such as "apply skills that have been learned in the university," "ask a supervisor for a specific project or a task," "establish contact with supervisors," "contribute to a good work atmosphere," and "enhance skills in workshops and training courses."

Over 200 students planning an internship participated in the study, which was in four steps. In step 1, participants were asked to imagine that they had accepted an internship and instructed to list all of the alternatives that they could think of to benefit as much as possible from that internship. In step 2, participants were given the master list of the 31 alternatives and asked to check each alternative that they considered personally relevant. In step 3, as participants often choose different words for listing their alternatives from those on the master list, they had to match each of their alternatives to the corresponding type of alternative on the master list. In step 4, all of the alternatives either personally generated in step 1 or initially recognized in step 2 were ranked in terms of significance, which we defined as the likelihood that the individual would pursue the alternative during the internship. On average, individuals originally generated 6.66 distinct alternatives and they recognized 11.27 additional alternatives on the master list. So, for this important personal decision, individuals created only about a third—37 percent—of the possible alternatives later recognized as relevant and important to them.

Perhaps surprisingly, individuals were unable to personally identify at least a half of their highest-ranked alternatives. Specifically, only 44 percent of the participants personally identified the alternative that they ranked as their most significant. Of their personal top-five-ranked alternatives, participants identified only 1.86 on average. Of their top-ten-ranked alternatives, participants personally identified only 3.50 on average.

Pitfalls in Creating Alternatives

Before discussing procedures to stimulate your thinking and creativity to generate better alternatives, it is worthwhile describing common pitfalls that result in inadequate attention being spent on the creation of alternatives. The basic cause of not creating alternatives for decisions when it would be worthwhile to do so is that the decision-maker's

> **The main reason leading to a less than desirable set of alternatives for a decision is not allocating time to create better alternatives.**

mind is never fully engaged in this activity. This pitfall can take many forms.

Not Allocating Time to Create Alternatives. Too often a decision-maker does not consciously recognize the possibility or the potential value of creating alternatives. Thus, no effort is allocated to this endeavor. The decision-maker may feel that the alternatives are, essentially, obvious or that he or she has no role to play in creating alternatives. The decision faced is simply to choose the best of those already available. In planning a three-day summer camping trip to the mountains, a couple decided to go to the same place as last year. That trip turned out to be pretty good, and it would be easier going there again this year. This alternative might work out if the intent is to have an okay time with little effort. However, it may be a poor choice for individuals with different aspirations.

Sometimes no time is spent creating alternatives because the decision-maker just wants to "solve the problem" and move on. If you and your spouse plan to take a two-week trip to Alaska this summer, you may face a decision of choosing a summer program for your ten-year-old child for the period of time when you will be gone. Some parents may select the first program they find that meets the single objective of "take care of our child at the appropriate time." This is the "solve it and move on" approach. Other parents would find this approach inappropriate, and would identify a few alternative summer programs and select one based on additional objectives for their child in terms of engaging in interesting activities, building skills, and having an enjoyable experience.

Stopping the Search for Alternatives after One Alternative Is Identified. Imagine that a friend told you that her company had a position to be filled and thought that you would be an excellent prospect. Would it make sense to seriously consider that position and, if it was offered, decide between just it and your current job? If you were willing to leave your job for another position, it would seem to be very useful to also pursue other job opportunities on the strength of your values. This might provide you with a larger and better set of alternatives from which to choose.

It is fine—in fact, advantageous—to have alternatives suggested by others for your decisions. It is not so desirable to rely only on alternatives suggested by others. It may save you some hard thinking and work. However, your alternatives are there to satisfy your values, and you are the expert on your values. Accordingly, it should be worthwhile to think about potential alternatives for any decision worthy of thought that you face.

Sometimes you may face an important decision for which you cannot seem to identify any viable alternatives. One such decision is faced by many doctoral students, namely the selection of a dissertation topic. The principle discussed below applies to any decision where realistic alternatives are difficult to identify.

► Selecting a Dissertation Topic

A new doctoral student, for good reasons, may not have much of an idea about what would be a good dissertation topic, or what would even be a dissertation topic. One promising idea would be to speak to potential advisors about possible topics that they find interesting. The student rejects some on various grounds, such as "I do not think that I could do it," "It's too hard and too time-consuming," "I am not sure what I could do on that topic," or "It is boring." Essentially, an implicit threshold is used to reject potential topics. Then, eventually, a topic is suggested that is above one's threshold. "Eureka! I've got a topic. The pressure is off." You have just chosen a topic that was the first one you found that met your minimum standard as a result of a search process—but that is not a decision process.

Selecting a dissertation topic with no realistic alternatives is not really a decision. Nor is it a good way to proceed. You rarely want to choose anything that is important without being aware of at least some alternatives. If you believe that your initial idea is appropriate to choose, a simple comparison with the subsequently created alternatives should support your judgment by indicating that this is the case.

After identifying a first alternative, you should continue to create other alternatives. This is usually easier than coming up with the first alternative, as you now have some experience and less pressure, since you already have a contender that can be your chosen alternative if necessary. Create at least four or five alternatives. If you end up choosing between five real alternatives, the chance that your originally identified alternative is best should only be about 20 percent. You are more likely to produce a high-quality dissertation, and have a productive and enjoyable experience producing it, if the topic results from a decision process rather than a search process. ◄

There are many important decisions where you may be tempted to select the first possible solution. In all of these, some effort spent creating alternatives that provide a nudge for your decision will likely be a wise investment. Examples include purchasing a car or a condominium, finding a new primary physician or a specialist, choosing a firm that will manage some aspects of your small company (e.g., taxes, payroll), or selecting an individual as the main contractor to build or remodel your house.

Thinking Too Narrowly about Alternatives. Too often we do not push our thinking to identify some harder-to-find alternatives. We identify alternatives that are easy to find, the so-called "low-hanging fruit." The result is that our creation of alternatives takes place inside the proverbial box, which limits the range of alternatives that are identified and, subsequently, considered. Several common decision-making habits limit our thinking.

Frequently we operate using "business as usual" procedures. This means that, when we face decisions that appear to be similar to past decisions, we consider the same alternatives we considered then. Suppose that out-of-town friends who you have not seen for a couple of years are visiting your city and you are planning to take them out for dinner. You routinely frequent three restaurants, so you consider these and choose one. However, this dinner is not a routine dinner. It may be an opportunity for the guests to dine in a new place where they've never eaten before. Asking them what their values are for the dinner restaurant, or even thinking about their values, may lead you to a different and better choice.

Inappropriately Using Constraints. The intent of constraints is to focus our thinking on the realistic alternatives. But constraints can also seriously limit our thinking. There are three major shortcomings of the manner in which constraints are commonly set and used. First, they are often defined too stringently, which can exclude high-quality alternatives. Second, constraints typically refer to only one objective relevant to the decision. An alternative that was excellent on four of five relevant objectives, but just missed the constraint on that fifth objective, would not be considered. Third, after alternatives are identified that satisfy the constraints, there is rarely any verification as to whether these alternatives are good enough so that no alternative that violates one of the constraints could be better.

Suppose that the couple with out-of-town friends for dinner used constraints to guide their thinking about possible restaurants. They wanted the restaurant to be within 10 miles of their home and cost between $50 and $100 per person. With other values equal, such as the quality of food, service, ambience, and parking, a review of all restaurants within 10 miles of their home indicated that Anne's Restaurant, 8 miles away and costing $85 per person, was the best. To verify the appropriateness of the constraints, they should consider whether any restaurant very close to their home costing more than $100 per person could be preferred to Anne's. Suppose the answer is "No." They also should consider whether any restaurant more than 10 miles away that cost $50 could be preferred to Anne's. Here, they judged that a restaurant 13 miles away for $50 per person would be equivalent in desirability to them as Anne's. Hence, they should consider restaurants between 10 and 13 miles from their home and costing between $50 and $85 per person. If nothing better is found, Anne's would clearly be the best choice for dinner.

In any thought process, individuals may anchor their thinking to an idea that had previously occurred to them.[4] This results in successive ideas being more similar to the existing ideas than they would have been without anchoring. Your family may have an annual budget for the amount of money you plan to spend for different categories of expenses, such as clothes, food, housing, entertainment, transportation, and reserves. It is common that setting this year's budget will likely begin with last year's budget as an anchor, and only small modifications will be made. This incremental approach may be inferior to a broader approach that begins with looking at what your family's potential plans are and events that will require funds this year.

The Conventional Advice for Creating Alternatives: Think Outside the Box

The conventional advice widely offered to create better alternatives is "Think outside the box." The spirit of this advice is worth following, but what does it mean and how should it be followed? All of the pitfalls above constrain productive thinking about creating alternatives. This thinking is limited to looking for alternatives in a constrained space, referred to as "the box." For each decision, that constrained space is defined by sets of assumptions, only some of which may be explicitly stated or consciously recognized. The reasoning for the advice to think outside the box is that the box is too small, so it constrains thinking about alternatives too much. Many desirable alternatives may exist that violate the constraints of the box, so they will not be recognized by just thinking within the box.

With this reasonable advice, it is natural to think that one should not think inside a box. However, the basic limitation is not due to thinking inside a box but with thinking inside a box that is too small—often much too small. All of the alternatives in a small box are the standard, well-known alternatives that are usually somewhat similar to each other. This small box often does not include innovative alternatives that may best solve the decision. Those alternatives are located outside the box. However, "outside the box" is everywhere else, which is a very large space to search for anything. You cannot effectively or efficiently look everywhere for alternatives. You need to focus your effort, since most of what is outside the box would be a terrible place to look for alternatives for a specific decision.

My Advice for Creating Alternatives: Think Inside the Right-Sized Box

It would be worthwhile to have useful guidance about where to look for good alternatives. You want to look for alternatives where high-quality alternatives might be found and not spend any effort looking where no realistic alternatives exist. The practical advice and procedures that follow provide guidance to do this.

You definitely want to search for alternatives by "thinking outside *the* box," but not "outside *a* box." You should "think inside the *alternatives box*." There is a right-sized alternatives box for every decision, meaning the box of all realistic alternatives relevant to that particular decision.

So, how in practice can you describe the alternatives box for a particular decision? The alternatives box for a decision is completely specified by the objectives of that decision. Any alternative that can contribute to the achievement of any of the objectives for the stated decision is a legitimate alternative to consider.

> **Thinking inside the alternatives box for relevant alternatives effectively focuses the search for high-quality alternatives.**

Figure 6.1 illustrates the idea. The intuitive thinking for alternatives often occurs inside the proverbial box. Next to it is the alternatives box, which should be many times larger than the proverbial box, visually indicating that there should be many more realistic alternatives in the right-sized alternatives box. Because the alternatives in the small proverbial box contribute to the values for the decision, those alternatives are also included in the right-sized box. Outside the proverbial box is everything not inside it, which is an extremely large space that includes all possible boxes. Except for the alternatives box, all of these are irrelevant places to look for alternatives for your decision, and any search there would be a waste of time. Thus, focus any effort to create alternatives by looking inside the alternatives box, as alternatives outside that box do not contribute to the achievement of any objectives of the decision at hand.

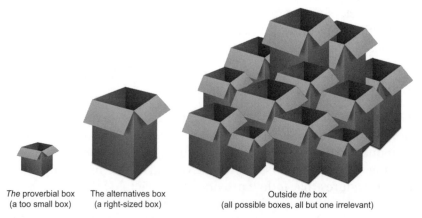

The proverbial box   The alternatives box   Outside *the* box
(a too small box)   (a right-sized box)   (all possible boxes, all but one irrelevant)

Figure 6.1 The Right-Sized Alternatives Box

This importance of the idea of an alternatives box is worth illustrating with a real case.

► Coordinating a Joint Project
A colleague, who lived in a city 800 miles away, and I were finishing a joint consulting project. We discussed the final steps and decided that meeting together for two days would be sufficient to complete the final report for that project. Hence, we intuitively characterized the set of all our alternatives for the decision statement "decide when to have a two-day meeting."

What are the assumptions of this decision statement? One explicit assumption is that we needed a meeting. A second explicit assumption is that the meeting needed to last two days. Implicit assumptions that we both had were that those two days needed to be consecutive days and that the project should be completed within a month. We both reviewed our availability, and found out that there were no two-day periods that we both had available in the next month. Hence, there were no alternatives for our decision as we had implicitly perceived it. The box we had initially created was too small, and empty. Because of this, we were forced to broaden our decision.

Upon reflection, we realized that we had implicitly assumed that our meeting needed to be two consecutive days. We removed this assumption, so our set of potential alternatives became some-what larger. However, it turned out that we did not find any two single days to conveniently meet to complete the project.

Finally, we realized a significant shortcoming in our think-ing. We had been using alternative-focused thinking, and had spent our time trying to create a viable alternative without having clearly thought about our values for the decision. We therefore switched to being value-focused and did what we should have done at the beginning. We explicitly listed our values for complet-ing the project to characterize our alternatives box. Our funda-mental values were to provide a high-quality product, useful to the client, and delivered on time. In addition, we each wanted to enjoy the process and minimize disruption to other aspects of our lives. These values characterized our alternatives box and identi-fied what we wanted to accomplish in order to complete the project. Using these five values, we created alternatives that involved each of us individually working on components needed to finish. We then decided appropriate times to effectively com-municate to each other. This allowed us to complete the work in the near future and have it be a high-quality product. As it turned out, we did not physically need to meet to do this. Overall, this alternative was better for both of us and for our clients than any of the alternatives that would have included meetings, which we had presumed were necessary by our initial, inappropriately con-strained boxes. ◀

Since the initial step to address any of our important deci-sions is to identify our values relevant to that decision, we have a way to define the right-sized alternatives box for that decision.

What we do not yet have is guidance for our search through that alternatives box to create alternatives. As explained below, the answer is that using your values to create alternatives is much better than just using time, or more time, to generate more alternatives.

The Usefulness of Spending Time to Create Alternatives

A natural question is whether simply using more time to create alternatives leads to better alternatives. An experiment involving the creation of alternatives to solve the significant parking problem at Bayreuth University in Germany examined this possibility.[5] Specifically, the decision statement was "decide how best to substantially improve the parking situation at the university." We experimenters, with input from others, first developed seven values for the decision: cost efficiency, sustainability, environmental friendliness, stakeholder satisfaction, more efficient use of parking lots, an increased area available for parking, and reduced parking demand.

Participating subjects were students at Bayreuth University, who were well aware of this parking problem. They were randomly included in two groups. All participants were asked to create alternatives in three sequential eight-minute periods with a short break in between periods. In each period the control group was given only the general guidance to think hard and create new alternatives or improve existing alternatives. In the first period the other group was provided some of the values and asked to use them one at a time to stimulate the creation of alternatives. All seven values were then provided in the second and third periods and guidance suggested using them initially two at a time and then all together to create alternatives. At the end of each period participants would construct a list of their best-five alternatives, and begin the next eight-minute period with this list.

The results were interesting. Comparing the first two periods, the participants using values made an average of 2.80 changes to their first best-five alternatives list and those in the control group using the same amount of time without values made 2.23 changes. Comparing the best-five alternatives of the second and third periods, those using values made on average 2.61 changes, whereas those using only time made 1.14 changes. All 44 of the participants with values made improvements in their best-five alternatives list going from the second to the third period. Only 11 of 22 from the control group without values made such improvements.

In a subsequent experiment, a group of 122 individuals evaluated several sets of 12 randomly chosen pairs of participants' best-five alternatives. For the control group, comparing participant's sets of alternatives from the first and second periods, the first set was preferred 109 times and second set 99 times. For the 11 of 22 participants in the control group who made any changes in their best-five alternatives list during the third period, comparisons indicated that the second and third sets were each preferred 48 times to the other. In contrast, the group that used values improved the quality of the best-five alternatives significantly over time. The sets of participants' alternatives of the second period were preferred 231 to 173 times to those of the first period and the alternatives of the third period were preferred 249 to 149 times to those of the second phase.

The results of this experiment show that only using more time to create alternatives can increase the number of the alternatives, but it does not improve the quality of the best alternatives. However, using values to stimulate the creation of alternatives is an effective use of additional time. This produced new alternatives that were included in the best-five alternatives list, and these new lists were independently judged to be of higher quality.

Using Values to Create Alternatives

The source of the alternatives for your decisions is your mind. Creating alternatives requires hard thinking, creativity, and sometimes soul-searching. As shown below, guidance to direct this thinking will produce more and better alternatives. As the intent of any chosen alternatives is to achieve what you value, decision-makers should use their values to guide their creation of realistic alternatives. But how should these values be used?

Creating desirable alternatives is a challenging endeavor. With dedicated and focused effort, you can identify more and better alternatives from which to choose.

One experiment that addressed this question was conducted as part of the MBA internship study at the US university that included values discussed in Chapter 5.[6] Prior to any mention of values, the MBA students were asked to list as many alternatives as they could to enhance the benefits of their internship in the summer between the two years of their studies. Subsequently they listed their values for their internship and then checked additional values from the master list in Table 5.1. Finally, after completing some other parts of the questionnaire unrelated to their internship decision, participants were provided with the alternatives each had initially created and a list of their values that they had personally identified or recognized on the master list.

The 295 participants were placed into two separate groups. Individuals in one group were told to use their values to stimulate the identification of as many additional alternatives as possible so as to enhance the benefits of their internship. Those in the second group were asked to do the same task, but with the additional guidance to use each of the values separately in order to stimulate their thoughts about potential alternatives.

In their initial lists of alternatives identified prior to any mention of values, participants generated an average of 5.36 alternatives. After being given the list of their values, participants asked to just use their values created on average 3.73 additional alternatives. Those in the group asked to use each of their values separately created an average of 5.69 additional alternatives, which more than doubled their number of alternatives. This experiment shows that using a list of values to stimulate thought produced additional alternatives, and using those values one at a time produced both significantly more and significantly more appealing alternatives.

A Practical Process for Creating Alternatives

An easy-to-use three-step process can help you create more and better alternatives for your decisions. First, you must define the decision that you face. Second, identify your values for the decision. Third, use the values to create relevant alternatives. Since the first two steps are discussed in detail in the preceding two chapters, only the third step is discussed in detail below.

Before beginning your process to create alternatives, put yourself in a positive frame of mind for the endeavor. Whether you begin with no specific alternatives in mind or you already have identified some alternatives, believe that there are better alternatives that you can create. If you already have identified a good alternative, believe that you have a decent chance of finding one or more better alternatives with dedicated effort. If you do not find a better alternative, you still have your very good one.

Step 1. Define Your Decision. Chapter 4 discusses how to think about and establish a clear decision statement for the decision that you want to face. Clarity in defining your decision is important for both identifying values and creating good alternatives for your decision.

Step 2. Identify Your Values for This Decision. Identify as many of your values as you can for this decision. The procedures in Chapter 5 should be very helpful in this process. Although not essential, it will likely be useful to state your values in the form of objectives, so as to clarify their meaning and help you better understand what you want to achieve by facing your decision. This, in turn, should enhance the creation of alternatives.

Step 3. Create Possible Alternatives. Any value can spark your thinking of an innovative idea that leads to a great solution to your decision. So, consider each of your values separately and try to think of alternatives that might contribute to achieving that value. Then use pairs of values, and/or larger subsets of values, to produce more thought about realistic alternatives. This thinking tends to produce a new alternative that is a combination of the potential alternatives created using only one objective, one

> **Because your values indicate what you hope to achieve by making a decision, they provide a probing guide for your thoughts to create better alternatives.**

that better contributes to the combination of values used. Collectively, these procedures will focus your search for alternatives throughout the entire alternatives box, without wasting your time searching outside that right-sized box.

Having done your own thinking first, now ask others for suggestions of alternatives. Others could include family, friends, and colleagues who you feel may have useful suggestions about your decisions. In other situations, individuals with specific expertise regarding the substance of the decision may offer useful alternatives. For example, physicians and investment counselors may know of alternatives for medical and financial decisions that you would not be able to create on your own.

After having generated several distinct alternatives, create additional alternatives by combining aspects of existing alternatives that can be implemented simultaneously. When elemental alternatives are created by thinking of single values, they should be expected to contribute well to this value. If compound alternatives are created from elemental alternatives that focused on different values, you would expect that the compound alternative would contribute well on each of the relevant individual values. Hence, this step to create compound alternatives may be particularly beneficial.

For the first decisions that you address with this procedure, you will definitely create alternatives. However, the experiments described earlier in the chapter suggest that you will likely have generated only about half the possible alternatives, and the average quality of the alternatives that you have not yet recognized is probably about as good on average as those that you have identified. If this is the case, the best of your alternatives is likely still among those you have not yet identified. Hence, challenge yourself to create a specific number of additional alternatives, perhaps as many as you already have. It can be done, and, with focused effort, you can do it. Prove this to yourself and help yourself with this nudge for your specific decision while doing so. Fortunately, but not surprisingly, recent research indicates that using objectives to prompt the creation of alternatives is effective regardless of the amount of experience and knowledge that one has about the decision being faced.[7]

► Volunteer Activities
When Jeff graduated from college he had not given much thought to the type of job he wanted; he just wanted a job. He was energetic and personable, so he found one, and then another, and another. After four years of moving from job to job and changing cities a couple of times, he recognized that he wanted to be in sales at a major company where he could contribute, advance, and become a respected member of that company.

Now 30 years old, Jeff is established in an enjoyable and exciting position in a great company. Recognizing all of the difficulties that he had in his earlier work years, he wants to give back and help younger versions of himself encumbered in work situations similar to those that he once experienced. He wants to decide what his volunteer activity should be.

He first identified the six objectives in Table 6.1 for his volunteer activity. Some implications of each of these objectives for creating alternatives are also indicated in the table. For instance, his first objective is to help individuals with an important problem, and his judgments of important problems included finding and flourishing in a career and adapting to "adult living" on your own. For the objective to use his skills, he felt that he was good at meeting people, establishing relationships, working with others, and contributing to teams.

One obvious alternative that Jeff identified was to join an existing volunteer organization that helps young professionals adjust to post-college working and living. Most of these organizations have regularly scheduled meetings that would not satisfy his objective to control his time commitment, which was important because individuals in sales need to adapt their time schedule to those of potential customers. This suggests a second alternative for his volunteer activity. He could propose a special position for himself in the established organization. Members who attend scheduled meetings of the group may recognize that an attendee has

Table 6.1 Objectives for a Volunteer Activity and Their Implications for Alternatives

Values (stated as objectives)	Implications of objective for alternatives
Help others with important problems	Problems concern employment and adapting to adult living
Help others who are trying to help themselves	Beneficiaries must put in effort in order to benefit
Use my skills	Good at meeting people, establishing relationships, working with others, and contributing to teams
Avoid wasting time	Avoid tasks requiring significant preparation
Be in control of my time	Contribute my effort on my own schedule
Avoid personal financial costs	Minimize commuting and infrastructure needs

difficulties that Jeff may be particularly suited for and effective at addressing. These individuals could be given Jeff's contact information to arrange a private meeting.

A third alternative would be to become an individual mentor and coach for individuals who could be helped by Jeff's knowledge and suggestions. Jeff could communicate with several volunteer organizations and/or human resources departments in various businesses about his volunteer efforts and suggest that they refer appropriate individuals to him. A fourth alternative, which Jeff thought was appealing in terms of many objectives, would be to create a volunteer role as a mentor at his current company to help younger employees who might benefit from his knowledge and experience. There are two versions of this alternative. One is an external program not affiliated with or a part of the company. The other is to include his volunteer activity as an internal service offered by the company.

In considering these alternatives, Jeff thought about the learning that would occur during his initial efforts at helping individuals. The information learned might indicate a previously unrecognized advantage of one of the alternatives. Thus, it may be useful to include the flexibility to easily change from one alternative to another as an objective for the original choice of an alternative. This highlights a general point when you create alternatives. Thinking about a newly created alternative may uncover relevant values that you had not previously identified. These newly recognized values might then nudge you to tailor existing proposed alternatives to make them better. ◄

An anecdote about volunteer activities and the usefulness of creating alternatives may be amusing. It concerned participating in a one-day event rather than an ongoing effort. I was once asked by an individual who led a major state agency in California if I would be the main speaker at a large meeting about risks and decision-making on a Friday in the state capital, Sacramento. He explained that there would be no fee for the presentation. Then he said that my travel expenses for a 200-mile round trip in my own car could not be reimbursed, but he would be able to take me to the conference lunch. I was a bit surprised that the modest travel expenses would not be reimbursed.

So I asked who would be attending the meeting. He explained it was a retreat for about 100 individuals from his agency. Then I asked if he and the other 100 employees were getting paid for that Friday, and he said they were. Then, rather than simply responding to his request with a "Yes" or a "No," I created a third response alternative. I told him that, if the meeting were changed to be on Saturday and he and all of the other participants came to the meeting without pay or travel reimbursement, then I would be pleased to come and make the requested presentation. I was subsequently not contacted about this wonderful opportunity.

Once you have explicitly used your values to guide the creation of alternatives for several decisions, you will definitely know how useful it is and your ability to use it will increase significantly. You will understand the benefits that you can expect for the time allocated to this activity. With this skill and knowledge, you will be able to use the three steps in a more integrated manner. You will see how the parts fit together and, with this larger picture, use the ideas more effectively and with less effort.

This recommended procedure to create alternatives may be different from techniques that you have used in the past. If you have a personal style that helps you create good alternatives for decisions that you confront, certainly keep using it. The process here should be a complement, and you should use it separately from and in addition to your current style. Then alternatives created from your personal style and from the process discussed here can be combined into what will be a better set of alternatives.

Motivating the Desire to Create Alternatives

Experience and common sense suggest that the more an individual wants something, the better his or her chances of achieving it. That notion is summed up in the well-known idiom "Where there is a will, there is a way." Having a will to identify or create a great alternative does not guarantee that such a great alternative exists. However, it likely does increase your chances of identifying or creating a great alternative if it does exist. Dedicated effort wisely spent creating alternatives has a much better chance of finding a great alternative than other passive "procedures," such as hope, divine guidance, or taking a "wait and see" attitude. Therefore, a useful way to improve your chances of identifying a great alternative for your decision may be to increase your will do so.

Where There Is a Way, There Is a Will. One way to enhance the identification of better alternatives might be summarized by this transposition of the famous idiom. For decisions, the transposed statement means that, if you believe there are excellent alternatives for your decision, you will have a stronger motivation to find them. It is easier to search for something if you believe that it is possible to find it. The following informal experiment illustrates this idea.

> If you believe that better alternatives exist, you have a better chance of creating them. Therefore, assume that better alternatives exist; they often do.

In a homework assignment in a graduate class on decision-making, I posed the following problem. Three young college students were messing around while playing pool one evening. As the result of a challenge, one forced a pool ball into his mouth. Then he could not open his mouth wide enough to remove it. It was stuck. Write down all the alternatives you can think of that might remove the ball other than calling someone else for help.

There was an additional, different comment given to students in each of two separate groups. Group 1 was told that "I know of three good alternatives to remove the pool ball." Group 2 was told to "be creative and identify any good alternatives to remove the pool ball." Those in group 1 did a much better job at finding alternatives. As it happens, I did not know of any good alternatives; but I soon did. Because of my statement, members of group 1 believed there were good alternatives. This seemed to motivate these individuals to think harder and more creatively, as well as more easily find reasonable alternatives. Examples of creative alternatives were: (1) place a very large rubber band behind the pool ball with ends out of both sides of the mouth and pull; (2) with an appropriate saw, cut parts of the pool ball away in the mouth and sequentially remove them; and (3) use a muscle relaxant to allow the jaw to open much wider.

Setting a Goal for Creating Alternatives. As a means to finding a great alternative for a specific decision, we want to create as many realistic alternatives as possible. Of course we want the alternatives to be as good as possible as well. However, it is better to separate the creation process from the evaluation process.

If you are thinking of possible alternatives for a delightful weekend trip, you could decide to write down as many alternatives as you can think of, or to write down at least eight alternatives. With the former guidance, there is no clear end to the task and no way to indicate success. With the goal of creating eight alternatives, success is obvious. If you stop any time before creating eight alternatives, that may suggest failure in the creation task.

The MBA internship experiment discussed in Chapter 5 mainly concerned the generation of values, but it has some results relevant to creating alternatives. Recall that we asked participants to list their values, as many as they could, for an internship. The 295 participants initially listed 6.4 values on average. Because we experimenters had created a master list of 32 possible values, we were quite sure that the students had not thought of several of their personal values. So we conducted a further experiment that set expectations that values important for their decision were yet to be identified. We divided the participants into groups and asked them to improve their lists of values. One group was given the standard advice, namely: "Examine your list of values and add any values that are missing." Four other groups were challenged: "Experience suggests that individuals typically identify less than 50 percent of the relevant values on the first attempt and that their missing values are just as important to them as the ones they listed. With additional thought, individuals can identify more of their values and more of their most important values." The four groups were then given different information. One group was requested to add as many additional values as its members could. The other three groups were given goals to add three, six, or nine additional values. The first group with no challenge added an average of 0.55 values. Participants in the group asked to add as many additional values as they could added 2.77 more values on average. Those groups with specific goals to add at least three, six, and nine values added on average 3.08, 3.90, and 4.87 values respectively.

The point is that believing that several relevant values were missing was helpful in motivating the generation of additional values. In addition, the goals clearly helped. Moreover, the level specified by the goal is important, as individuals generated more values with higher goals. However, if a goal were set to add 20 additional values, individuals may think that this would be impossible and/or ridiculous, and do worse than with a goal of nine additional values. In summary, realistic goals motivate better achievement in many settings. This experiment, which is very similar to creating alternatives, suggests that setting goals can have an important role in stimulating the creation of alternatives for your decisions.

Influencing Others to Create Alternatives for You

A 28-year-old woman had a responsible position in a public relations firm in New York for six years after college. She and her husband then moved to Austin, where he accepted a great work offer. They also were planning to have children, and she was going to take a hiatus from employment to participate full-time in the children's early lives. A year after arriving in Austin she had twins. When the children began attending school, her intent was to again work full-time, at an Austin public relations firm.

Before leaving New York for Austin she asked colleagues if they had friends or connections in the field who lived in Austin. She contacted each of them after arriving there and became friends with a couple of them. She also routinely attended professional events with the local public relations crowd, to help remain relatively up to date in the field and widen her professional relationships. She sought out and completed a few assignments while her twins were in preschool when a company needed a little extra help. All of this was partly for enjoyment and interest, but also to help establish professional standing with local public relations professionals, because she anticipated returning to full-time employment in the future.

How can you influence whether you are offered high-quality employment alternatives? The answer is essentially the old adage that you need to be in the right place at the right time. But you need not leave this to luck or hoping, which are often thought to be necessary. There is a lot that you can proactively do to enhance your chances of getting the alternatives that you want.

The Right Place to Be Is in the Minds of Others. For people to offer you an alternative, the initiating spark is to recognize a personal need or a desire that may be fulfilled by offering that alternative. They must make the connection between you and their need or desire.

Being in the right place at the right time facilitates connecting you to the needs and desires of others. However, the common meaning of the phrase "Be in the right place at the right time" refers to *physically* being in the right physical place at the right time. With this meaning, it is impossible to be in more than one place at any one time. Fortunately, in many situations, it is *thoughts* about you and your interests that need to be in the right place at the right time. The right place to be is in the minds of individuals

> **Several good things that have happened to you might be attributed to being in the right place at the right time. To enhance others suggesting alternatives and decision opportunities for you, the right place to be is in the minds of others and the right time to be there is always, and you can influence both.**

who are in a position to offer, or facilitate the offering of, alternatives to you, and the right time to be there is always.

Obviously, you can be in the minds of more than one person at the same time. What you want to do is seed ideas in the minds of others for alternatives that you would like. The direct way to do this is to tell individuals of your desires. If you communicate with many people that you are interested in a particular type of alternative, you greatly improve the chances that a connection will be made to help create such an alternative.

The following personal example illustrates that the use of this idea is relevant in numerous organizational situations.

► Contributing at Duke University

In the spring of 2002 I accepted a five-year faculty position at Duke University's Fuqua School of Business, beginning July 1. My appointment would involve nine months of work time each year, but it did not include regular teaching assignments or tenure. My title for the position was research professor.

My main responsibility would be to contribute to the quality and reputation of the school by initiating and publishing research, mentoring younger faculty and doctoral students, providing professional service (e.g., professional societies, national committees, and journals), and contributing to all other school objectives except teaching regular courses. I planned to do this while living in San Francisco and spending a week each month on Duke's campus in Durham, North Carolina.

When opportunities arose at Fuqua to which I could contribute I wanted the appropriate individuals to think of me as a potential contributor, whether or not I was physically at Fuqua that week. To increase the chances of this routinely happening, it was important to be in the right place at the right time. The right place to be was in the minds of the deans and my colleagues on the faculty at Fuqua, so my name would pop up when a task needed to be done, and the question arose of who was available to do it.

To help facilitate awareness, as well as plan to meet colleagues when on campus, I would always email them a week before I was going to be on-campus. Then, on my first day on campus, I would visit them to say "Hello" and let them know that I had arrived. Also, rather than email others in the building, I would walk through the halls to some-one's office to ask a question, arrange a future meeting, work together, or propose lunch. Visually seeing me at Fuqua reinforced that I was a colleague. This seemed to have a positive effect, as indicated by the following comment. One day a faculty member saw me in the Fuqua cafeteria at lunch and said: "You're here again this week? You were just here last week." In this case, I knew I had not been physically on campus for three weeks, but realized that, since I was frequently seen when I was there, it seemed like last week.

Over my ten years at Fuqua (as I was reappointed for an additional five years) I was able to jointly work on research and publications with many faculty members and several doctoral stu-dents, as well as contribute to many other activities that are collec-tively done by the faculty. I think my strategy to make it easier for colleagues to think of me as an active faculty member of Fuqua and Duke was helpful. ◄

Whenever you are involved in any group or activity where contributions are needed, they are usually welcomed. In your effort to contribute at least your share, you can create strategies that will make this both easier and more enjoyable. If you identify many ways to contribute, you can choose the ones that are more impor-tant and more enjoyable for you to do. If you have to self-generate all of the alternatives, you will likely not become aware of many good alternatives of which others were aware. Enable others to create alternatives for you. Being in the minds of others when possible alternatives occur will certainly help provide interesting opportunities.

Value-Focused Brainstorming

Brainstorming is a well-known approach to create alternatives, based partially on the idea that two or more people should have more ideas than one. Brainstorming involves multiple individuals interacting in a group meeting to generate alternatives and fosters creativity by welcoming all ideas and avoiding any evaluation of potential alternatives during the generation process.[8]

Traditional brainstorming has two shortcomings for creating alternatives for decisions. First, little guidance is given to participants about the characteristics of the alternatives that are desired. Second, the usual interactive process of creating alternatives has one person speaking and all others listening at any given time. Hence, the listener's thoughts gravitate to the ideas of the speaker. It is also difficult to do one's own deep thinking when listening or speaking.

The four steps of value-focused brainstorming are given in Table 6.2. Note that the first three steps are exactly the steps used for an individual to create alternatives given above. The first shortcoming of traditional brainstorming is addressed in step 2, which provides guidance for creating desirable types of alternatives. The values frame the breadth of the brainstorming session that should occur, by defining the right-sized alternatives box for thinking about desirable alternatives. The values can be established by an initial "brainstorming session" with the same participants, or a subset of them, in the session to create alternatives, or they can be initially provided by whoever convened the

> **Value-focused brainstorming first identifies the values for the decision and then uses them to guide the creation of alternatives. It enhances participation and creativity by having individual brainstormers identify alternatives prior to having the group work on creating additional alternatives together.**

brainstorming session to create alternatives. The second shortcoming is addressed in step 3. Each individual does his or her own thinking and creating of alternatives prior to pursuing the traditional interpersonal aspects of brainstorming in step 4.

Table 6.2 Steps of Value-Focused Brainstorming

---

1. State the decision to be solved.
2. Identify the values of the decision.
3. Individually generate alternatives.
4. Collectively generate alternatives.

As a formal process, value-focused brainstorming is more frequently relevant to business and organizational decisions. Less formally, a family or other group could use value-focused brainstorming for an important personal decision facing the group or a member of it.

The following case summarizes a significant application.[9] It also provided a test concerning whether articulating the values intended to be achieved by the alternatives would enhance the standard brainstorming process. Specifically, would explicitly using the values to create alternatives result in more and better alternatives that could nudge decision-makers to make better decisions with better consequences?

▶ Evacuation from Large Buildings

After the terrorist attacks on the World Trade Center in 2001, one of numerous federal recommendations was to improve emergency evacuation from large buildings. One task to fulfill this recommendation was a two-and-a-half-day invitation-only workshop held in 2008 that I facilitated to create potential alternatives that may improve the evacuation of large buildings. Over 30 individuals knowledgeable about different aspects of emergency evacuation actively participated. Collectively, their experience covered firefighting, architecture, building standards, building codes, communications, building construction, materials science, handicapped individuals, human behavior, and emergency management.

Since all participants were very knowledgeable about evacuation, I initially asked them to list all of the alternatives that they thought would improve evacuation. This was to ensure each participant that their original ideas for alternatives would not be lost. Next, each participant was asked to list all of his or her values regarding the evacuation of buildings. Then I told them that they could surely identify more values and provided specific suggestions for evacuation decisions based on the general ideas to stimulate additional values shown in Table 5.2. Suggestions included "consider what might have contributed to an inadequate evacuation" and "think of cases where individuals were trapped in the building; what improvements might have avoided this?." After all the values had been listed, individuals were asked to state their values as objectives, which facilitated our understanding and the combining of objectives.

A total of 32 individuals provided lists of values. Collectively, this resulted in 205 objectives on the first list and 156 on the second. Some objectives, naturally, were on the lists of many individuals, such as "save lives." The average numbers of objectives were 6.4 for the first list and 4.9 added objectives for the second list for each participant.

In the evening of the first day two coworkers and I constructed a comprehensive list of all objectives. Common objectives of different individuals were included only once, and objectives were organized into the 12 categories of means objectives and seven categories of fundamental objectives shown in Table 6.3.

On the second workshop day participants were asked to use the individual objectives on the group's comprehensive list to stimulate the creation of any alternatives that would facilitate

Table 6.3 Categories of Objectives for Evacuation of Large Buildings

---

Categories of fundamental objectives
    Save lives and prevent injuries to occupants
    Save lives and prevent injuries to firefighters/responders
    Minimize property damage
    Minimize impact on property operations
    Minimize economic costs
    Reduce stress
    Reduce grief

Categories of means objectives
    Enhance detection
    Maximize situation awareness
    Make people feel safe
    Minimize response time
    Enhance communication
    Enhance safety
    Facilitate responder access
    Isolate fire
    Minimize evacuation time
    Improve knowledge about the system
    Improve education and training
    Provide easy evacuation procedures

---

evacuation. Then they were asked to create any additional alternatives by considering pairs or other combinations of objectives. Thirty participants generated alternatives on the first workshop day prior to listing objectives, 21 individuals created additional alternatives on the second day using individual objectives on the comprehensive list, and then 18 created alternatives based on pairs or combinations of objectives. Then an hour was allocated for groups of two to four individuals to generate alternatives that were different from those that the individuals in the respective groups already had generated.

A total of 221 alternatives were identified on the first day. On the second day 81 more alternatives were created by considering single objectives, 48 more considering pairs and combinations, and 50 by groups. As the number of participants was smaller on the second day, the averages were 7.4 alternatives per person prior to listing objectives, and 8.5 additional alternatives per person using objectives, assuming 21 people. On the second evening of the workshop duplicate alternatives were deleted and the remaining alternatives were organized into categories, as shown in Table 6.4.

An important question concerns whether some of the alternatives created by the value-focused brainstorming were innovative and of high quality. A preliminary evaluation of 37 selected alternatives was performed by the nine groups of two to four participants on the third day of the workshop. Three values were used for this evaluation: usefulness, referring to an alternative's contribution to improve evacuations; feasibility, referring to the likelihood the alternative could be implemented within ten years; and creativity, ranging from a standard, well-known alternative to an alternative that was completely new. Some of the most useful and feasible alternatives were very creative and previously unrecognized among this very experienced group. This suggests that using values to stimulate the generation of alternatives in brainstorming processes can produce some very desirable alternatives that will nudge the decision-makers to make better decisions. ◄

There is a strong message for creating alternatives in brainstorming sessions from the case above. A group of professionals who were all very knowledgeable about and had significant experience with the evacuation of large buildings were each able to create a reasonable number of new alternatives to improve the evacuation process for large buildings. When subsequently

Table 6.4 Categories of Alternatives for Evacuation of Large Buildings

---

Alternatives involving:

Sprinklers or active suppression systems
Protection in place or areas of refuge
Building construction changes
Building material changes
Fire service
Elevators
Societal, regulatory, and legal changes
Facilities and equipment external to the building
Communication
Information systems
Pre-event planning
Efficient use of evacuation systems
Enhancement of stairwell evacuation
Improvement of the design process
Reliability of building systems
Event procedural changes
Improved event detection

---

stimulated by the objectives that they had created for evacuation processes, they were on average able to double the total number of alternatives they had identified. This doubling occurred for a decision that was well understood and had occurred thousands of times in the past.

You can adapt the value-focused brainstorming process for important personal or professional decisions. Suppose that you are at an important crossroads in your career or life. You may feel that there are few guidelines for what to do and have an open mind about what you should do. You could ask a special group of friends or family to participate in a value-focused brainstorming process to generate some useful ideas. Prior to this you should carefully define your decision and then specify as many relevant values as possible. The value-focused brainstorming group could also be asked to suggest any additional values before proceeding to steps 3 and 4. Note that the second and third steps also could be done individually before getting the group together. This alone may provide useful alternatives. Step 4, if it is done, does require a joint meeting, which may be arranged as part of an enjoyable gathering of friends.

Value-focused brainstorming can be used more directly and less formally with a small group who will all jointly experience the consequences of an alternative. There may be a leader with responsibility for the decision or a group may need to collectively choose an alternative. Examples include partners in a successful small professional firm that must move from its present location, a group of friends planning a hike in a remote area, and a family planning for the temporary care of a family member recuperating from a major surgery. One of my favorite examples illustrates the idea.

► One Family's Important Vacation

A gentleman came up to me after I had spoken at a conference and said he would like to thank me for some thoughts of mine he had read. Specifically, he referred to a comment about the usefulness of using value-focused brainstorming on family decisions. I had mentioned that children could positively participate in specifying values and alternatives for some family decisions that interested them.

His family included his wife and three daughters, aged eight, ten, and 13 at the time of the story. Unfortunately, his wife had been diagnosed with breast cancer two years earlier, and each family member had been severely affected. For several months his wife received regular medical care so the family naturally remained near home. As a result, the family had not taken a vacation for over two years. There was some good news though. The medical circumstances were improving and the parents thought for the first time that the husband and children could and should go on a vacation.

The man telling me the story said that his family lived in the Washington, DC, area and that, prior to his wife's breast cancer, the family usually vacationed in Maine near the ocean. He said that he and his wife both initially thought he should take the children on a familiar vacation. He mentioned that reading an article that I had written on value-focused decision-making stimulated his thinking. He decided to ask each child to write down what she would like on a nice vacation, and he wrote down his values as well. Values that were written included "exciting," "great outdoors," "near the ocean," "new," "place we have never seen," "everyone would have great stories to tell mom," and "make mom happy." The next step was to generate alternatives, which was not too difficult. The list included travel to Maine, the Carolinas, the Texas Gulf Coast, California, and the Pacific Northwest of the United States. After discussing these alternatives in terms of their values, a trip to the Pacific Northwest was chosen, and they had a wonderful vacation. Each evening they telephoned mom at home and reported everything. She was happy and invigorated because of the experiences her family were able to have. They were all looking forward to a trip to the Northwest with mom in the future. ◄

Enhance Your Preferred Alternative

You are in the process of making an important decision. You have clearly stated your objectives, created several alternatives in addition to the obvious ones, and preliminarily examined the pros and cons of each alternative. Having done this, you feel confident that you have identified what you think of as your preferred alternative. Before selecting and implementing that alternative, it takes only a few minutes to try to make it better yet. There are several different techniques to facilitate this process

Suppose that your preferred alternative is excellent in terms of achieving most of your values, but is somewhat inferior on a couple of them. An examination of the reasons for these relatively poor achievements may lead you to think of how to modify that best alternative to make it better.

Here is an example. You are building a cabin in the mountains that you plan to use in summer and winter. Your values include "having wide-open outdoor areas with views that are accessible in all seasons," so the initial cabin design includes a large covered balcony extending from the cabin. You now recognize that it would sometimes be too cold or windy to enjoyably use.

> After identifying a preferred alternative, but before implementing it, consider how well you expect it to satisfy each of your objectives. Then stimulate your thoughts to see if you can modify it to improve performance on any of those objectives.

An easy modification is to glass in the balcony. Such a design feature may be permanent or flexible, to allow easy installation for colder seasons or just for the days and weather conditions when you want to use it.

Some compound component alternatives involve a series of elemental alternatives sequenced in time, such as vacations, business trips, and shopping for a day with many required tasks. The order of the tasks can sometimes be modified to improve an alternative. Suppose that you are planning a two-week trip to Norway, where you will visit Oslo and Bergen for the first week and then take an ocean liner up the coast, with stops, and end in Trondheim for three days at the end of your second week. Then you will fly back to Oslo and return home.

You are excited about going, but you find out that Bergen has a major European conference on the days that you plan to visit. The large number of visitors at this conference would seriously degrade your visit to the city. To avoid this, you could modify your trip to immediately leave Oslo after arriving and travel to and visit Bergen straight away. Then take your one-week journey north on the ocean liner. After visiting Trondheim, fly back to Oslo for a four-day visit and then travel home. Another alternative would be to take the original trip in reverse. Fly to Oslo and visit for four days and then fly to Trondheim. After visiting Trondheim, take the ocean liner south to Bergen for the end of the second week. Then travel to Oslo and return home.

Sometimes you can just remove a constraint on your alternatives and create a much better one. Suppose that you are searching for the perfect Christmas present for someone very special. Your values include that it should be "useful," "affordable," and "just what the special person would like." You find the perfect present: a beautiful watch that you believe the recipient will love. But the watch is too expensive. For a price that you can afford to pay, you have found another nice watch, but it is not as special as the beautiful watch. How can you lower the price of the original watch? One alternative that might be much better involves eliminating the implicit constraint that the present needs to be given on Christmas Day. You know that the price of the watch will be significantly lower a couple of weeks after Christmas. Your "gift" on Christmas Day can be a card, perhaps with a picture of the watch, announcing the gift. In early January you can either purchase the watch or go shopping together to make sure your loved one gets the watch he or she really wants.

Another way to enhance alternatives is by what I refer to as *add-on alternatives*. The idea is simple. Implementing an alternative usually requires the use of resources, often money and/or time. You want to think about other decisions that might, in essence, share those resources, so you get more benefits and enjoyment for your investment. If you have a business trip to Washington, DC, many of us would give some thought to whether there are any other business purposes that might be easily accomplished in Washington on this trip. However, we might not think of pursuing other business purposes much closer to Washington than our home or pursuing personal activities such as visiting a friend, who lives somewhere not too far from Washington, on Saturday before flying home on Sunday.

► Selecting a Consultant

You work in a large consulting firm and have just been selected by the president to lead a major project for a client. One immediate decision that you face is to select an outside consultant with the specific expertise to provide an analysis within six months, as required by others on your project team. Your values for this decision are to have "high-quality work," "provided on time," and "for a reasonable cost." Furthermore, you want the president to appreciate your decision and management skills. In recent years, when a project has required this special expertise, one particular individual has always been selected. You check on his past performance, and his work is described as "sufficient." You decide to thoroughly search for others who could do this project and come up with six additional candidates. After reviewing the work experience of each and then having meetings with the top three, one of these was clearly better than the other two. So you feel there are two final alternatives: the individual who has regularly worked on company projects requiring this expertise; and the new individual.

Based on all of your company's experience, you understand the quality of work that the regular individual will provide. Also, you believe that the new person would probably do a better job and be less expensive, but, because you have no experience working with her, there are uncertainties about performance. Articulating what you mean by uncertainties, you feel there is about a 20 percent chance that her performance will be subpar compared to the regular consultant. During the project, if this were occurring, you would recognize it halfway through the six-month effort and could compensate for any initial shortcomings before the results were needed with an additional effort and cost. Financially, your preferred individual will save about 15 percent of the cost compared to the regular consultant, and it would be 25 percent higher if her initial performance turned out to be subpar.

Accounting for the possibility of an inferior performance, you still believe that it is better to hire the new individual. To potentially reduce the chance that the president perceives that your decision management skills are not the best if the new person's performance turns out to be subpar, you discuss this decision with the president before making your decision and present your reasoning as to why this alternative seems best. Its main advantages, in your judgment, are an 80 percent chance of providing a better product than the regular consultant for 15 percent less cost, and also the identification of a second expert who your company can hire for similar future projects. Now the president can understand the reasoning prior to the consequences occurring, and the president naturally understands that most important decisions have uncertainties that the decision-maker does not control. In addition, the recognition of potentially having a second qualified individual for future contracts requiring the specific expertise is definitely worthwhile to the firm.

It is useful to recognize a subtle but important point. The alternative of simply selecting the new individual as the consultant and the alternative of discussing the logic with the president and then selecting the new individual as the consultant are different alternatives and have different potential consequences. The alternative that included the discussion essentially costs nothing extra, and the consequences are better for both the decision-maker and the organization. ◄

The message is that, after any alternative is chosen, but prior to its implementation, it is often worthwhile to look into how to improve this alternative. The examples above illustrate the breadth of applicability of declaring a decision opportunity to improve prospective alternatives and the potential benefits of such efforts.

Additional Thoughts for Decisions in Organizations

When an organization faces an important decision, the creation of an alternative better than any currently contemplated is obviously very worthwhile. Each of the ideas in this chapter definitely is useful for creating alternatives for organizational decisions.

Organizations often fall into the same traps in creating alternatives that individuals do. Time is frequently not dedicated to creating alternatives. This may occur because nobody has an explicit responsibility to create alternatives but someone does have the responsibility of solving the problem. The focus on the solving puts pressure on choosing the best of the available alternatives now, rather than initially trying to create better alternatives that will add value and be better for the organization.

When time is spent thinking about different alternatives, there is often the constraint of thinking too narrowly. Everyone thinks about possible alternatives inside that little box that is too constrained. The full set of values that the organization has for this decision needs to be articulated to define the larger, alternatives box to guide thinking about alternatives.

> **For organizational decisions, multiple individuals should identify the appropriate values and then create alternatives, first individually and then as a group. The overall process follows the steps of value-focused brainstorming.**

For most organizational decisions, more than one individual should contribute some effort to try to create alternatives. The practical guidelines for creating alternatives are the first three steps of value-focused brainstorming. Each individual should use the values that define the alternatives box to stimulate his or her creation of alternatives. The collection of possible alternatives from these individuals is the initial set of alternatives for the organizational decision. Then additional alternatives can be created by anyone in the organization and by blending previously created alternatives by combining the best aspects of each.

In cases when additional creativity is desired, particularly when knowledge from different disciplines is needed to identify creative alternatives, the fourth interpersonal step of value-focused brainstorming should be used to generate additional alternatives. Often many organizational alternatives are created by individuals in a specific division of the organization and/or with training in a particular discipline. These alternatives may not recognize relevant issues known by individuals in other divisions or disciplines. Hence, various sets of alternatives created within different divisions or disciplines may need to be integrated into a new, more realistic and desirable alternative. When the values for a decision include multiple objectives best understood by individuals in different disciplines, it is useful to have a team of individuals collaborate to create better alternatives.

Given the positive results of using values to create alternatives for the well-understood decision to improve the evacuation of large buildings discussed earlier, imagine what would happen when an organization faces a complex decision that is unique, or unique to it. It should be easier to identify the values for such a decision than to identify alternatives for it with no guidance. The benefits of using the values that the organization wishes to identify to guide the thought process to create alternatives should be great.

7 IDENTIFYING DECISION OPPORTUNITIES

The distinction between decision problems and decision opportunities is very important, but it is not recognized by most decision-makers. Decision problems are decisions that you must face as a result of others' decisions and/or circumstances beyond your control. I refer to decisions that you create for yourself as decision opportunities rather than decision problems.

The concepts of a *decision* and of a *problem* are interrelated in everyday use. Once a problem occurs, we frequently say: "I have a decision problem." Since most individuals believe that solving a problem is the only reason to make a decision, it is not surprising that creating decisions is not something most individuals want to do. After all, who needs another problem? But a key idea of this book is that you can greatly benefit from recognizing and pursuing more decision opportunities. Decision opportunities are not problems to be solved, but opportunities to pursue.

Most decisions are made to solve problems. But other decisions do not concern problems. If you lose your employment because of a reorganization at your company, that creates a problem, which requires a decision (or several decisions) to address the situation and find a new job. If you receive an unexpected personal inquiry about a better job from another organization that you believe would be a step forward in your career, you will need to make some decisions, but is this really a problem? It is not a negative situation, so it is not a problem, but it is a decision problem, since the decision occurred as the result of someone else's decision, and you have to respond.

Who should be making your decisions? This is not a trick question, and the correct response is obvious. *You* should be making your decisions. So, who should be making the decisions to select which specific decisions you will face? This is a much more challenging question. My response is that you should be making some of them, and likely more of them than you currently are making. Your decisions empower you! They provide the only way that you can purposefully influence the quality of your life, or the well-being of others and our planet. Take advantage of that power.

Proactive versus Reactive Decision-Making

You do not choose the decision problems that you must face due to the actions of others and circumstances beyond your control. Addressing these decisions usually relies on reactive alternative-focused decision-making. On the other hand, you do have complete control to identify any specific decision that you want to face. This requires proactive value-focused decision-making.

> **Do not just solve your decision problems caused by others. Create decision opportunities to improve your life and avoid future decision problems.**

Let me illustrate the distinctions of the approaches above in a personal context important to each of you: your health. Suppose that your health is fine now, and you don't even think about it. This is a desirable situation, but it likely won't remain so forever. There will be times when you become ill and need to make a decision about whether to see a doctor. If you do visit a doctor, subsequent decisions need to be made by physicians and medical personnel about the specific diagnosis of your ailment. Next, you and your doctor need to make decisions about appropriate treatment. As illustrated in Figure 7.1, all of the decisions made once you become ill are clearly reactive responses to decision problems. Hopefully, as a result, you will recover and be as healthy as you were before your illness. If you are only a reactive decision-maker, you will make the necessary decisions and hope for the best.

Reactive alternative-focused decision-making

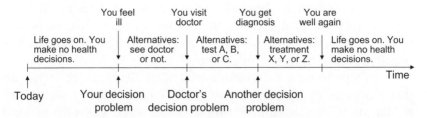

Proactive value-focused decision-making

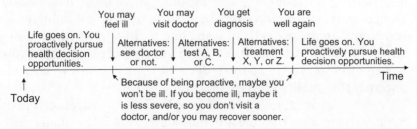

Figure 7.1 Proactive versus Reactive Decision-Making for Health Decisions

What would be different if you were a proactive decision-maker? While you are feeling just fine, you could create a decision opportunity for yourself. Suppose that you create the decision opportunity of "decide how to improve my health." Creating this decision opportunity is a significant nudge, which will often lead to a good decision that will improve your life.

By pursuing this decision opportunity, the direct short-term benefits are that you will be healthier, likely feel better, and be able to comfortably participate in more activities. Thus, as indicated in Figure 7.1, you may prevent the occurrence of the medical decision problem and not become ill. Furthermore, if you become ill, being healthier may reduce the seriousness and/or the recovery time.

A long-term benefit of addressing this decision opportunity now is that you may not subsequently face some decision problems concerning illness or accidents. Being proactive in this case may result in trading the current decision opportunity concerning how to become healthier for future decision problems, such as where to have triple bypass surgery and how to modify your life after having had a serious heart attack. If you end up facing such decision problems, they may have less severe consequences because of your better health. Also, if such a decision problem occurs, it may happen further in the future, and better medical alternatives to address such decision problems may have been developed.

Depending on your circumstances, alternatives to pursue this decision opportunity may include eliminating unhealthy habits such as smoking, eating a better diet, exercising regularly, getting annual flu shots, having appropriate periodic health exams, eliminating distractions while driving (e.g., texting, putting on makeup), and drinking alcohol in moderation. The point is not to alert you about such healthy alternatives, as you know them as well as I do, but to illustrate in an easily understood context that it is within your power—and only your power—to decide to address decision opportunities that will improve the quality of your life.

It seems natural for many people to think of decision opportunities to enhance their health and safety. That is the main reason why I have used this health context to distinguish between proactive and reactive decision-making and illustrate the key role of decision opportunities. I want you to understand the concept of a decision opportunity and recognize that it is a good idea that you can readily use in any decision context. In some contexts, such as employment, personal relationships, and living your life, it may not be so obvious how decision opportunities can be useful. Yet creating decision opportunities in any context is a good idea. Comparing Figure 7.2 to Figure 7.1 illustrates how analogous proactive decision-making is for employment decisions and health decisions.

A Key Distinction between Decision Opportunities and Decision Problems

Pursuing a decision opportunity that you created usually improves your life, whereas solving a decision problem that occurred usually does not improve your life. Solving a decision problem

Pursuing a decision opportunity is done to improve your quality of life. Solving a decision problem is done to return your quality of life to what it was prior to the occurrence of the decision problem.

Reactive alternative-focused decision-making

Proactive value-focused decision-making

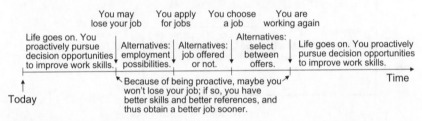

Figure 7.2 Proactive versus Reactive Decision-Making for Employment Decisions

attempts to restore your quality of life to that you had experienced before the decision problem occurred, back to the previous status quo. Pursuing a decision opportunity should improve your circumstances relative to the current status quo quality of your life.

This important distinction is illustrated in Figure 7.3, which indicates your quality of life over a period of time beginning today. In the top panel of Figure 7.3, something occurs that creates a serious decision problem a week from now. In the bottom panel, you proactively decide to address a useful decision opportunity a week from now. In both cases, your quality of life is the same during this first week. After that one week, due to the decision problem, your quality of life drops, as shown. You begin to address that decision problem and implement an alternative a few days later. Your situation should improve, but, depending on the specific decision and the alternative chosen, the path of improvement can vary greatly. Figure 7.3 illustrates two cases for both decision problems and decision opportunities.

As represented by the solid line for a decision problem, not much changes for a while, but then the consequences of your alternative begin to restore the quality of your life. After some

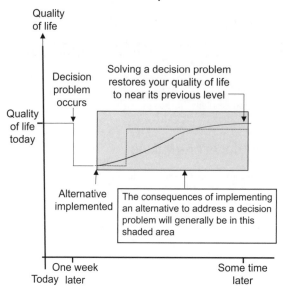

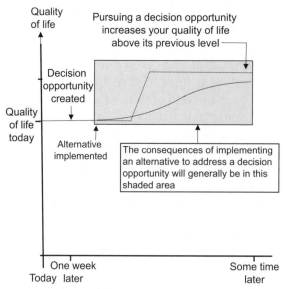

Figure 7.3 Impact on Your Quality of Life of Decision Problems and Decision Opportunities

time it is roughly back to where it was before you experienced the decision problem. An example might be your recovery from an injured back that you chose to address with physical therapy. The dotted line in the figure represents a different situation, where the improvement occurs at a single time in the future. An example is when your vehicle was damaged and not operable because of an accident. You chose to repair it and, when it was finished, it was almost as good as before the accident.

After you begin pursuing the decision opportunity in Figure 7.3, your quality of life in each of the two cases doesn't improve much immediately because the consequences require time to occur. The solid line represents a case where your quality of life slowly improves and ends up after some time to be significantly better than it was prior to pursuing the decision opportunity. An example is when you pursue a decision opportunity to strengthen your core body muscles by taking a four-month exercise class. The dashed line produces rapid improvements after some time period. An example is when you proactively pursue a decision opportunity to expand certain skills relevant to work and take a specific course to do so. The rapid improvement in your quality of life begins when you can implement what you learned in the course at work

The time frames and the increased quality of your life over time due to implementing an alternative for your decision can greatly vary. The improvements over time could follow any path within the shaded areas in Figure 7.3. If your decision problem is due to getting the flu, your quality of life drops a little and likely recovers within a week. If your decision problem is due to a serious accident, your quality of life may significantly drop and recovery could take a year, and it may not return completely to the quality of life you had prior to the accident. If the decision opportunity involves enrolling in the special six-month corporate business skills program, your quality of life due to a better job may accrue in about a year, and the level of improvement over your previous quality of life could vary greatly depending on many circumstances.

The improvements in your quality of life from what it was when you addressed your decision problem or decision opportunity may be either essentially permanent or temporary. With decision problems, the intent is almost always to make permanent improvements to restore your previous quality of life. You definitely want the consequences of solving decision problems concerning a job loss, a serious accident, or your child's poor academic performance in school to be permanent. With decision opportunities, decisions to enhance your ability to enjoy life, such as those concerning advancing your education, developing long-term friendships, and improving your decision-making skills, are meant to have a permanent effect. Decision opportunities to take a special vacation, voluntarily accept a challenging assignment at work, or help someone in need are mainly intended to have temporary effects, although there is often a long-term residual improvement in your quality of life.

Why Most Decision-Makers Underutilize Decision Opportunities

Recognizing and pursuing a decision opportunity is a very desirable nudge. As a result, your life will almost surely improve, and often in several ways, as illustrated with the health and employment decisions

> **Creating a decision opportunity is a powerful nudge, because pursuing that decision opportunity can have a positive influence on the quality of your life.**

discussed above. Facing a decision opportunity is a positive happening.

So, why don't decision-makers routinely create decision opportunities? Basically, most decision-makers do not have the conceptual framework to do this. The distinction between a decision problem and a decision opportunity is rarely made, at least in part because there has been no proper term or definition for what I have defined as a decision opportunity. This obviously hinders any routine use of this beneficial concept.

Many individuals make New Year's resolutions and/or create bucket lists of items that they desire to do or achieve. These resolutions and bucket items are not decision opportunities, but each could be the basis for defining a decision opportunity. Depending on your conception, achieving resolutions or accomplishing items on your list may rely on hope or desire. Hope is a positive emotion, but, with just hope, you have no influence on whether a resolution or bucket item will be fulfilled. To fulfill any hope or desire requires a decision to choose and implement an alternative.

Interestingly, almost all of us have unknowingly identified and pursued many decision opportunities for routine decisions, but we did not recognize them as such. Many of the things that we end up voluntarily doing in life are the result of an informal process akin to explicitly defining decision opportunities. Examples include deciding to go to a movie some evening, to create a dinner party for friends, to apply for a better job, to learn another language, to develop a new hobby or skill, or become an active fan of a sport team. We are in control of deciding to consider such activities, and our lives are usually improved as a result of doing them.

Selecting Your Next Important Decision

Suppose that your life is going well and you are not facing any important decisions at this time. You are enjoying your life. However, there is surely a decision opportunity that you could recognize that should make your life a bit better still. This decision opportunity is to decide whether the next important decision that you face will be a decision opportunity or a decision problem.

If you choose to make your next decision a decision opportunity, you create that decision opportunity and begin pursuing it to improve your quality of life from where it is today. If you do not decide to choose a decision opportunity, the default alternative is simply to do nothing and wait for the next decision problem. You solve it when it occurs, to get your quality of life back to what it was prior to that decision problem occurring. The decision opportunity is the better choice, because it very likely provides you with a higher quality of life than waiting for a decision problem. Recognizing this fact should strongly nudge you toward consciously creating more decision opportunities.

Some of your more important decisions are about which decisions you should face. Just as important to the quality of your life are the decisions that you did not think of or did not think of at the appropriate time. One example is remaining in an unsatisfying job because of the paycheck, and never recognizing the decision to search for a better job possibly with higher pay. Another case is not thinking soon enough about whether you would like to have children,[1] then not having the possibility to do so after you finally decide that you would like to have a child. Decision opportunities to address such situations could have been created, and addressing them might have avoided such negative circumstances.

Purposefully Creating Decision Opportunities

Your initial thoughts that lead to a decision opportunity are often about something that you would like or would not like in your future. Table 7.1 indicates several types of initial thoughts and the corresponding overall objective for a decision opportunity to improve your situation.

Many businesses and homeowners have considered a decision opportunity of what to do with specific waste materials. A general question to consider is whether the current waste could be useful as

Table 7.1 Illustrative Thoughts that Stimulate the Creation of Decision Opportunities

Initial thought	Objective of the decision opportunity
I want to achieve X	Achieve X
Something is bothering me	Eliminate the bother
I need more information to make a good decision	Identify the information useful for the decision and collect or create it
I'd like to do Y, but I can't because of. . .	Eliminate the reason why I can't do Y
I'm impressed by Graham's skill S	Develop skill S
I admire Diana's personal habit H	Develop habit H
A friend or family member is experiencing a serious difficulty	Help that friend or family member
Recognizing the usefulness of improving your decision-making skill	Improve my decision-making abilities
Experiencing Z would be great	Experience Z
Professional accomplishment P would help my career	Accomplish P

a resource. The potential alternatives are not limited to using it for the purpose that created the waste or only by the business or home that produced the waste. The potential uses can include different products, as well as selling or giving the waste to others who could productively use it.

Once you have chosen to face a decision opportunity, you may understand it well enough to identify one great alternative and actively pursue it. In such cases, recognizing the decision opportunity provided enough clarity about what action you should take.

► Converting Waste into a Resource

Kenneth "Hap" Klopp was the president and CEO at the North Face, headquartered in Berkeley, California, for 20 years after purchasing it as a local retail store. During that time he built it into a recognized world leader manufacturing and selling outdoor clothing, skiware, and camping equipment. Many of the North Face clothing and tent products were made in one of several colors using nylon cloth. As the company grew, even though cutting procedures minimized the amount of scrap cloth, the amount of scrap material became significant. Mr. Klopp recognized a decision opportunity: decide what could productively be done with all of the scrap material. Alternatives were developed that considered both single-color and multicolor uses, as well as the status quo "do nothing" alternative of discarding the current scrap material. The chosen alternative was to design and produce a multicolored duck down parka made from pieces of scrap. These parkas were extremely popular and sold at a premium compared to single-colored parkas in certain markets. ◄

For other decision opportunities, you may find it useful to construct an unambiguous decision frame of that decision opportunity. The steps of the process, which are the same as those for any decision problem that you face, are discussed in Chapter 3 and summarized in Table 3.1.

The first step is to state your decision opportunity clearly by beginning with the word "Decide" and ending with your intended overall objective or purpose. For example, for the intended objective "achieve X," your desired statement would be "decide how to best achieve X." As each decision opportunity is intended to make your life, or some aspect of your life, better, the second step is to define what you mean by "better" in this decision context. For this, you need to specify your values for this decision statement, because they indicate what you care about. The procedures in Chapter 5 will help you specify your values. These values are then used as a basis to create alternatives for the decision opportunity that you have chosen to address. Details on this process are provided in Chapter 6.

You can also consciously develop decision opportunities by beginning with your values. The following case illustrates the process to do this.

► Improving Your Social Life

Kathy is young and talented and recently moved to a large city over 500 miles away to begin working at an established firm. The job turns out to be terrific, but as of yet her social life is not satisfying. She has recognized the decision opportunity to improve her social life.

To define her decision opportunity, she first identified what she was particularly interested in regarding her social life. After serious thought, she defined her decision opportunity as "decide how to enjoy more activities with friends." To create alternatives, it is worthwhile to be more specific about the activities she was particularly interested in pursuing. Three main types of events were specified, namely going on local trips, exercising more frequently at her athletic club, and attending thought-provoking events.

Next, she wanted to understand why this shortcoming in her social life was occurring. The general answer was clear: mainly, not enough free time. However, the specific reasons for this were not so clear. After some introspection she concluded that her shortage of available time resulted chiefly from two habits. She was staying at work too late too often, mainly just to chat with coworkers. Second, she was spending a large amount of her current free time on social media.

Now she figured out how much time she was spending on these two time-consuming activities. She concluded that she could leave work more promptly and save six hours a week with no downgrading of her work performance. She was both surprised and irritated to realize that her current social media time was about 26 hours per week. So she set a limit of one hour per day for social media use, which freed 19 hours per week for other activities. She soon experienced the benefit of using the 25 additional hours per week interacting with friends and felt much happier. ◄

An important class of decision opportunities is when you decide that you want advice from someone. Often this advice is from professionals such as doctors, accountants, nutritionists, or lawyers about what to do in a certain situation. We all have pursued such decision opportunities. A less common related group of decision opportunities is when you want advice from someone who you respect concerning a decision you are facing, or perhaps should be facing. If I'm facing a difficult decision, after some time of thinking about it in person I frequently describe my decision to friends or family members and ask what they think my objectives should be, and/or what alternatives they can think of that I might like. I also sometimes ask senior colleagues about what I should professionally include in my next couple of years or what skills I should develop or enhance. Their responses suggest potential decision opportunities for me.

► **Relationships with Family Members**

Suppose that your grown daughter in her late twenties lives and works about 25 miles from your home. After high school she went to a university across the country and returned to the local area to begin a career four years ago. During that time you routinely have had several events together: the traditional holidays and birthday celebrations, some local excursions, a weekend trip each year, and numerous simple family dinners at your home. However, you have become aware that the difficulty of planning such get-togethers has increased and the frequency has decreased. You are not happy about this and do not know how or why it happened. This suggests several decision opportunities. One is to find out about your daughter's perceptions and preferences for the changed circumstances that you have just described. If you find out, or happen to know, that she prefers more frequent meetings, another decision opportunity is to find out what she thinks the basis for the current situation is, and change it.

She may feel that you had somehow signaled to her that you were not interested in meeting so frequently, a perception that suggests the decision opportunity of how to correct it. The alternative of just declaring that it is not true may not be the best alternative, as actions speak louder than words. You may also find that she is having additional constraints on her availability because of a critical project at work or because she has met an interesting friend. Another decision opportunity is to decide how to have family times that are less constraining and/or more interesting to her. ◄

The general point is that, if you have a personal problem with someone you care about, defining decision opportunities to address the situation is the only way you can improve the situation for them or for you.

Each of us naturally likes to help family and friends. They likely are not consciously aware of the concept and power of decision opportunities. This suggests that your decision opportunity is to help them recognize decision opportunities that could change a hope into a reality and make their lives better.

► **Helping a Friend Pursue Personal Goals**
Several years ago my wife and I were having dinner with our close friend Alan, who is a physician. My wife's book, *How to Get a Job in the San Francisco Bay Area*, had just been published and I had recently published a few professional articles. Alan knew of this, and in the discussion said something like: "I would really like to publish an article someday and see it in print." Janet and I replied, in unison and emphatically, "You could publish an article." Alan had great ideas. His main medical interests had always been wellness and causes of and corrections for dysfunctional medical work environments. We mentioned that he just needed to decide what he wanted to write, the professional journal in which he would like it to appear, and then write the article. We also mentioned that he might need to rewrite it a few times and should identify a couple of alternative journals that would also be appropriate for publishing his article. Alan had no trouble recognizing his decision opportunity and vigorously pursued it. Since that first article he has published over 100 peer-refereed articles in professional journals, and he is now a well-recognized authority on his interests and has lectured on these topics all over the world. ◄

Out-of-the-Blue Decision Opportunities. You want to be attuned to recognize decision opportunities at any time, as they can occur unexpectedly. The proverbial place for decision opportunities to occur in this manner is in the shower. An idea seems to pop into your mind, suggesting something you would like to do, experience, or accomplish. It could range from visiting Estonia, writing a book, being more pleasant to a particular person, talking to your boss about concerns at work, avoiding social media for a weekend, or being more proactive in finding a partner – possibly for life. Similar thoughts can occur while daydreaming or relaxing. You can give yourself a nudge that should improve your life by identifying a decision opportunity that your musings or daydreams suggest.

Other out-of-the-blue decision opportunities can be triggered by something that has just occurred or has been said. Suppose that your spouse is on a business or personal trip for a few days. You are making dinner at home or out alone in a restaurant and you have a flash feeling that this dinner would be a lot more enjoyable with your spouse. As the proverb says, "Absence makes the heart grow fonder." That feeling may stimulate a thought of a decision opportunity, namely to do something special to express that feeling to your spouse when she or he returns home.

Your friend, teacher, or family member may say something that suggests a decision opportunity. For example, suppose that you are on a walk in the local park with your ten-year-old daughter and she says: "I really like walking with you in the trees, daddy." An opening such as this might trigger the decision opportunity to have a family overnight camping trip in a forest with your daughter. For this decision, there are many alternatives: when, where, how long, how remote, and with whom.

Converting Decision Problems into Decision Opportunities

We each face some decision problems without any particularly appealing alternatives. You just received an offer to attend a professional conference including several important individuals in your field for three days at the end of next month. You definitely want to go to the conference, but you have a conflict. For those same three days, you previously agreed to visit your college roommate, who lives 1,000 miles away and you have not seen for about two years. It is early December, and yesterday you had a medical exam and today you found out that you have a lump in your breast. You live in a country with universal medical coverage and called in your area health center to arrange appointments for a biopsy to assess whether the tumor is malignant, and, if so, to have the tumor surgically removed. Because of the impending holidays, there is no available time for these appointments during the next six weeks.

There is a strong tendency to address decision problems such as these in the given narrow frame: just solve the problem by choosing the best of the available alternatives. Cancel your trip with your roommate with sincere apologies. Accept the first available appointment to get the biopsy, and, if necessary, a subsequent operation. Directly addressing these decisions is not appealing, but you believe that it needs to be done and the appropriate alternative seems clear.

It is important to recognize that, once such a decision problem occurs, there may be a more appealing decision opportunity that can replace the need to address that decision problem. The basis for converting decision problems into more appealing decision opportunities is the frame for your decision problem, which is discussed in

> After a decision problem has occurred, you can sometimes replace it with a decision opportunity or modify it to be a decision opportunity.

Chapter 3. The three components necessary to construct that frame are a statement of the decision you face, your values for the decision, and the alternatives that you want to consider. If you change any of these components, your decision problem will be altered, so it is a different decision. Since you created that different decision, it is a decision opportunity.

The following two cases illustrate the conversion of decision problems into decision opportunities by expanding the statement of your original decision problem, adding additional values relevant to the decision, and/or increasing the number of alternatives under consideration.

► Managing Conflicting Time Commitments

On facing the decision problem about whether to visit your college roommate next month or attend the professional conference, the readily available alternatives are clear: one or the other. Given the choices, you may feel that it is necessary to cancel the agreed-upon visit with your college friend. Again, think of your values. You definitely feel it would be enjoyable and professionally very important to attend the professional conference; you want to experience a great time with your college roommate; and you want your college roommate to have a great time. Based on these values, you would like to both attend the professional conference and visit your friend the same weekend; but you can't. However, you can do better. Just eliminate the constraint of "the same weekend," so your decision opportunity is to "decide how to attend the professional conference and visit my friend for a weekend."

Rather than just canceling a visit with your friend by saying "We have to plan something for some other time" and leaving it at that, think of what your college roommate really would like. You know her well, so this should not be a difficult task. Then create other alternatives to get together with your college roommate. With some serious thinking of what you both like, you may create some alternatives, such as a three-day visit to Québec City, a visit to your college for the weekend of the annual homecoming, or a trip to New York to see some theater and enjoy the city. You then explain the situation to your college roommate and offer her a choice of these three alternatives that you think she would like. One, or perhaps more, of these three alternatives may be preferable to the current planned visit by both your college roommate and you. For sure, the demonstrated thought and offer associated with the necessary cancellation of the original visit will be appreciated. ◄

► Arranging Appropriate Medical Treatment
Regarding having a lump detected and a biopsy required, many individuals would consider that the alternatives are to check the nearby medical facilities and make an appointment at the one with the earliest opening. In the situation described in this example, the mother of a friend of mine found that the earliest opening for a biopsy was approximately six weeks away. My friend, his mother, and the family strongly felt that the implications of this wait were very undesirable and could be dangerous. Therefore, they addressed the decision opportunity to find a facility that could do the biopsy and any necessary subsequent treatment (e.g., surgical removal of the tumor, with possible other steps) much sooner.

They enlarged the geographic region that they considered, which included many additional alternative state medical facilities that could provide the services needed. One facility was found that could do the biopsy in two days and any subsequent treatment in the next week. They chose that option. The biopsy indicated that the tumor was malignant and involved a fast-spreading cancer. Based on this information, my friend's mother chose to have the tumor removed soon with a subsequent protocol of chemotherapy. The physician later said that it was significant that this cancer was detected when it was, because each month could make a difference. In checkups since the full range of treatment, my friend's mother has been declared free of cancer. ◄

Add-On Decision Opportunities

You work in Atlanta and have just been informed of an upcoming business trip scheduled for two weeks from now in mid-September to Calgary, Alberta, with meetings on Wednesday through Friday midday. You now have a decision problem concerning the arrangements for the trip. Because you are pressed for time, you ask your company's travel officials to recommend flights, and they suggested the least-cost non-refundable ticket. Their proposed itinerary has you changing planes, both going and coming, in Salt Lake City. With roughly four-hour stopovers both ways, you leave Tuesday at noon and arrive at 8:30 p.m. local time and depart Friday at 4:00 p.m. and arrive in Atlanta at 5:15 a.m. on Saturday morning. This itinerary is terrible and would disrupt your entire weekend.

► Better Air Travel Accommodations

You readily pursue the decision opportunity to find a more convenient airline itinerary. That evening you checked and found much better connections through Chicago, where you could depart from Atlanta at roughly the same time and arrive in Calgary at 5:30 p.m. local time. Returning, you could depart on Friday at 2:30 p.m. and arrive in Atlanta at 11:00 p.m. that evening. And the total additional cost was approximately $40. Naturally, you booked this itinerary. ◄

It is often worth recognizing the decision opportunity to investigate various flights on the basis of your values. Once you know the origins and destinations of a planned flight itinerary, just 15 minutes of thought and effort can often avoid the loss of much more time due to hassle and inconvenience for relatively little or no cost. Compared to the flight plan booked by your company's travel office, the Chicago option offers an evening in Calgary and approximately eight hours less total travel time and avoids an overnight flight to get home. For most travelers, 15 minutes of thought invested to save eight hours of essentially wasted time is a bargain, even without any other advantages.

The implementation of any alternative for a decision involves the commitment of resources such as time, money, and effort. When making such a commitment, it may be useful to consider whether any other decisions might be pursued that could share the use of these committed resources. A common example where this occurs involves a business trip set up for a specific purpose. It may be relatively easy to add on other business purposes, such as meeting with additional customers or clients, or achieving a personal desire, such as visiting friends, a renowned museum, or a special sports event. The concept of an add-on decision opportunity can nudge you to better use any commitment of resources.

Before booking an airline reservation for a business trip, it is frequently a good idea to consider a decision opportunity by expanding the values to include personal interests. The decision opportunity is to decide whether and which business/pleasure trip might be better than the strictly business trip option. You cannot be worse off by recognizing this decision opportunity, and you might be much better off than if you didn't recognize it.

► A Special Weekend

Suppose that you could easily arrange to have no commitments in Atlanta on the weekend that you return. Take time to ask yourself what else you could add to your Calgary business trip. The Canadian Rocky Mountains and Banff National Park are a beautiful part of North America only 80 miles from Calgary. It may be worth adding a visit there to your plans for a few days. Perhaps your spouse or a friend could join you in Calgary after lunch on Friday.

Even if you had to return for work next Monday, if you have never seen that part of the Canadian Rockies, two days would be very enjoyable, and would certainly inform you whether you should plan a longer trip to that area in the future. You can often give yourself a nudge that improves travel alternatives in this fashion by adding activities worthwhile to you. Recognizing these, the question that remains is whether the additional time and cost are worth it. ◄

The Value of Learning in Any Decision. Adding an objective about learning in any decision problem converts it to a decision opportunity.

Companies have much more experience concerning the hiring process and employment offers than almost any individual.

If an organization offers you a job, the hiring team naturally believes the benefits to the organization are of greater value than the total costs. Having received a job offer, you may not know much about the difference in value of the perceived benefits and costs of your employment to the firm. But you can learn something about that difference.

If you suggest an increase in your offered salary, the company's response may help you learn about this difference. Your suggested increase may not make too much difference to the firm and it may end up improving your offer. You may find out that your salary cannot be increased, but that a separate desirable perk can be added to the offer. Or the firm may respond with "We can't do that now, but I understand your situation and maybe in the future. . ." If you present your suggestion diplomatically, it should rarely result in the withdrawal of the original offer, although it may not change the offer. You also gain some experience in negotiating for yourself concerning future career positions. In any potential employment discussions, you should always have the objective of learning how to do it better, as what you learn may be very useful in your future.

► Negotiating an Employment Offer
Allison had a great job with a well-respected local company for three years, and then the situation began to change when her firm was purchased by a national organization. Within three months some of her friends had left, and there were many new rules and company policies to follow. Going to work was no longer enjoyable and she didn't feel that customers were being treated well. She decided to look for better opportunities and has now received attractive offers from two different companies, A and B. In most ways, they are similar in meeting her objectives, and both salaries are essentially the same. She would be pleased to accept either, but the offer at company A is slightly preferred to the offer at company B because the neighborhood near company A is more interesting. Treated as a decision problem to select a new job now just requires the choice between the two alternatives. But Allison thought more deeply.

Allison has not taken a real vacation for a year and she would like one. However, both companies are hoping she will start without a break, since the high season for their business is upon them. Allison has identified some appealing decision opportunities to expand her decision. She could inquire at company

A whether their offer could include a three-week vacation at a specific time after the high season is over. She might request this with or without pay or with some earned days off because of extra work during the high season. She might say that she would definitely accept the offer if she received this time off with pay.

Separately, because of her financial circumstances, Allison may know that she would prefer the offer of company B if it were exactly as offered except that the annual salary was 10 percent higher. With the offer from company A in hand, she is risking nothing by suggesting an additional 10 percent annually from company B and politely explaining why this is so important. It could be funds to pay off college loans and become debt-free, helping an aging parent, or any of many reasons that do not make it sound as if it is only money that matters to Allison. It isn't the case, so she should be able to make that clear. If the salary of company B is raised by 10 percent, she could accept the offer, or she could then make a proposal to have her salary raised at company A. ◄

Benefiting from Decision Opportunities

By routinely identifying and pursuing decision opportunities, you have the possibility to make things better and can significantly enhance the quality of your life. To convert this potential into a reality requires you to make the effort to pursue four steps.

1. Understand thoroughly the concept of a decision opportunity and how it is different from the decision problems that you regularly face. Pursuing decision opportunities can improve your life, whereas addressing decision problems can only restore your quality of life to where it was prior to when the decision problem occurred.

2. Recognize that you have the exclusive power to identify your own decision opportunities. Any limitation on your ability to do this must be due to a lack of understanding of the concepts and procedures to identify decision opportunities or a lack of effort and time commitment to identify them.

3. Allocate time and effort to consciously identify appealing decision opportunities. There are many procedures to create decision opportunities from scratch, to convert decision problems into decision opportunities, and to

add on decision opportunities to other decisions that you are considering.

4. Begin using decision opportunities regularly in both your personal life and your professional life. Use them for any decisions worthy of thought, not just your life-changing or very important decisions. Your experiences will not only provide worthwhile benefits but will serve as practice to help improve your skill in routinely identifying and implementing decision opportunities for any of your decisions, including those of great importance.

By following these four steps, you can make identifying and using decision opportunities a lifelong habit that greatly contributes to the quality of your life.

Additional Thoughts for Decisions in Organizations

Decision opportunities are important for any business or governmental organization. For businesses, being proactive and routinely searching for decision opportunities leads to alternatives that improve your business and can keep you ahead of the competition. Focusing all of your decision effort on decision problems can maintain your business as it is and, at

> **In businesses, being proactive and routinely identifying and pursuing decision opportunities promotes creativity and innovation.**

best, allows you to keep up with the competition. The distinction relates to the often repeated question: do you want to lead or do you want to follow? The leaders must identify decision opportunities and implement alternatives to take advantage of them.

▶ Customer Acquisition at American Express

American Express is one of the largest and most respected companies providing charge cards and credit cards to customers worldwide. In the 1980s and through 1995 American Express made many of its strategic decisions with the sole objective of maximizing profit. A key strategic decision concerned the recruitment of potential new cardholders. Annually, American Express would select millions of individuals to contact about applying for an American Express card. Selecting the individuals to contact was based on the results of a sophisticated analytical model that calculated the expected contribution to the net present value of profits for prospective cardholders.

By 1995, mainly because of the rapid growth of rivals Visa and MasterCard in the 1980s and early 1990s, the American Express share of the total market for charges on such cards had been decreasing for over a decade. American Express recognized that it had a decision opportunity to address how to rebuild its market share. The company added the objective of increasing market share to the original objective of maximizing net profit when evaluating prospective customers. So, what had been a model with a single objective was expanded to become a model with two objectives. I worked with American Express executives to construct a two-objective evaluation function that could consistently evaluate and compare the relative importance of any change in expected profits or in market share to American Express.

This model was initially implemented in late 1995 to select which of 50 million prospective customers to contact. As a result, targeting strategies were altered to focus on customers who would constitute both a higher-usage and a higher-risk group. This significantly increased customer acquisition volume, exceeding business goals of acquisition in 1996 by a large number. In the first six months of 1997 the American Express market share of the domestic card market increased from 18.31 percent to 18.90 percent, whereas it had lost market share in each of the corresponding six-month periods over the previous ten years. Using the multiple-objective evaluation function, the relative importance of this increase in market share was calculated to be equivalent to an additional profit of $447 million in 1997 dollars.

The Wall Street Journal published an article on this impressive improvement.[2] In the article, H. Spencer Nilson, the publisher of the Nilson Report,[3] said: "You've got to give credit to American Express for overcoming huge obstacles to growth through creative marketing and excellent customer service." Also in the article, Kenneth I. Chenault, the then president of American Express, who became the chairman and chief executive officer, was quoted as saying: "Market share has been a very key focus of our card business over the last three years and I think what you're seeing is that we have had a very strong effect in increasing spending on our card products and our cards in force." ◄

The motives of governmental organizations are different from those of private organizations. Government organizations have a responsibility to address the problems that beset the citizens who they represent. The typical way that they address such a problem, once it is recognized, is to create alternatives, choose one – hopefully a good one – and implement it. However, the problems that governments face typically recur.

Examples concern how to improve traffic, better educate students, train individuals for jobs, feed and house the needy, communicate better with constituents, and maintain infrastructure. For such situations and services, governments can proactively create and pursue decision opportunities to decide how to improve efforts in the future when similar problems occur and decide what proactive steps might avoid or lessen the frequency and magnitude of such future problems.

The process for creating decision opportunities within any organization is similar to that of an individual, as the initial spark for creating any decision opportunity must occur in the mind of an individual. However, an individual in an organization (e.g., a president or a manager) can solicit the assistance of numerous others working for him or her to proactively create decision opportunities that may be worthwhile to meet a specific purpose. A manager who does this is pursuing a decision opportunity that he or she created, namely to generate useful decision opportunities. He or she could also pursue a decision opportunity to elicit suggestions for alternatives to pursue that decision opportunity. In both of these situations, the manager will get much better responses if the values that he or she hopes to achieve are clearly specified in the request for suggestions.

In the cases above, the manager asks for specific assistance and then receives useful ideas. However, the stimulus for ideas need not come from a specific request of some manager in an organization. Why be so limiting in this way? An organization could establish a systematic process to stimulate proactive ideas from anyone for a decision opportunity that might benefit the organization. It may also be desirable to acknowledge and reward, financially and/or otherwise, great decision opportunities that result in significant contributions to the organization.

8 OBTAINING AUTHORIZATION TO SELECT ALTERNATIVES CONTROLLED BY OTHERS

You certainly have the authority to make your decisions. But does this mean that you have the authority to choose any alternative that you can think of for your decisions? Unfortunately, it does not. There are important decisions for which you do not have the authority to implement some alternatives that have great appeal to you. Someone else, who I refer to as the authorized decision-maker, controls whether the alternative that you prefer for a particular decision can be implemented. The good news is that there are reasonable ways to remove such restrictions, which is the focus of this chapter.

You are a salesman for a software firm selling a product useful for any city or municipality. Your region of responsibility includes several southwestern states, and your office is in Phoenix. For personal reasons, mainly easy access to skiing and camping, you would prefer to have your office in Salt Lake City. Your manager is the authorized decision-maker, with total control over whether such a move is authorized. Another example is a city with regulations for building or remodeling houses that might block the views of neighbors. Neighbors have the right to review your construction plans and file a complaint within a specified time. If there are no complaints you can build as planned. If there is one or more complaint, the city official will review each complaint and make a decision on what can or cannot be built. Your neighbors and the city official are all authorized decision-makers for this decision. A third situation is where you share the decision-making authority with other individuals. They can choose not to accept the alternative that you desire, which will, essentially, block your implementation of this alternative. A simple example is when you want to go on a weekend outing with your good friend. If he does not choose to go, you can't have an outing together.

An Alternative that Can't Be Refused

For some decisions, you may think of a very desirable general alternative. However, an authorized decision-maker has the authority to accept or reject any specific alternative that you propose. Prior to implementation, you need to create a specific alternative that includes the general features of your desired alternative and additional features to make that specific alternative attractive to the authorized decision-maker. You want to make that specific alternative so attractive to the authorized decision-maker that it can't be refused.

Creating such an alternative is a powerful nudge that leads to a good decision—one that will often improve your life. The immediate influence of this nudge is on the authorized decision-maker. As a result of this nudge, a specific version of your desirable general alternative becomes viable, enabling you to choose it. Hence, creating the specific alternative that can't be refused can be considered as an indirect nudge of yourself that allows you to select a greatly desired alternative.

The process of creating and proposing an alternative that can't be refused is what I think of as a *phantom negotiation*. You are negotiating both for yourself and for the authorized decision-maker, who is not directly involved at this time, and possibly not even aware of the process. It begins when you think of something that you would like. This thought itself may be an alternative, or, almost immediately after the thought, you will envision an alternative that would provide what you desire. I refer to this as your *dream alternative*, which is represented in Figure 8.1. However, you recognize that this alternative is worse for the authorized decision-maker than the status quo as shown. The challenge for you is to design your proposed alternative to include the key features of your dream alternative as well as to improve matters for the authorized

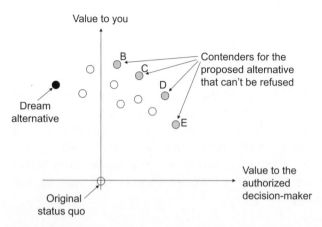

Figure 8.1 Creating an Alternative that Can't Be Refused

decision-maker, who must authorize your alternative. You want her improvement relative to the status quo to be significant enough to be an alternative that can't be refused. You might even figure out an alternative that is better for you than your current dream alternative and also positive for the authorized decision-maker.

Once you create an alternative that you think can't be refused, you propose it to the authorized decision-maker. From her perspective, without any warning you are proposing an alternative that will change her current situation from the status quo. If this change represents an improvement to her status quo, she will likely authorize it. If it does not, you should find out why and modify your proposal to address her concern. You are not doing anything inappropriate in this process, because who would not like to receive an offer that was so good that it could not be refused? I am open to such offers, and I hope you are too.

Suppose that you create the additional alternatives described by the circles in Figure 8.1. Note that, of the ten alternatives created, only the four shaded circles represent contenders for the proposed alternative that can't be refused. Two of the other alternatives are worse for the authorized decision-maker than the status quo and four are worse for both you and the authorized

> **If someone else has authority over whether the alternative that you desire can be implemented, use the authorized decision-maker's values to modify your desired alternative to please both of you.**

decision-maker than at least one of the four shaded contenders. You might propose alternative B, because it is better than the status quo for the authorized decision-maker and the best of the contenders for you. However, if the authorized decision-maker did not recognize that the possible benefits were perhaps overbalanced toward you when proposed, she may recognize it later. For this reason, and perhaps based on your concept of fairness, you might propose alternative C or D, which both have a better balance of benefits and a better chance of being an alternative that can't be refused.

A significant personal example of creating an alternative that can't be refused should clarify the concepts and process and demonstrate its value.

► Writing a Book Together

As a graduate student in operations research at the Massachusetts Institute of Technology, I had arranged to have Professor Howard Raiffa of Harvard University as my doctoral thesis advisor, and wrote my thesis on the theory and practice of using objective functions incorporating multiple objectives. By the spring prior to graduating I had completed all of the degree requirements and had the time to think about my life after graduation and decision opportunities that would enhance both my personal and professional life. One such decision opportunity with great appeal to me was to write a book on decision-making with multiple objectives with Howard. He was a world-renowned leader in fields now called the decision sciences, and a delightful person.

Co-authoring such a book was a dream alternative for me. It was obvious that it would be a joy, I would learn a great deal, and it would greatly enhance my professional career. However, it wasn't so clear that such a collaboration would be a good deal for Howard, since he had numerous other professional commitments and an active personal and family life. I needed to propose this joint book to Howard, the authorized decision-maker, and I really wanted a positive response.

I thought hard about what Howard's values might be for such a project. I knew he would like to have such a book published, because it would communicate his many ideas on the important topic of how to think clearly about and do an analysis of decisions with multiple objectives. This book would promote more informed decisions in such circumstances and provide a basis for educating future students on the topic. I knew

Howard always wanted to help young professionals, and he certainly would recognize that the joint book would greatly help me. He also would even further increase his intellectual impact if the proposed book was of high quality, since no comprehensive book existed on this important topic at that time. These values concerned the pluses of such a book for Howard. But what about the minuses?

The disadvantages were clear. They mainly concerned Howard's time commitment and the subsequent inconveniences that might render it not worth his effort. These could result in opportunities that he subsequently might not be able to pursue, and there was always the possibility of the need arising to cancel the book project.

To develop an alternative that I hoped Howard couldn't refuse, I decided to outline a proposed book that provided an unambiguous description of our task. It included material that Howard thought was important and yet not widely known or understood. I tried to make this an outline of a book he would be proud to co-author.

I realized that I could not eliminate his time commitment, but I could significantly reduce the negative implications of that commitment. I proposed that we write the book with a flexible timeframe, one that could be adjusted to avoid as much negative impact on any of his other activities as possible. For necessary meetings and communication, we could have these any time of day or night and anywhere convenient to Howard. And he could cancel or postpone such meetings as needed with, essentially, no notice.

In June we had a meeting, at which I proposed the joint book project and presented the outline. I stated the obvious advantages to me and then mentioned what I thought were the pros and cons to him. I then spelled out all of the guidelines that would minimize the negative impacts to him. As a summary, I mentioned that he definitely cared about the topic and wanted such a book to exist, but he probably would never write that book alone as he had too many other interesting projects and activities. On the other hand, I said that I would have nothing more important to pursue professionally and I would do all that I could to make our joint book a reality. Finally, I stated the obvious: "If at any time you feel that the book is not measuring up to your quality standard, you can cancel the project." At the end of our meeting, which included a lot of discussion, Howard enthusiastically agreed to the project.

I was delighted. The flexibility on timing that was part of our alternative turned out to be critical, as Howard soon became immersed in work on creating the International Institute for Applied Systems Analysis near Vienna, and subsequently served as the first director of IIASA. During that time period we were also able to apply the methodological ideas in the book to many important decisions involving multiple objectives. Including several of these applications in our book improved it relative to what we would have been able to achieve with a more compressed schedule. Our book, *Decisions with Multiple Objectives*, was published, and it is still in print.[1] ◄

It is worth recognizing that the crucial features of my dream alternative were to co-author a high-quality book with Howard about decision-making to which I could make a substantial contribution. Knowing these crucial features, my task was to design a specific alternative that not only maintained the crucial features of the dream alternative but was also better for Howard, the authorized decision-maker, than his current status quo.

This example illustrates the two activities necessary to create better alternatives for an authorized decision-maker. The first is to identify the values of the authorized decision-maker, and the second is to identify features for potential alternatives that improve the degree of achievement of those values. Then, add such features to the dream alternative to make it an alternative that you believe can't be refused.

A common circumstance that can be crucial for creating an alternative that can't be refused is present in this example. Sometimes the main disadvantages of your dream alternative to the authorized decision-maker arise from the process of implementing the alternative rather than from the alternative itself. These disadvantages often result from the commitment of time, effort, or money, which render other future activities either inconvenient, difficult, or impossible. Hence, the values of the authorized decision-maker regarding implementation may be the key to constructing an alternative that can't be refused. The role of providing flexibility for implementing the alternative to eliminate inconveniences, constraints, and hassle for the authorized decision-maker was very helpful in this example, as it is in many decision opportunities.

Identifying the Values of an Authorized Decision-Maker

To modify your dream alternative to make it appeal to an authorized decision-maker, you do not need to know all of their values relevant to the decision of concern. Even if you know only one of the authorized decision-maker's values, you still may be able to modify your dream alternative enough to be acceptable. However, the better you understand the authorized decision-maker's values, the easier it will be to create an alternative that cannot be refused and the more likely it will lead to the authorized decision-maker's agreement.

To identify the values of an authorized decision-maker, someone needs to articulate them. There are three possibilities: you, the authorized decision-maker him- or herself, or others. In many cases the authorized decision-maker is someone you know, and you can generate a list of many of his or her values from your knowledge. In the example above, I had worked with Howard for a couple of years as a doctoral student and was able to articulate many of his values that were relevant to this decision.

The authorized decision-maker is, naturally, an excellent source of his or her own values, and sometimes you can directly inquire about these. If you already know the person, it should not be difficult to arrange to do this. Most people are willing to discuss what they care about, including their values regarding something that they care about accomplishing.

► A Summer Internship

Suppose that you have a summer internship at an organization and you want it to be worthwhile; who wouldn't? But you realize that your concept of what is worthwhile is vague, so you think hard about your values for this internship. You would like a project that would make a contribution both to the work of your supervisor, who is the authorized decision-maker in the situation, and to the organization. You want it to offer you the opportunity to demonstrate your skills and to improve them. These skills include professionally interacting with others, writing effectively, and being creative, thoughtful, and thorough. Finally, you would like to earn a very enthusiastic reference for use in the future.

You need to talk to your supervisor about a project. First, you should inquire about the values that your supervisor would like to see achieved by such projects. Next, you could discuss potential projects that, if carried out well, would achieve these values. Then you could request a day to carefully think about which project will allow you to best achieve your supervisor's values. During this time you could also consider how well each of the projects will meet your internship objectives. You might also be able to create a new alternative project by modifying a suggestion of your supervisor in a way that you feel is better for the supervisor, the organization, and you. You describe your preferred project to your supervisor and, essentially, say: "I prefer project A, because it allows me to best contribute to the values that you care about and it also allows me to make a positive contribution to the organization." If it is convincingly offered, it should be hard to refuse, partly because the supervisor has little to lose and you have described the benefits. ◄

You are relatively new at your company and become aware of a standing committee whose members routinely meet to gather and manage ideas from employees for improving operations at or the products of the company. You identify a decision opportunity and decide that you would like to be a member of that committee to meet others throughout the company, and to learn about the activities and functioning of parts of the company more quickly. From colleagues, you learn that the committee reports to a vice president and that she selects members for the committee. You have never met the vice president, who is the authorized decision-maker, and want to understand her values regarding the committee. In this case, you may need to develop these values from others.

You find out who is currently on the committee and arrange discussions with a couple of these members. In addition, you learn about a committee document describing the reasons for its existence. From these sources, you can discern many of the values of the vice president for the committee. These include values for the employees and values for the company. The values for the company are to receive and act on employee ideas efficiently, enhance the work environment, and improve its products. Values directly affecting the employees are to demonstrate that the company management values its employees, cares about the quality of their work environment, considers the suggestions of all employees, implements many of their ideas, and recognizes individuals for their good ideas.

Creating Alternatives that Are Desirable to the Authorized Decision-Maker

Designing an appealing alternative for an authorized decision-maker uses the same thoughtful processes as creating good alternatives for yourself, which are discussed in Chapter 6. You separately consider each value of the authorized decision-maker and think about what elements to add to or modify your dream alternative that improves it in terms of that value.

> **Use the values of the authorized decision-maker to improve an alternative for that authorized decision-maker and retain the current features that you want.**

An important mental attitude in this design process is to believe that there are specific alternatives that can be created that include your crucial features. You can succeed with effort and creativity, as your eventual proposed alternative can include anything that is positive for the authorized decision-maker. You can even combine unrelated decisions that are desired by the authorized decision-maker into your alternative.

► Coaching a Soccer Team

Suppose that you and another child's parent are the co-coaches of a grade school soccer team. At the beginning of the season you both had agreed to attend all practices and games. Now something has occurred, so you really want to skip next weekend's game, but you recognize how difficult it is for one person to manage all aspects of the team during a game. You feel as though you need the other coach's authorization to miss the game, and you don't want this to be grudgingly given.

You might create an alternative that the other coach could miss a game or a couple of practices if desired. You may also realize that your two families will end up hosting a season-ending team party, and perhaps know that the other coach would not enjoy being responsible for that. You could include in your alternative that you will be solely responsible for all aspects of that party. He may find this alternative to be great. You can also combine your desire to miss next weekend's game with an unrelated decision. You may own a summer cabin in a recreational area a couple of hours away from where you live. You can simply offer the use of your cabin to him for a weekend as part of your desired alternative.

The point is that there are numerous possibilities, and creative thinking can unearth how to make what you propose more positive for the other individual. ◄

This general idea of combining decisions is particularly important when the feature you want is clearly a negative to the authorized decision-maker. In such a case, you both cannot simultaneously benefit in terms of your crucial value; if you gain, the authorized decision-maker loses, and vice versa. A decision to raise your salary has such a feature, especially in the case of a very small company.

If you decide that you definitely want a 20 percent raise, you may be able to combine this request with many other possible aspects to create an alternative that can't be refused. You could offer to take responsibility for something in addition to what you currently do. You may enjoy that and look forward to enhancing your skills. You may have thoughts on how the company could be more efficient and effective at reducing expenses. You might offer to take responsibility for identifying how to do this. You could propose, depending on the circumstances, that your desired increase in salary be paid for from one-half of such savings and occur only when they are documented. Also, you may have ideas to increase revenue. The bottom line is that, if implementing your proposal improves the quality or profitability of the company, it is much easier to authorize an increase in salary.

Uses of Alternatives that Can't Be Refused

Obtaining the approval of an authorized decision-maker is very useful in at least three general circumstances: making dreams come true, avoiding nightmares, and overcoming constraints. Its use for making dreams come true is discussed above. The other two uses are described and illustrated below.

Avoiding Nightmares. A nightmare is an undesirable situation that you are currently in because of someone else's decision. That individual, who is the authorized decision-maker, has made a decision that will have a detrimental effect for you. We all find ourselves in such situations once in a while. An example is when your manager assigns you a boring task that will require a month of your time and effort. Figure 8.2 illustrates the general situation, where your original status quo prior to the other's decision and the new nightmare status quo are indicated.

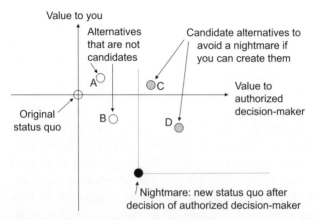

Figure 8.2 Creating an Alternative to Avoid a Nightmare

To get out of this nightmare, you need to create an alternative that has higher values for both you and the authorized decision-maker than this new status quo. Hence, only new alternatives to the upper right of the dashed lines in Figure 8.2 will likely be acceptable. The thought process and procedures that you use are the same as those for making your dreams come true. In Figure 8.2, alternatives A and B are not better for the

> When you are in an undesirable situation as the result of another's decision, that decision-maker can let you out of this situation. Create and propose an alternative that is better for the decision-maker that includes getting you out of this situation.

authorized decision-maker, so these would not be potential candidates. If you could create an alternative C, suggest it. If not, alternative D would also be an improvement for both you and the authorized decision-maker. Even though alternative D is less desirable to you than the original status quo, it is much better than the nightmare.

If your manager has assigned you a nightmare task, you may be able to identify a task that would be more valuable to your boss and the organization that you would like to do. Then propose to your boss that you do this more valuable task instead of the nightmare task. To facilitate acceptance of your proposal, you might also suggest other ways that your boss could easily have the nightmare task accomplished. Maybe it could be outsourced effectively, maybe another manager at your boss' level has an employee with available time, and maybe the task would be useful for a college student's internship that existed or could be created. Any of these ideas, or a combination, may get you out of doing the nightmare task with no negative consequences, and maybe some positive consequences for creatively thinking of a better way to handle the task.

Sometimes potential nightmares can be anticipated and avoided. A common case is when a group of, say, five individuals has agreed to do something that requires the completion of several tasks that will be done individually but must be integrated together. Two specific examples concern a team at work requested to produce a written report and friends preparing for a week-long wilderness hike. You like all of the individuals in both cases, but some of them tend to procrastinate and you know that a great deal of time will be spent discussing the numerous small problems that will inevitably come up in the process of completing the work. You find such discussions boring and a waste of time and you have some other important upcoming responsibilities.

To avoid such a potential nightmare, you can first identify a substantial task that will provide more than your fair share of the effort to produce the desired result. Then propose to the group that you do this task soon and explain that you feel it would be your contribution to the effort. Since it both gets the process started and reduces the effort required by the others, they should each view it as an alternative that can't be refused. To be collegial, you could add that you are willing to consider contributions that require some time to finalize the overall preparations. Your proactive effort will have removed you from the boring discussions and wasted time that might follow and yet you will be contributing more than your share of the joint project work.

Overcoming Constraints. Sometimes you think of an alternative that you would like to implement and then learn you can't implement that alternative because of some constraint, rule, or guideline. The constraint was established by some authority such as a government, business, school, or your parents. The purpose of the constraint may be to establish or maintain quality related to alternatives such as the one you are interested in pursuing. Examples are a university that limits enrollment in a particular class or a company that sets a constraint that limits telecommuting to one day a week.

Typically, some individual has responsibility for enforcing the constraint, such as the instructor in a limited-enrollment course or one's manager regarding telecommuting. These individuals often have the authority to disregard the constraint in specific instances, and, if they don't have such authority, they probably know who does. There are two things you must do to have the constraint waived for your alternative. You need to design your alternative so that it is reasonable to implement and so that it provides benefits—or, certainly, no disbenefits—to the authorized decision-maker. Thus, the authorized decision-maker can justify waiving the constraint for you and not others and also avoid complaints about not appropriately enforcing the constraint.

A key to justify the disregarding of a constraint is to create your alternative so that it achieves the intent of the constraint, even though it violates the specific guideline. The intent of a class limit of 20 students in a college class is to ensure high-quality individual attention for students in the class. Other factors also influence this, such as the arrangement of the classroom, tangible material brought into and from each class, and the processing of material necessary for each class. If you ask the instructor to join an already full class and offer to take charge of some tasks such as these, the instructor could avoid some onerous tasks and focus on teaching. This would improve the quality of the class and provide a rationale for disregarding the class limit constraint in your case. You would likely become the twenty-first student in the class and have as much interaction with the instructor as you would like. Moreover, if necessary, the instructor may be able to describe you as a volunteer teaching aide, thus technically avoiding breaking the guideline.

The same idea applies to getting approval to telecommute whenever you want. In this case, you can at first follow your company's one-day-a-week constraint. Try to use the two hours per day that you might save by telecommuting to do more and/or better-quality work. Be able to document the specifics of what you did to make a greater contribution when telecommuting. When you discuss your desire to telecommute two and sometimes three days a week, explicitly mention that interacting with colleagues at work is important to your productivity and that you would certainly physically be at the office whenever it was useful and/or requested by your boss or colleagues. Your productivity record while telecommuting provides your boss with a clear justification to disregard the telecommuting constraint for you, and, since you are more productive, it makes his work life better. It also sets a high standard for anyone else who wishes to telecommute more frequently than the constraint allows.

▶ Obtaining a Reservation in a Sold-out Hotel

In 2013 the University of Bayreuth in Germany invited me to be a visiting professor for a week to work with my colleague Johannes Siebert, teach a short course on value-focused decision-making, and present a university seminar. Bayreuth is the home of the famous Bayreuth Festival, which features Richard Wagner's work every summer. In February the week for my visit was chosen as May 20 to 24. Under normal circumstances, all hotels in Bayreuth are only about half full during this period of the year. With an online search, I found the hotel where I wanted to stay. The Hotel Goldener Anker is historic, owned by the same family since its origin in 1753, and it is centrally located.

Johannes said he would make my reservation for six days, from Sunday May 19 to Saturday May 25. At the hotel, he learned that no rooms were available, because May 21 was fully booked. As it happened, May 22 was the 200th anniversary of Wagner's birth, and there was a one-day special event that attracted numerous opera fans to Bayreuth. On the other five days that I wanted, the hotel was less than half full. Since the hotel had more than 50 rooms and the event was about three months in the future, it was reasonable to anticipate that one or more reservation would be canceled. Perhaps more relevant, the hotel certainly had kept a few rooms available for "future circumstances." Johannes also learned that the standard rate for a single room was about €100 per night at this time of the year, but on May 21 the nightly rate was €200.

With this information, Johannes subsequently spoke with the receptionist and explained that booking a reservation for me for six days would bring in €600 at €100 per night compared to €200 for a May 21 booking and an empty room for the other five nights. The receptionist said she did not have the authority to book such a reservation as no rooms were available on May 21. Johannes thanked her and asked to speak to the manager. The manager recognized that making a six-day reservation for me was definitely in the interest of the hotel and had the authority to do this. It turned out to be a very enjoyable place to stay. ◀

Two aspects of this case are noteworthy. First, there was no need to create a different alternative in order for the constraint to be disregarded. The alternative of the specific six-day reservation remained the same, as it was a much better alternative for the hotel than following the constraint. Second, the receptionist who initially enforced the constraint did not have the authority to override it. Finding the authorized decision-maker who did have that authority was obviously critical.

Value-Focused Negotiations

You have likely been involved in numerous negotiations in life, although a majority of these "negotiations" may not have been formally recognized as such. A teenager and parents may negotiate about the use of a vehicle for an evening. You and a coworker have a month to complete an important project, so you jointly develop a project plan and negotiate who will do what parts and a project timeline. If you have been involved in purchasing a new or used vehicle or a home, you recognize many of these as negotiations. For most high levels of employment, there are negotiations concerning responsibilities, resources, and compensation.

Many books have been written on negotiations.[2] This section does not try to repeat what other authors have said so clearly. Instead, it states and illustrates how value-focused concepts can play a significant complementary role in preparing for and creating nudges to benefit from negotiations. The illustrations involve negotiations with two parties, you and the individual I refer to as your negotiation partner, although the ideas are relevant to multi-party negotiations. Your negotiation partner is an authorized decision-maker from your perspective, as he or she must accept any alternative that you like in order to implement it.

Understand Your Negotiation Partner's Values. The influence that you have in any negotiation results from the individual decisions that you make in that negotiation, whereas the consequences that accrue to you as a result of the negotiation result from the joint decision to accept a particular settlement for that negotiation. And why would you possibly care about these decisions? The answer, which is the same as with any decision that you face, is your values. You would rather have better consequences than a worse result from your negotiation, and your values specify what you care about in that negotiation. You could not successfully negotiate anything if you did not know what you wanted to achieve by the negotiation. Thus, it is essential to understand your values for any negotiation.

The distinctive feature of your decisions in a negotiation is that the consequences you experience depend on the decisions of your negotiation partner as well as on your own decisions. Even though you negotiate for yourself, obviously, and your negotiation partner negotiates for him- or herself, it is important that you understand your partner's values. In order to achieve something that you want from the nego-

> In negotiations with other parties, it is important to thoroughly understand their values. Knowing their values, you can create an alternative that provides what you desire and also is beneficial and acceptable to them.

tiation, your partner must agree. His or her decision on whether to agree depends on how well a proposed negotiated agreement achieves his or her values. Hence, one of your values for the negotiation should be to please your partner enough so that he or she can accept the negotiated agreement that also provides what you want for yourself.

The better you understand partners' values, the more able you are to appraise how desirable an alternative you are considering is for them and whether it is better than their current status quo, and hence potentially acceptable. You could also recognize if an alternative being considered is a terrific deal for them. If so, you can likely create a revised alternative that is better for you and somewhat decreases their benefits. This revised alternative might better balance the benefits of the negotiation between you and them and be acceptable to both of you.

Creating Alternatives Involving Tradeoffs between Values. In most important negotiations, each negotiator will have multiple values. Also, your negotiation partner may have some values that you do not care about at all. However, if your partner cares about something, you should care about it. The existence of and your recognition of such values may be the key to a negotiated agreement

> If your negotiation partner has a value that you do not care about, you should. Recognizing that value may be your key to achieving a desirable negotiated agreement.

that provides all that you desire and satisfies your negotiation partner too.

► Purchasing a Used Car

Suppose that you have been searching for a used car for your son when he goes to college in two months. You do not want to pay more than $6,000, but hope to pay about $5,000. You have looked for over a month and found nothing appropriate in your price range.

However, yesterday a neighbor informed you that a coworker had just accepted a transfer to the corporate headquarters in London. He will be leaving in a month and is selling his car before leaving. Your neighbor helps you contact him and you check out the car. It's exactly what you want, except the seller wants $6,800, more than you want to pay even though you think it is worth more than $6,800.

You think about his values, and it seems that his life during the next month would be very difficult without a car. In your discussion, you casually ask what he would do if you bought his car, and he mentioned that he probably would have to rent one. You believe that the cost and inconvenience would be worth more than $800 to him. You don't care when you receive the car as long as it occurs within the next two months, when your son goes to college.

With this information, you create what you hope will be an alternative that he can't refuse. You offer $6,000 for the car and say the sale and transfer can take place at any convenient time for him prior to his departure for London. The seller says: "I hadn't even thought of such an arrangement. That sounds good and very convenient to me; it's a deal." ◄

Note that you did not care when you received the car, but it mattered a lot to the seller to keep his car this next month. Thus, it was relevant to you because you could create an alternative that satisfied him better on a value irrelevant to you and, in exchange, he could accept a decrease in the purchase price, which was very important to you. In fact, it was essential to find a negotiated agreement.

This same concept applies even if you both care about a particular value. The crucial feature is that the importance of given changes of consequences on a specific value are different for you and your negotiating partner. Suppose that you did have a preference for receiving the car now rather than in a month, but this was not too important. To clarify how important, you thought about the relative importance to you of getting the car now for

$6,800 or in a month for $6,000. It seemed that saving $800 was about five times more important than getting the car a month sooner. So, getting the car now compared to in a month is worth about $160 to you. Yet selling the car in a month rather than now is worth at least $800 to the seller.

Even though your offer to purchase the car in a month for $6,000 may be a little less desirable to you when timing matters, this agreement is still a good deal for you, as it meets your $6,000 guideline and you feel the value of the car is greater than that.

The Folly of Constructing Alternatives by Addressing Each Value Separately. It is usually quite inferior to construct a proposed negotiated agreement that attempts to separately balance the desirability of each value for each negotiator. The example above is useful to illustrate this significant but common error.

Given that the range for the sale price of the car was the seller's price of $6,800 and the buyer's maximum of $6,000 that he wanted to pay, one might select $6,400 as fair, since it is halfway between the bounding costs. The range of the sale date ranges from today, preferred by the buyer, to a month from now, preferred by the seller. Assuming a month is four weeks, the same seemingly equitable splitting procedure would lead to transferring ownership of the car in two weeks. Put together, we have a proposed alternative of $6,400 for the car to be transferred in two weeks' time. The seller would likely say "No" to this, as he desired a higher price and still would have to go through the inconvenience and cost of renting a car. The buyer would also reject such an alternative, as it is more than he can afford to pay.

Such an inferior procedure does not account for the fact that the difference in cost between $6,800 and $6,000 may be valued very differently by the two negotiators. Moreover, the difference in transfer time may be valued very differently. It is such differences in value that render most negotiations worthwhile to each party. The greater these differences are, the easier it is to identify negotiated agreements that are better for each party, and the amounts better for each can be greater. This explains why the alternative of $6,000 for the car transferred at the end of the month is better for both individuals than $6,400 transferred in two weeks.

Creating Post-Agreement Improvements. Suppose that you had initially decided that you could pay up to $7,000 for a car that was excellent in terms of your non-cost values (e.g., safety equipment, operating quality, body condition). You examine the car for sale by the individual moving to London, and it is perfect and the asking price is $6,800. You offer to purchase the car, because it costs less than you are willing to pay, and you will then be done searching for a car for your son. The negotiated agreement is signed, a check passed, and you own the car.

Both you and the seller are better off with this agreement, as illustrated in Figure 8.3. You may now find it useful to consider a bit more negotiation, which may again improve each of your situations relative to the negotiated agreement. You use the same process described earlier to find a win-win alternative, only now you are considering alternatives relative to the status quo of the negotiated agreement, which is that you drive the car home having paid $6,800.

You might ask what the seller will do for transportation this next month. The story is the same as above; he will have to rent a car. You know that you don't really need the car this coming month and offer to have the sale occur in a month for $6,000, and the seller may accept. If he does, he returns your $6,800 check, and you have a contract to pay $6,000 when you pick up the car in a month. This would result in additional improvements for both you and the seller, represented by the point defined in Figure 8.3 as the situation with post-negotiation improvements.

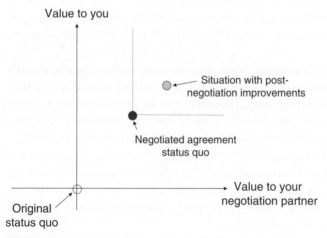

Figure 8.3 Creating Post-Negotiation Improvements to Negotiated Settlements

You may wonder why, in this example, the buyer might not initially make an offer of $6,000 and transferring the car in a month without first agreeing to the purchase of the car for $6,800. The big reason is that the buyer really wants the car, and agreeing to purchase at the offering price of $6,800 guarantees that the most important aspect of the negotiation is finalized without hassle or missteps.

Initially offering $6,000 and possession a month later may have sounded like a bad deal to the seller, as it is well below his $6,800 asking price. Furthermore, he may then get the idea that he will be able to sell his car for more than $6,000 with possession to take place in a month to someone else. However, if he has already sold the car for $6,800 with possession taking place today, his reference—represented by the negotiated agreement status quo— is different from the original status quo. It may be that the $800 for the convenience of driving his own car and not paying for renting another is a good deal. Even if this post-negotiation offer is not accepted, you still have the car, and that is what you value the most. Your values should guide the decisions that you make in the negotiation process as well as those about any post-agreement improvements.

Positive Pre-Negotiation Influence. Prior to negotiations there are often meetings between the potential negotiation partners to see if they have enough compatible interests to warrant a negotiation. An example includes potential employment and hiring meetings between an individual and a company. If negotiations are pursued, how you communicate your values can often positively nudge the relative quality of any employment offer.

For larger organizations, discussions to finalize the details of an offer often take place with a member of the human resources department. He or she may ask what you hope to achieve in your job and, sometimes specifically, how important the salary is to you. There is a tendency to not want to sound overly driven by money, so your response may be that contributing, teamwork, and learning are the most important aspects of the job, and then good working relationships and maybe fun, and money is relevant but not on a par with the other items. As a result, you may receive an offer that you like, or at least accept.

However, a different representation of your values might work better. First, recognize that the human resources person can have little effect on any of the values above, such as contributing, learning, and fun, except for the starting salary. In addition to all the values above, you may say something along the lines of "Salary is also very important, because I have significant debt from paying for my education," or "It is essential to help support my parents," or "To be able to afford living reasonably near work." This signals to the human resources person that, if the company wants to increase the chances that you accept its offer, it perhaps should propose a salary at the higher end of the possible range.

Alternatives for Group Decisions among Friends or Family Members

With friends and family, I usually think of a joint decision as a group decision rather than a negotiation, although the structure of each is similar. In a negotiation, the participants tend to be mainly concerned with satisfying themselves. In a group decision, each participant is usually also concerned with satisfying each of the other participants. Still, each participant is an authorized decision-maker from the perspective of the others, as each could, basically, veto any alternative that the entire group might pursue.

A common class of group decisions concerns instances when a few friends or colleagues must jointly choose an alternative that will personally affect each of them. By "a few," I mean two to five individuals, although the ideas discussed below may sometimes be useful for slightly larger groups. Examples of decisions would include what activity to jointly do, where you will jointly meet for a weekend gathering, and how to organize a required task.

A simple example is illuminating. Suppose that two people are going to decide where to have a nice dinner together. One asks the other what type of food she would like to eat. It should on the face of it be easy to respond, but, to a thoughtful person, this response may not be so easy after all. The complexity results from the fact that the responding individual has two values, namely to please herself and to please her friend. Her friend probably has the same considerations with his values. Suppose that she thinks her friend would likely prefer to eat at a French restaurant, which is not her first choice but still okay, so she suggests a French restaurant. Her friend interprets this suggestion as her preference, and, even though it would not in fact be his first choice, he amicably agrees and they go to a French restaurant. Over dinner they talk, and find out that each would have much preferred a Thai restaurant.

When friends or colleagues face a common decision, inferior alternatives are often suggested and subsequently chosen, because each individual cares about pleasing the other(s). Although each individual is very knowledgeable about his or her own values and preferences for potential alternatives, they often do not know the other's preferences very well. They certainly do not know the other's preferences as well as the other person does. So, give yourself a nudge and use a straightforward way to avoid this shortcoming and make better, and often much quicker, decisions in these situations. The key is to separate two considerations necessary for making an informed group decision: first, obtain each group member's preferences for the alternatives; then, combine those preferences to provide a group evaluation.

► Selecting a Restaurant

In the restaurant example above, one person could have said something such as "Let each of us think first only of our own values for what we personally prefer, and then rank our top three or four types of restaurants for our dinner tonight." Once we have this information, we can easily choose where to eat.

Following this alternative, suppose that the woman's ranking was Thai, Italian, Japanese, and French. The man's preferences were Moroccan, Thai, French, and steakhouse. Clearly, Thai is preferred to French by both individuals. Also, no restaurant except possibly the Moroccan, the man's first choice, could be preferable to the Thai restaurant, given the ranking information. Unless the man thought there was a large gap in the desirability between the Moroccan and Thai restaurants to him, he would likely say the obvious: "Let's have dinner at a Thai restaurant." ◄

If a group of several friends or family members or a school group faces such a joint decision, the process and procedure are only slightly more involved. First, each individual generates his or her ideas of desirable alternatives from a personal viewpoint only. Combine their suggestions into a list of all alternatives, and then each individual ranks the

> **The fundamental information that you need to make a sound group decision is each group member's personal preferences for the alternatives under consideration.**

alternatives on this list, or perhaps just their top five alternatives, in terms of personal preference. "Personal preference" means what the individual would prefer without considering any of the others' judgments or feelings. As each individual is the expert on his or her personal preferences for the alternatives, these rankings represent a summary of all the information needed to make a sound group decision. Using these rankings, and a little common sense similar to that in the restaurant example above, one alternative may clearly be the best. Otherwise, it should be possible to eliminate several poor alternatives and identify a relatively short list of contending alternatives. A discussion of the pros and cons of these contenders should provide the basis for a decision that can be jointly agreed upon, and often please each of the individuals. This process allows for full participation, with appropriate consideration of all viable alternatives, and is simple to use and understand.

Additional Thoughts for Decisions in Organizations

In businesses, institutions, and government organizations, most people report to someone. Frequently, much of the work to choose an alternative is done by an individual or group at one level. The result is often a recommended alternative sent to a manager, the authorized decision-maker at a higher level. In other words, the lower level recommends the alternative to implement and the

> **Many decisions in businesses and organizations are examined and evaluated by teams that report to an authorized decision-maker. Understanding the values of that authorized decision-maker prior to addressing the decision will significantly increase the influence of that report.**

higher level accepts or rejects that recommendation. A rejection may involve starting a subsequent analogous decision process at the lower level with a little more information and guidance or the implementation of an alternative modified from that being recommended. That guidance should definitely include the complete set of objectives that the authorized decision-makers want to achieve by making this decision. In addition, any alternatives that these authorized decision-makers think should or should not be considered in creating recommendations would be very useful to know.

It is well understood that negotiations occur frequently in organizations. There are internal negotiations between individuals, such as those involving the hiring, promoting, or dismissal of a key individual. There are negotiations between groups within the company, such as product development, sales, and marketing for a soon-to-be-released product. Some may refer to these interactions as discussions, although they, naturally, have many features of negotiations. All groups in such a situation may have a common strategic objective, such as to have a tremendously successful product, but the groups may have different specific objectives that contribute to this strategic objective, and these objectives will at least partially conflict with each other.

There are also numerous organizational negotiations between organizations. A company will naturally negotiate with its suppliers and with certain large customers. A national government agency may negotiate with several state agencies concerned with similar activities. At a high level, negotiations between organizations consider contracts, mergers, or other significant ways to work together for a common purpose.

For all of the organizational decisions involving other parties, the intent is the same as with any internal organizational decision: to identify and implement good alternatives. What is different when other parties are involved in the decision is that such an alternative must also be a good alternative for that other party as well as for your organization. It is, of course, essential to thoroughly understand your values in any such situation. In addition, you will be in a much better position to identify and implement great alternatives if you make the effort to understand the values of the other party, or parties, as well as you can. With such an understanding, you will be able to create better alternatives for them and for yourself, anticipate better their actions and reactions to your proposals and actions, and react in a more productive manner throughout any decision-making process.

9 BECOMING A VALUE-FOCUSED DECISION-MAKER

Value-focused decision-makers understand that they can influence the quality of their lives by using their power to make decisions. They actively and proactively use specific value-focused concepts and procedures to nudge themselves to make better decisions. In order to routinely use value-focused decision-making to nudge yourself to make better decisions, you need to develop skills to apply its four key concepts. These concepts, which are not a part of most decision-makers' skills, are the following.

1. Identifying values. Allocate time and effort to create a complete list of what you care about regarding any decision that you face.
2. Creating alternatives. Do not accept just the obvious or given alternatives. Try to create new alternatives that are better than any currently recognized alternatives.
3. Generating decision opportunities. Proactively create decision opportunities that will make your life better and possibly avoid future decision problems. Do not just wait for problems to occur.
4. Designing alternatives that satisfy others. The authorization of someone else is frequently required in order to implement an alternative you want. Understanding that other person's values and modifying your desired

alternative to include benefits to him or her in terms of his or her values is important. It is this newly developed win-win alternative that may well be implemented.

Mastering the Skills of Value-Focused Decision-Making

To master the skills of value-focused decision-making it is necessary that you learn to use these four key value-focused concepts and techniques in your decisions. Repeated use of these concepts will result in better decisions and provide practice applying them. With more practice, you will naturally become more proficient at value-focused decision-making and routinely nudge yourself to make better decisions. Two recent studies have indicated that individuals who take the initiative to improve their lives and who are proactive in developing and using the value-focused decision-making skills above enjoy both higher satisfaction with their decisions and more satisfying lives than others.[1]

This process of learning and practicing to improve your value-focused decision-making skills is analogous to the learning and practice necessary to develop any other skill, such as playing a sport or a musical instrument, writing, or cooking. Conceptually, you could learn what you should do to perform each of these activities well by reading about them, but you would not be proficient at these skills without significant practice. That is why medical students have lengthy internships to practice what they have learned. Who would prefer to be operated on by a surgeon who had learned everything relevant to the operation but had no practice?

> To improve your decision-making skills, you need to continually learn how to better make decisions and keep practicing what you have learned.

To develop each of the four value-focused skills listed above to improve your decision-making requires three steps:

1. learn and understand the concepts and techniques necessary to implement them;
2. practice using these concepts and techniques on familiar, less important decisions; and
3. apply the value-focused concepts and techniques on your decisions worthy of thought to improve your

decisions and continually improve your abilities to apply value-focused concepts.

Chapters 5 to 8, which collectively address step 1, provide details about each of the four concepts and how to use them to improve your decisions.

This chapter presents material to guide you in pursuing step 2. To develop the skills to use the concepts, it is beneficial to initially practice using each one separately. The next four sections present several basic decisions, similar to decisions that you have previously faced, to practice using each concept. You can personalize these basic decisions to represent a decision that you do or will likely face. By applying the concepts to these decisions, you will understand the information that you create by applying them. This should help you develop the initial skill to begin applying relevant value-focused decision-making concepts to any of your decisions.

> To improve your decision-making, you need to learn the concepts and techniques that are the foundation for important decision-making skills and use them on familiar decisions to become proficient. Then you can routinely apply these skills to all of your decisions worthy of thought.

Step 3 is what you will naturally want to do: apply your newly developed value-focused decision-making skills to important decisions that you are facing. Aside from improving these decisions, it also serves as practice to keep improving your skills. What you learn from how you make each current decision is relevant to how well you make other decisions in the future.

Each use of any concept of value-focused decision-making in a decision nudges you to make a better choice. But, when you begin to routinely use all of the appropriate concepts on your decisions, the benefits compound in a way analogous to the compounding interest of a financial investment. By better understanding your values for some decisions, you will be able to identify your specific values for other decisions more quickly, which reduces the time necessary to make a good decision. By knowing your values for a specific decision, your ability to create better alternatives is enhanced. Hence, you can make better decisions that lead to better consequences. As a result, the frequency and severity of future decision problems are both reduced, which saves the time and hassle of addressing those decision problems that otherwise would have occurred. Partly because of these interrelationships, improving your decision-making skills will improve your life.

With practice, you will master value-focused decision-making and it will become the natural way for you to address your decisions. As you become more proficient, it will essentially become a habit. You will quickly focus on the values that matter in any decision worthy of your thought and recognize the appropriate steps necessary to proceed to a sound decision.

Developing the Skill to Identify Your Values

Making a high-quality decision requires you to thoroughly understand your values for that decision, which describes what you want to achieve by making it. So, in any decision situation you should think about your values first, meaning no later than soon after consciously recognizing that you are going to make a decision.

To begin developing your skill to identify your values, Table 9.1 presents six basic decision situations to use in your initial attempts. You should be able to modify each of these basic decisions to make them directly relevant to you.

Now select one of those decisions that you believe should be relatively easy. Make a list of all of your values for that decision that come to mind. When you have no more thoughts of additional values for this decision, write down a list of your values for the other five decisions. Keep your records separate for the different decisions so that you can more easily complete the following tasks and recognize your progress.

Now check to see how complete your lists are; are they missing any of your values? Take two of your lists and challenge yourself to double the number of your values. Spend at least six minutes thinking hard about additional values relevant to each decision. Take two other decisions and use the devices in Table 5.2 to stimulate thoughts of additional values. With the final two decisions, show your lists of values to a few friends separately and ask them to identify any additional values that they think may be relevant to you. If any are relevant, or stimulate your thoughts about other values that are relevant, add them. For each of these six decisions, you should have been able to identify additional values with the processes suggested.

Table 9.1 Basic Decisions for Identifying Your Values

---

1. You are selecting a restaurant for an important dinner meeting with your manager, someone who may hire you, a potentially significant other who you met last month, your book reading group, or someone else. What are your values for selecting the restaurant?

2. You will attend a personal or business event. To do this, you must select a specific round-trip airline itinerary between two cities that have no direct flights between them. However, there are numerous possible itineraries connecting in different locations and using different airlines. What are the values for selecting your airline itinerary?

3. You want to clean up and organize something that you consider to be a mess. It may be a desk, filing cabinets, a closet, a room, your garage, your garden, or anything else. For the mess that you choose, what are your values for the task?

4. You need a new, or possibly used, major product. It may be a kitchen appliance (e.g., refrigerator, stove and oven, or dishwasher), a clothes washer and dryer, a television, a computer, a vehicle, or another major product. Select a product and specify your values for purchasing that product.

5. You are planning a weekend trip sometime during the next few months. What are your values for the trip that, if well achieved, would make it a great success?

6. For your important meeting that you chose for the first decision above, consider what you hope to achieve during your meeting. Develop your list of values for this meeting. Note that this list of values should be different from, but may overlap with, the list of your values for the first decision.

At this stage you should have a reasonable list of your values for the six decision situations. You can likely improve the lists by clarifying what each value means and why you care about it. Do this for each decision separately and proceed one value at a time.

Look at each listed value and ask yourself: "What do I mean by this value?" Your thoughts may result in a clearer restatement of that value or indicate an additional value. Then go through your possible updated list and ask for each listed value: "Why do I care about this value?" Your thoughts here often indicate additional new values, where the original listed value is a means that influences the newly identified value. If you do identify an additional new value, put it to the question of why you care. Continue this process until no additional values are being generated. The result of this is what I consider to be your final list of values for the specific decision.

It is insightful to compare your complete lists for the six decision situations with your original lists. Unless you are remarkably introspective, I think you will be surprised about some of the values on your final lists that you missed in making your original lists. For a few of the new values, I expect you may think: "How was it possible I missed that?" It still happens to me sometimes, because specifying a complete set of values for any decision is difficult. If you worked hard on these tasks, and if your original lists and final lists of values are essentially the same, I would appreciate it if you could share your technique for identifying values with me.

To finalize the examples above, there are two more tasks with each set of values. The first is procedural. You want to state each value in the common format of an objective, which is a verb followed by an object. Numerous examples are presented in Table 5.3 to illustrate the idea. Examples for your airline itinerary decision above may include "minimize total travel time," "be well rested on arrival," "avoid missing connecting flights," "receive miles in an airline account," "avoid overnight travel," "arrive on time for the event," "enjoy the travel," and "minimize travel costs."

The second task is to organize your values for each decision. This involves dividing your objectives into two categories: means objectives and fundamental objectives. For each objective for a specific decision, ask yourself why you care about it. If the complete answer is that you care about the objective only because it has an influence on better achieving other objectives on your list, it is a means objective. Otherwise, it is a fundamental objective. As examples from the flight itinerary, suppose that the only reason you want to avoid overnight travel is to be well rested upon arrival. If so, "avoid overnight travel" is a means objective. If avoiding missing connecting flights is relevant only to minimize total travel time and to avoid overnight travel (which may be necessary if you miss a connection), "avoid missing connecting flights" is also a means objective. If the other listed objectives are each directly relevant for selecting a flight itinerary, they are fundamental objectives. Figure 5.1 illustrates a detailed example for how to separate the means and fundamental objectives for an important personal decision.

Creating a complete list of values for any decision is the foundation for value-focused decision-making about that decision. You can practice this skill almost any time and benefit from the practice. If you have "nonproductive" downtime, such as waiting in a line or a traffic jam, riding public transport, or having a coffee or a drink alone or with friends, you can reflect for a moment on what values you think are appropriate for a particular decision. These may be your current decisions or decisions you will face in the future, decisions of a group to which belong, or decisions facing your city or state or nation. Examples of public decisions include values for the city's decision to select a location for a new school or a new park, or for the local policies on homelessness. What should your country's values be for setting an immigration policy, establishing new personal tax laws, or reducing emissions of specific pollutants? Even for very minor decisions, the relevant values may be interesting to consider. As examples that offer useful practice, consider your values for where to hang your jacket in a public area, which locker to choose in a sports club, where to park when going to a particular venue or store, how to load your dishwasher, and which table to choose in a restaurant.

After completing the examples for the six basic decisions above, you will have acquired some knowledge and experience about identifying and organizing values. You should now be able to productively begin identifying values for your own more important decisions. Not only will this practice provide you with useful insights relevant to making these decisions, but it will also enhance your ability to identify and recognize your values more easily.

Developing the Skill to Create Alternatives

Creating alternatives is a critical decision-making skill. If you create—and, of course, then select—one alternative that is better than any of the alternatives you were originally considering, you have nudged yourself to make a better decision than you possibly could have by identifying and selecting the best of the original alternatives.

The potential importance of spending time to create desirable alternatives is under-recognized and underused. Chapter 6 presents several ideas to stimulate your creativity to develop high-quality alternatives for your important decisions. If you are considering the experiences and skills that you want to develop next year to advance in your organization, there are probably numerous alternatives to pursue this purpose. The effectiveness and enjoyment of pursuing the best of these would be much greater than pursuing alternatives that are only satisfactory and immediately obvious. If you are planning to renovate your kitchen or planning where to go and what to do on your vacation, there are many alternatives, and you likely do not know them all. For decisions such as these, it is usually worthwhile to spend some time to create a set of good alternatives before making your choice.

Before proceeding, I should mention that there are certain decisions for which it is not useful to create alternatives. For these decisions, it is easy to identify all possible alternatives. If you are deciding which television of a specific size to purchase, the set of alternatives is given by those for sale. If you are deciding when to take a specific one-week vacation from work next summer, the complete set of possible alternatives includes all of the weeks beginning in June through September.

Table 9.2 presents six basic decisions to use for practicing the creation of alternatives. With each of these, make any adjustments to the decision that personalizes it to reflect a specific decision that is or soon will be relevant to you.

You can, of course, address the six decisions in any order that you choose. However, I suggest decision 1 be considered first, as you already have the values for this decision from the previous exercise to create values. For each of your specific decisions, sequentially go through five separate activities.

1. List as many alternatives as you can think of for the decision.
2. Create a list of your values for the decision and then use these values one at a time to stimulate the creation of additional alternatives.

Table 9.2 Basic Decisions for Creating Alternatives

---

1. You are planning to take a personal trip on a weekend sometime in the next several months. What are some alternatives that seem appealing?
2. Assume that you own the property where you live even if you do not. You decide to remodel one specific room. Select the room and create alternatives for the renovation.
3. Suppose that you work in an office building. You would like to work from home two days per week, but you are concerned that your productivity may drop. What are some alternatives that might improve your productivity at home to be as high as or higher than that in the office?
4. You often seem too busy to exercise regularly at a sports facility. What are some alternatives that you could integrate into your daily schedule and life that would provide some exercise and be much better than none?
5. You have an upcoming interview that will influence whether you are offered a professional position that you would like. This interview may be for a different job where you are currently employed or for an internship or job with a different organization. Choose one of these situations that could be relevant to you and create alternatives for how you should manage the interview (i.e., what you do and say) to increase your chances of being offered the job or internship.
6. A family member or a very good friend has been having a difficult time recently. You would like to do something for him or her that might begin to change things for the better. Pick a person who you would like help in this manner, and then create a set of alternatives for that purpose.

---

3. If it has been at least five minutes since you generated your last alternative, take a break. Then come back and challenge yourself to come up with at least three more. There almost surely will be that many additional good alternatives.

4. Review each item on your list of alternatives. In addition to being an alternative itself, various combinations of these items could likely be integrated together, perhaps with some modifications, to be an additional alternative. Construct some of these that seem particularly appealing.
5. As a check on your completeness, show two decisions, each with a few of your corresponding alternatives, to some friends or coworkers. Challenge them to create different additional alternatives for both decisions.

Once you have finished the six decisions, you can use your results as part of the basis for a value-focused brainstorming exercise. For both decisions 1 and 2 in Table 9.2, imagine that it involved one or more family members or friends. For one of these decisions, separately guide each of the other individuals through the first two activities above. To represent the intent of value-focused brainstorming, it is best if these other individuals are not informed of your personal results prior to their effort. Then combine their and your sets of values and alternatives for the decision. Comparing the combined sets of values and of alternatives to yours and each of the other individual's is an indication of the usefulness of value-focused brainstorming for decisions involving multiple individuals.

Developing the Skill to Generate Decision Opportunities

By generating and pursuing decision opportunities, you can make your life, or an aspect of your life, better than it is now. And, obviously, if you make one aspect of your life better and other aspects remain the same, your life is better.

There are a great many decision opportunities that you can generate. Some of these directly affect the quality of your life. Some directly affect your environment, which can affect your quality of life. Still others affect the quality of lives of others who you care about, which indirectly affects the quality of your life.

A decision opportunity has the same structure as a decision problem. The sets of relevant values and alternatives define each. The difference is that you decided to face the decision opportunity— it's a good situation—whereas you did not choose to address a decision problem—which, usually, is not a good situation. As mentioned in Chapter 7, each of you has previously recognized some decision opportunities. If, without being forced, you invite someone to an activity, a dinner, or to have a coffee or drink together, you are actually pursuing a decision opportunity. Whether explicitly or not, you created the decision of whether to extend the invitation and then decided to do so. However, the process of creating a decision opportunity is not clearly recognized by many people. As a result, they are unaware of the potential of decision opportunities to enhance their lives. To become familiar with the concept and its usefulness, Table 9.3 provides eight categories where you can proactively nudge yourself by creating some decision opportunities. Four of these categories affect you directly, and two each affect people you care about and your environment.

For each of the categories in Table 9.3, create several decision opportunities. To do this, place the category after the words "What can I do to." So, for instance, with the first category, this yields "What can I do to improve my life at home?." Your responses could be broad or narrow. List each decision opportunity as a decision statement beginning with the word "decide." For example, a broad decision opportunity would be "decide to keep the home more organized," whereas a narrow one would be "decide to routinely dispose of the waste in full waste baskets." There should be many alternatives for each decision opportunity. Considering why you would be interested in a narrowly stated decision opportunity may suggest a broader decision opportunity.

After you create a set of decision opportunities for each of the categories, choose one decision opportunity in each category

Table 9.3 Categories for Generating Decision Opportunities

1. Improve my life at home.
2. Improve my life at work or school.
3. Participate in more worthwhile activities.
4. Learn something of interest.
5. Improve the life of a specific family member (e.g., spouse, child, parent, sibling).
6. Do something special with a specific friend.
7. Make a positive impact on my local community.
8. Lower my carbon footprint (i.e., greenhouse gas emissions attributable to me).

that is particularly appealing to you. For each of these decision opportunities, identify your values for pursuing it. For instance, suppose that one of the decision opportunities that you created to improve your life at work was "decide to improve my skills relevant to my work." Think about and write down your values for the decision to improve your work skills. Now, for each of the selected decision opportunities, use the corresponding values to identify a set of alternatives, using the procedures discussed in the previous section, that would each be potentially worthwhile to pursue that decision opportunity.

Develop the Skill to Design Alternatives that Satisfy Others

As discussed earlier, the authorization of another individual is sometimes required in order to implement a desired alternative for your decision. If that desired alternative has worse consequences for the authorized decision-maker than the status quo, it will likely not be authorized. To overcome this limitation, you need to modify your desired alternative to be better than the status quo for the authorized decision-maker. When you propose this win-win alternative to the authorized decision-maker, he or she will recognize it as a superior alternative that should be authorized.

You have already practiced creating alternatives to meet your values. What is different here is that the proposed alternative must also meet the authorized decision-maker's values. This requires something that we have not previously practiced, namely developing a list of values for another individual. Fortunately, you do not need to understand all of the authorized decision-maker's values, because you can create alternatives that are improvements relative to the current situation using only some, or perhaps just one, of his or her values. Once you have a list of some or all of an authorized decision-maker's values, constructing an alternative to meet them requires the same thought process as constructing an alternative to meet your values.

Table 9.4 presents two decision situations with an authorized decision-maker who controls whether an alternative that you would like can be implemented. There are two versions to each decision situation, so you have four distinct decisions designed to gain some practice specifying the values of others, which is

Table 9.4 Decision Situations with an Authorized Decision-Maker

---

1. You have decided that you want to go on a one- or two-day weekend trip with a specific individual. There are two versions, one with a specific family member and the other with a specific friend. Your initial plan with your friend is that each individual will pay for their own expenses and joint expenses will be shared. From your perspective, the other individual in both versions is an authorized decision-maker. If he or she does not want to go on the proposed trip, your desire of a trip together cannot happen.
2. You would like to work at a job located in one city and live in another which is more than 500 miles away. One version is a temporary arrangement for telecommuting three days a week for a particular three-month period beginning in six weeks' time. The second version is to establish a permanent arrangement to only come to the office once a month and for "all hands" meetings. Your manager is the authorized decision-maker for whether your proposed alternative to work in one place and yet live far away is accepted.

---

relevant to creating alternatives that will be authorized by the authorized decision-maker.

For decision 1 in Table 9.4, first select a specific person for both versions. There are six questions to be addressed separately and in order for each of the two versions of the decision. The questions are the following.

1. Thinking just about your values, write down some desirable alternatives for the trip.
2. Without speaking to your prospective trip partner, list what you believe his or her values are for going on the trip.
3. Use these values to create any new alternatives for your joint trip.
4. Have a discussion with your trip partner. First explain the idea of the weekend trip, and then guide him or her to express his or her values for such a trip. The ideas in Chapter 5 for stimulating the creation of your own values can be used to guide him or her in expressing his or her values.

5. Use the values expressed by your prospective trip partner, who is the authorized decision-maker, to create additional alternatives for your trip. Note that these additional alternatives may be modified versions of the alternatives that you previously developed.

6. Thinking of both your and your partner's values, and viewing the lists of alternatives produced with questions 1, 3, and 5, eliminate any alternatives that you both find inferior to at least one other alternative and construct a list of the alternatives that you think are competitors for your joint trip.

Note that you created your values and alternatives for a weekend trip when you responded to decision 1 in Table 9.2. These alternatives should be close to those you produced in your list of alternatives responding to item 1 above. Also, you will get insights when you compare your lists of the values of your trip partner that you created without his or her involvement, responding to item 2 above, and then with him or her in discussions, developed in response to item 4. Finally, compare the sets of alternatives prepared in response to items 1 and 6. You will notice that having more explicit information about the values of your trip partner usually leads to better alternatives, as indicated in your response to item 6.

For decision 2 in Table 9.4, there are five questions you want to specifically consider for each of the two versions of the decision. The questions are the following.

1. Write down the alternatives that you may use to ask your manager about the possibility of working where you do now but living elsewhere.

2. List all of your values related to why you want to work there yet live elsewhere.

3. Use your values to stimulate ideas, and write down any additional alternatives that you might suggest to your manager with the hope of gaining approval.

4. Identify and make a list of all of the values that you think your manager will consider in his or her decision of whether to approve your work/home alternative.

5. Considering these values, write down any additional alternatives that you may use in asking your manager to authorize your request.

Note that your values in item 2 should be quite similar to those you developed in responding to decision 3 in Table 9.2. Specifically, did some of your values listed in item 2 pertain to what you want to contribute to your organization? Also, compared to the alternatives you generated in item 1, were you able to create any additional alternatives using values in item 3 and again in item 5? Do you feel that items 3 and 5 both generated better alternatives? The answers to both these question should be "Yes," unless you were able to intuitively consider these values prior to explicitly articulating them.

Practicing the Use of Value-Focused Decision-Making

By now you should have a good idea of how value-focused decision-making can be used to improve your life and what you must do to benefit from it. You can now begin using these concepts to create better decisions to face and to help make more informed and better decisions. This should provide direct benefits to you. It will also provide indirect benefits, because each use provides more practice and improves your skills.

Practice will further your learning, both about the concepts themselves and about how to effectively use them. Especially at the beginning, you should include explicit practice on less complex and less important decisions, for two reasons. First, there are many of these decisions worthy of thought, so you can get more practice. Second, you can gain useful insights with less effort to see how the value-focused decision-making process works and benefits you. As you become more adept at using procedures to provide information, such as a more complete set of values for a decision, you can naturally tackle more complex decisions more effectively.

> **Initially, practice using value-focused decision-making ideas and procedures on your less complex and less important decisions. There are many of these, and each use requires less time and effort. As you increase your skill you can begin applying the procedures to your more important decisions.**

You need to commit yourself to practice in order to master your use of value-focused decision-making. Practicing involves intellectual exercise and can be useful and fun. But especially in the beginning, when you are thinking hard to come up with ideas but they remain elusive, the effort may seem more like work than fun. Hence, it may be helpful if you design your practicing to be more like playing a game with a friend or personally doing a thought-provoking puzzle. Both are, typically, more fun. Ideas for doing this are included in what follows.

There are different ways to practice the use of value-focused decision-making. They are categorized below as individual practice, playing games to practice with friends, and acting as a consultant for others facing decision situations.

Practice on Your Own. A natural way for you to initially gain some experience with developing your skills necessary for value-focused decision-making is to use the concepts on some of the simpler decisions that you face in your day. Since identifying values and creating alternatives are essential aspects of every decision problem and every decision opportunity and any decision where the desirable alternatives require authorization by another, it is useful to initially practice on identifying values and creating alternatives on decisions that matter to you, but are not too complex.

When you have some spare time, you always can give yourself a nudge by recognizing the decision opportunity of how to use that time, whether five minutes or longer. You can exercise your mind by practicing concepts of value-focused decision-making on decisions to which you normally do not give much thought but which may be interesting to think about. The beginning of your day may include eating breakfast, loading the dishwasher, commuting to work, running a meeting at work, and meeting a colleague for lunch. For any of these activities, you have choices about how to do them, including doing them without thinking. You can recognize any decision and think about the values that you want to achieve by making it. Then try to create as many alternatives as you can. For any of the hundreds of small decisions you make in a day, it can be a thoughtful and useful exercise—at least for a few times—to identify values and alternatives for it. Practice on readily available decision situations, and your sensitivity to and skills for identifying values and creating alternatives will improve.

Suppose that you had hoped to have the cooperation of one individual in your work meeting in order to develop a recommendation for your manager. That cooperation did not happen. Retrospectively realizing that you could have done something before the meeting to facilitate this cooperation indicates a decision opportunity that either wasn't recognized or wasn't pursued by you. Then do the exercise of creating alternatives for that decision opportunity that you think would have led to more cooperation had you taken just a few minutes to do it. This process is in the spirit of what is common in professional sports. After the game, the coaches and players want to review film of the game to understand what was not done well, what could be improved, and how to build that understanding into future actions (i.e., decisions).

Every day you observe the results of a large number of decisions that others make. These range from the available products for sale, their prices, advertisements, traffic light settings, the locations of stations along a transit line, the managing of a sports team during a game, operating procedures of workers, and public problems that perhaps should receive attention. For any of these you can practice by considering what values were likely used for making the decisions that led to your observations. For example, what are the values that should be used in designing a particular product or for addressing an observed public problem? Sometimes the values may be clear, so what are some reasonable alternatives? This is productive daydreaming, in order to develop value-focused decision-making skills by thinking about interesting problems and opportunities.

Practice with Others. Each of the suggestions to develop value-focused skills on your own can also be used together with friends or colleagues—at least, those who are intellectually inquisitive or practically oriented.

You can work as a team, using the concepts of value-focused decision-making to identify values, create alternatives or decision opportunities, or design alternatives that cannot be refused by an authorized decision-maker. If it is appealing to you, you can make parts of these exercises into a cooperative or a competitive game. If you are in a college class with a friend, see who can list the most objectives, and the best set of objectives, for selecting the topic of a major term paper. Then use each of the objectives on the combined set of objectives to create potential topics for the term paper. An analogous situation concerns identifying the objectives for a client report that is the responsibility of colleagues at a consulting company.

It is often said that, once you can teach something to another person, you then have a thorough understanding of the material. If you have a readily available "student" of any age, you can try to teach him or her about the concepts of value-focused decision-making and their uses and usefulness. In the process, you surely will enhance your own skills for using these ideas.

Practice as an Advisor to Others. Descriptively, everybody seems to have some problems that they would prefer not to have. As the only way that these individuals can purposefully have a positive effect on their situation is by their decisions, you may be able to assist them as an advisor by applying the appropriate concepts of value-focused decision-making to provide a nudge to make a better decision. They also may have defined some decisions that you could help them address.

The individual may be a family member, friend, coworker, or perhaps the person sitting next to you in an airplane or chatting with you at a cocktail party. Your relationship with the individual, the time you will have with them, and his or her willingness to participate clearly influences what you can do. If he or she is willing to give some time and thought, perhaps only a few minutes, you have a good chance to have a positive effect.

If little time is available, just helping such individuals articulate their values is often useful. They may originally state just one value or perhaps a few. Likely, with a general understanding of their decision situation and your knowledge about values, you can generate at least a few more. Rather than directly ask if the values are relevant to the individuals' decision, try to lead them in the conversation to discover the additional relevant values themselves. Sometimes you can do this by pursuing means–ends relationships. For all of their originally stated values, ask them why they really care about them. For any response, point out that it is potentially another value that may be important to them in their decision. Then, for the response, ask: "Tell me a bit more about why that is important." This should bring them closer to understanding the fundamental objectives that they should use for creating and evaluating alternatives in their decision.

With a friend or a family member, you may have a lot of time, especially if progress is being made. Depending on the decision situation, any, and possibly all, of the value-focused decision-making concepts may be useful. Any of the procedures to implement these concepts discussed in Chapters 5 to 8 can be used. When this advisory involvement goes well, you end up helping the decision-maker, and you also gain knowledge and skills that enhance your ability to help yourself in the future.

An Important Perspective

Your initial attempts to explicitly use the concepts of value-focused decision-making should, and likely will, involve applying the concepts on several small decisions worthy of thought before you tackle your first important decision. But there will be your first attempt on an important decision that you face. The insights you gain and the help rendered in this decision-making process may end up being less than you had hoped. Should this be a surprise? Absolutely not. There is a reasonable chance that your first attempt to use value-focused decision-making on an important decision, if you review it after several other attempts with important decisions, will be considered one of your less beneficial attempts.

With value-focused skills, you will be noticeably better after just ten serious attempts to use it, and much better after 25 attempts. There is a sharp learning curve, because you are beginning from the initial point of zero experience with value-focused concepts. If you include the usefulness of what you learned in your early attempts to use value-focused decision-making, each of them should be a success. With early experiences using value-focused decision-making, working on any of your real decisions has both positive direct consequences and indirect (i.e., learning for future decisions) consequences.

Additional Thoughts for Decisions in Organizations

The material in this chapter is directly relevant to organizational decision-making. There are significant benefits if an organization clearly states and communicates the values relevant to its decisions. The organization should be interested in creating innovative and better alternatives. With an understanding of the relevant values, any member in an organization may generate better alternatives, as well as decision opportunities that will help achieve the organization's strategic objectives. The concepts of value-focused decision-making directly address the issues relevant to each of these situations. Hence, value-focused decision-making can be very useful in organizations. Each use can provide a nudge to make a better decision.

It is only by individuals that value-focused decision-making can be introduced and implemented in the organization. The individuals who have learned and understand the concepts of value-focused decision-making and how to use them can apply them to the decisions of the organization. Since they often will be working with coworkers on such decisions, they will be educating those colleagues about the concepts and use of value-focused decision-making.

> **Working with colleagues on business and organizational decisions, you can educate them about the concepts and use of value-focused decision-making and illustrate the benefits for the types of decisions being addressed.**

This chapter has provided several decision-making exercises to practice implementing value-focused decision-making concepts on other decisions that you face. The skill that you develop practicing on these individual decisions is relevant to any decisions faced by organizations. In addition, in any specific organization, someone or a group of coworkers familiar with value-focused decision-making could design an analogous set of examples that addresses typical decisions occurring in that organization. These examples would provide additional training for individuals planning to use the concepts on the organization's decisions. Each use results in additional experience and improved proficiency with utilizing value-focused decision-making.

10 ENHANCING THE QUALITY OF YOUR LIFE

The focus of this book until now has been on individual decisions that you do or should face. I now enlarge the focus to the collective set of all of the decisions that you make throughout your life. As Ralph Waldo Emerson said, "The only person you are destined to become is the person you decide to be."[1] You have the power to enhance the quality of your life and maintain it at a high level. The way you do this, which is the only way you can do this, is through the decisions that you face and the alternatives that you decide to implement for those decisions. The flip side of this is that, if you make no purposeful decisions, then you have no way to influence your quality of life.

Most of us would probably like a high-quality life, but we do not have a clear understanding of what that personally means. This circumstance was summed up very well by the comedian Lily Tomlin, who said: "I always wanted to be somebody, but now I realize I should have been more specific."[2] Answering the question "Who do I want to be?" is being more specific.

As you would like to live your life as well as you can, your all-encompassing life objective should be to maximize your quality of life. To pursue a high quality of life, you must define what the concept of "quality of life" means for you. This task involves articulating the objectives to describe what you want to achieve, contribute, and experience during your lifetime. These life objectives provide the guidance and consistency for all of your decisions.

Personal Strategic Planning

The decisions throughout your life represent your only way to purposefully influence the quality of your life. So: do you have a strategic plan to guide your decision-making for your life? Most people do not, but consider the following.

- Many individuals, after becoming an adult, have financial plans, health plans, and maybe death plans (e.g., wills, legal documents). Each of these plans helps address specific potential problems in our lives, but they provide little guidance for the opportunities of life or the life you wish to live. Few individuals have a life plan to help guide the future that they want to have.
- Most individuals believe that any significant organization, such as a corporation, a government agency, or a non-governmental organization (NGO), should have a strategic plan. When I have asked "Why?," typical reasons given are that the performance of any organization is important and a strategic plan promotes good performance. When I ask people if they think that their performance (i.e., what they do, experience, accomplish, and contribute) in life is important, they almost all acknowledge that their performance is important, but they rarely have a strategic life plan.

A strategic plan for an organization often includes implementing major alternatives that cannot easily or quickly be changed or adapted. An organizational strategic plan can be relatively rigid and difficult to change once the implementation of alternatives has begun. The strategic plan also indicates how parts of the organization should coordinate to achieve a common purpose. Such a strategic plan would be impractical for an individual.

Managing one's personal life has different features from managing an organization. One's life is multifaceted and dynamic. There are many separate strategies being pursued simultaneously. There may be strategies concerning one's health, love relationships, raising children, contributing to the community, being on teams, enjoying time with friends, dealing with work challenges, finances, and community affairs, keeping abreast of numerous topics, growing spiritually, and so on. Many alternatives for pursuing each of these are being planned and carried out at the same time. Events can occur that require the quick adaptation of alternatives, which can sometimes be carried out, since an individual is much more nimble than any organization.

You are making so many decisions affecting your quality of life that there is no reasonable way to develop a strategic plan that indicates the alternatives you should choose for all of the decisions that you may face in life. However, you can greatly benefit from a strategic plan that specifies your personal life objectives. Knowing your life objectives nudges your decision-making to be more creative, more consistent, and better in general, as well as reducing anxiety and the time required to make good decisions. Your life objectives also provide a checklist for creating specific objectives for any important decision you face. As your life objectives collectively include the full range of what you care to achieve, developing them and routinely considering them reduces the chances that you miss any relevant objectives in your creation and appraisal of alternatives for any important decision. This provides a nudge to make a better choice for each of these decisions.

With a clear specification of what you want to achieve in life, you have a better chance of achieving it—or, at least, more of it. The logic is simple. If you know what you want to achieve, you are more likely to think of ways to achieve it, more likely to pursue it, and thus more likely to achieve it. The American baseball player Yogi Berra cleverly

> **If you clearly understand what you want to achieve and contribute in your life, your thoughts and effort will be better focused on these aspirations.**

commented on this when he said: "If you don't know where you are going, you'll end up somewhere else."[3]

As the concept of life objectives is distinct, I will illustrate and explain my life objectives to provide a useful background for understanding the concept, and for the subsequent discussion of how you can develop and use your own life objectives.

My Life Objectives

Five strategic objectives describe what I ultimately pursue in my life and, essentially, define my quality of life. The first two—"to enjoy life" and "to be intellectually fulfilled"—describe what I daily desire out of life. "To have enriching experiences" refers to those experiences that affect my life over time and broaden my perspective, understanding, and character. The last two—"to enhance the lives of family and friends" and "to contribute to society"—concern my desire to positively influence the lives of others.

Each of the five strategic objectives can be defined by more detailed objectives. "To enjoy life" for me includes fun, joy, excitement, and emotions, which captures my feelings. "To be intellectually fulfilled" includes learning, knowing, understanding, and reasoning, which captures my thoughts. There are numerous relationships between these aspects. Learning leads to knowledge, which leads to understanding. Better understanding what is exciting and enjoyable can lead to better pursuit of those things.

"To have enriching experiences" evokes feelings and allows me to experience, truly understand, and cherish strong positive feelings such as love, inspiration, pride, wonder, delight, satisfaction, amazement, and thankfulness. Some of these enriching experiences go on for a lifetime, such as relationships with family members and best friends. Others occur in a much shorter period of time and become clearly etched in my mind and heart forever. They never blend in with or get mixed up with other memories. This provides the unique memories that allow me to relive the experiences in detail. Each time that I recall one of those memories, I can perceive the same emotions and feelings.

"To enhance the lives of family and friends" is fundamentally important to me, as it is for many people. Two major aspects of this objective concern my wife Janet and son Greg, as well as other family and friends. Regarding "to contribute to society," this includes my concerns for employers, organizations to which I belong, my professional field, my community, and colleagues, coworkers, readers, and other individuals with whom I have contact.

On the left of Figure 10.1 are the main means life objectives that contribute to better achieving my strategic life objectives. The means–ends relationships among my life objectives are illustrated in my life objectives diagram in Figure 10.2. For clarity, only the higher-level strategic life objectives listed in Figure 10.1 are included in Figure 10.2.

It is useful to examine the three constraints on freedom of choice illustrated in Figure 10.2 concerning health, financial well-being, and available time. I consider these to be the three essential means objectives necessary for a good-quality modern life. If I had

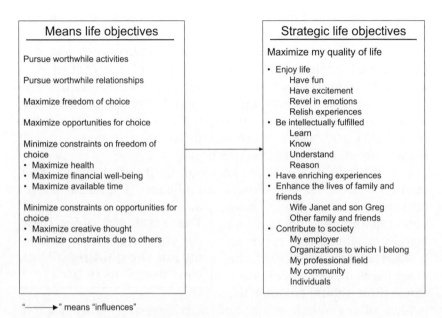

Figure 10.1 My Life Objectives

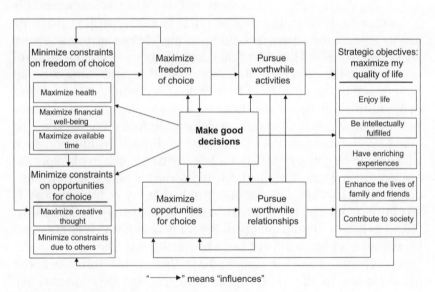

Figure 10.2 My Life Objectives Diagram

extremely poor health, or only enough money to avoid starving, or virtually no available time, I would not be able to pursue much of anything that I would like to do. However, if I have good health, enough money, and ample time, I could in theory do about anything that I would like to do, for myself or for others.

To benefit from this theoretical possibility, as indicated in the lower left of Figure 10.2, I need to proactively create good ideas about interesting things that I want to do and limit constraints from others and circumstances on my possible choices. Collectively, achieving these objectives will expand and enhance the alternatives that I can choose between and my freedom to choose them. It is then essential to make good decisions.

What I do in my life and who I do it with influences my quality of life to the degree that I can influence it. If I make poorer decisions, I will likely have poorer-quality relationships and activities, which will result in a lesser quality of life. On the other hand, if I make better decisions, these should enhance the quality of my relationships and activities, and hence lead to a higher quality of life.

> **The strategic objectives for your life are the foundation for guiding all of your decisions in life.**

In discussions with others about what is fundamentally important to them in life, I have often heard something like "My health is the most important thing to me." My health is also very important to me, so I have thought carefully about whether it is one of my strategic life objectives. Basically, I asked myself: "Suppose that I am incredibly healthy, but I have little enjoyment, am not intellectually fulfilled, have no enriching experiences, and do not enhance the lives of family and friends or contribute to society. Would I be living a high quality of life?" The answer is obvious: I would not. Such a life would be similar to that of a healthy tree, stuck in one spot for life. So, for me, good health is clearly a means objective to a high-quality life. However, this does not imply that my health objective is less important than any of my strategic life objectives, as I would be forced to have a limited quality of life if my health was very poor and I could have a high quality of life if my health was fine.

The framework in Figure 10.2 facilitates clear thinking about my decisions in life. It promotes value-focused decision-making, because my thinking focuses on how the potential alternatives influence achieving my values, as stated by my objectives in Figure 10.2. By routinely using my life objectives to guide all of my decisions, I am routinely nudging myself to make better decisions, ranging from those that are life-changing to those that may do no more than enhance my day.

Using Your Life Objectives

Your life objectives provide a roadmap to guide you to live the life that you desire. Since the only influence on the life that you end up experiencing is due to your decisions, your life objectives also provide the basis for coherence and consistency among all of your decisions in order to provide a high-quality life as you define it. In addition, specific objectives can facilitate a process for you to recognize differences between what you desire and what you have achieved and help you identify opportunities for improvement.

Since your life objectives provide the guidelines for living your life, they will change little, if at all, over time. Otherwise, they would not be your life objectives. If you identify what you think is a new life objective, this often does not indicate a change in your objectives. Rather, it likely indicates that you have gained a clearer understanding of one of your life objectives or that you wanted to highlight an important aspect of a particular life objective.

What *will* change over time is the set of realistic alternatives for pursuing your life objectives. For example, if you had a life objective to pursue meaningful and enjoyable relationships, the realistic alternatives to develop such relationships at ages 15, 25, 45, and 70 could be much different due to the different circumstances regarding your interests, health, financial well-being, and available time at those ages.

It is useful to comment in more detail about specific uses of your life objectives for defining your quality of life, guiding your decisions, providing a basis for consistency among your decisions, and proactively improving your life.

Defining Your Quality of Life. There is no standard for the meaning of "quality of life." Different people will have different concepts of their own quality of life. However, very few individuals have a clear definition of what they mean when referring to their quality of life, and even fewer have developed a comprehensive description of the quality of their life. This is a key reason why it is useful to create your life objectives. Your strategic life objectives define what you mean when you refer to your quality of life and provide a basis for how you should judge the quality of your life.

Guiding Your Decisions. Once you have created your life objectives, they can be used like a navigation system for your vehicle travel. The navigation system provides guidance for any travel, telling you how to get from where you are to where you want to be. Your life objectives can provide guidance for any decision to help get you from where you are to where you want to be. Many of your trips are familiar to you, so you do not need to use your navigation system explicitly, but your travel would likely be quite consistent with its suggestions. Many of your decisions are also familiar, so you may not explicitly check your life objectives. They are internalized and naturally used to guide your thoughtful decisions.

On an important trip to somewhere you have never been, you will likely use your navigation system to guide your travel, suggesting which decisions to make where and when. Similarly, for an important decision that has complex or unique features, you may want to explicitly use your life objectives to help you specify an appropriate set of objectives for that decision, develop better alternatives, and appraise which alternative to choose given the information that you currently have. If you miss a suggested turn on your trip, the navigation system will suggest to you how to make decisions to get you to your destination. Likewise, if a personal decision is taking you in a direction inconsistent with your intent, referring to your life objectives will help you recognize how far astray you are and help you decide how to adapt or replace your current alternative so as to better pursue your objectives. It is nice to have your value navigation system available to unobtrusively nudge you toward decisions that are aligned with achieving your life objectives.

Providing Consistency among Your Decisions. Your life objectives are the basis for coherence and consistency among all of your decisions in order to provide a high-quality life as you define it. The purpose of every decision that you make is to contribute to improving your quality of life, which includes consideration of others you care for. So, your life objectives, specifically those influenced by a particular decision, are those that ultimately are relevant to appraise the alternatives for that decision. Doing this explicitly would not be practical. Therefore, we choose objectives for each decision that more directly describe the consequences that eventually affect your quality of life.

Consistency between your different decisions can be promoted by referring to one's life objectives when specifying objectives for important decisions. Considering how that decision may influence each of your life objectives will influence the specific objectives chosen for that decision. This will give you an informal appraisal of how effective different important decisions are at contributing to your quality of life. If you have the time or money to pursue only one of two important decisions and you feel one of those will likely have a bigger influence on improving your quality of life, that is the one you should pursue. This helps you recognize how to get the biggest "bang" to your quality of life for your "buck" of money and time.

Proactively Improving Your Life. Addressing decision problems only maintains the quality of your life. If you want to improve the quality of your life, you have to identify and pursue decision opportunities. Chapter 7 presents information about how to create decision opportunities on the basis of recognizing something that you would like or not like in your future. Your life objectives provide a source to more systematically create worthwhile decision opportunities. For any of your life objectives, and at any time, you can ask yourself: "How could I improve my performance on this objective?" Answers that come to mind will provide the basis for creating a decision opportunity. Use of this idea, with examples, is discussed in detail later in this chapter.

Most people will benefit from articulating and understanding their life objectives. Such understanding empowers you to take more control over your own life, and it will result in an increase in the quality of your life. The rest of this chapter outlines methods and procedures to create, organize, and use your strategic objectives in guiding your life.

Creating the Objectives for Your Life

Few individuals have a thorough understanding about what they want in life. Yet each of us wants a good life as we define it. Understanding clearly what you believe would be a good life for you is the purpose of spending time to make your life objectives explicit. Since your effort on this task essentially begins with nothing explicitly stated, your chance of making useful progress to reward your effort is high.

Creating the objectives for your life is conceptually the same as creating your objectives for an important decision. Thus, the procedures discussed in Chapter 5 to identify objectives for a decision can also be used for identifying the objectives of your life. Practically, the process of defining and clarifying your life objectives is both more difficult and more important.

Generating an Initial List of Your Life Values. Creating your life values requires deep and prolonged thinking over time about what is important to you personally, and why. It incorporates your thoughts and your feelings, and also involves some dreaming about how you really would like your life to be. Fortunately, the process is interesting, enlightening, and rewarding.

The most challenging aspect of identifying your life values is to bring them to your consciousness, so that you can list and clarify them. Constructing your original list of life values is a creative process. In explicitly stating these values, there are no limits on what they are or on how you describe or list them. Do not be constrained in your thinking. Include anything that you feel may influence your quality of life. This is a wish list being created, not a list for what you will surely be able to achieve. If you have a thought about some potential value, such as "That's hoping for too much; I can't have that," simply forget the admonition and include that value on your list.

At some point you will be out of ideas, but your list is not done. Research discussed in Chapter 5 and experience have both demonstrated two important facts about an individual's ability to create values for important decisions. First, people typically identify fewer than half their significant values on the first attempt. Second, values that they do not initially identify are often just as important as those they did include on their initial list. Based on some experiences with asking both professionals and graduate students to identify their life values, I expect that individuals are no better at this more difficult challenge of creating the values for their lives. With focused guidance, adequate thought, and sustained periods of effort over time, you should be able to create a useful representation of your life values.

Your vision for your life as you would like it to be may stimulate your thinking about your life values. You can visualize it as a video of yourself as you travel a desirable path throughout your life. Alternatively, you could imagine it as an autobiography of the life you would relish to live. If your life vision included raising a wonderful family, you would want to think hard about what this means to you. This would help you characterize your values for having a wonderful family. Given that, you can think about means values that would contribute to creating a wonderful family. The thought process would also suggest numerous decision opportunities that would be useful to pursue in order to have a wonderful family.

Below are six additional suggestions that will help you identify more of your life values that have not been previously recognized.

1. Consider the activities (e.g., work and leisure) that you have spent a significant time doing. Ask yourself what you like and enjoy about these activities. Also ask if there are any unintended consequences you would like to avoid. Your answers to each of these suggests values.

2. Reflect on both very good and very bad decisions that you have made. For the good decisions, recognize what values were achieved that made that decision so good. For the bad decisions, recognize what values were either not achieved or even not considered that should have been.

3. Identify very good and very bad outcomes of some of your significant past decisions. For the good outcomes, identify values that were achieved. For the bad outcomes, identify which values were negatively impacted.

4. Imagine yourself at different ages in the future. Select about four different ages when you believe that your main concerns may be somewhat different from your concerns today. For each age, think hard about life values you may have then. To facilitate your thinking, you may identify friends, family, or acquaintances of those ages that you respect and admire today, and consider the values they likely pursue that gained your respect and admiration.

5. Think hard about what you might regret in the future if you had not included it in your life or had not enough time allocated to it. Review your life from today, and also 20 years from now, and identify any major aspects or experiences that are or will likely be missing. These thoughts should help you identify some important life values.

6. Inquire about the perspectives of your family and friends. What values might each of them suggest for

you? Think carefully about whether these suggested values are appropriate for you, and not just values that someone hoped that you would have. Include them if you decide that they are your values.

Add all of the newly identified values to your original list. Do not worry about any overlap or possible redundancy, as this causes no problems at this creative stage and is easily managed later in the process.

The real soul-searching comes next. Pursue the reasoning for each value that you now have on your list. For each value, consider if and why it is one of your life values. Thinking about this question requires you to delve more deeply into what you really want for your life. Repeatedly asking "Why?" for the response, and then for its response, pushes you to better understand what you truly want out of life. This process may indicate some new values to add to your list. It also results in a chain of means-to-ends thought that leads you to your strategic life values.

You now surely have a larger and more complete list of your life values. But you are still not done. Sleep on it, as they say—or, more appropriately, live with it while you are awake. Take weeks, or even months, and reflect on your life values from time to time. When you think of any new one, add it to your list. Reuse the guidance above on these new values. After you find that almost all of your thoughts about potential life values are already on your list, you are essentially done. I say "essentially done" because you can always add a new relevant value if one comes to mind or modify an existing value that you now more clearly understand.

Stating Your Life Values as Objectives. Going from no explicit documentation of what you care about in your life to having a list of life values requires a major effort. Stating any recognized value as an objective, which means stating the value succinctly as a verb–object combination, is much less challenging.

There are two reasons to state your identified values as objectives. The process often clarifies the meanings of stated values, and all values are then stated in a consistent format.

When a life value is stated as an objective, it should make sense in the following sentence: "My life will be better if I [place your objective here]." Examples include "please my spouse," "maximize my wealth," "contribute to my community," "improve (or maintain) my health," and "make time for art." Recognizing that you want to end up with your life values stated as life objectives, you may choose to write down some of these values as objectives when you initially identify them.

Refining Your Life Objectives. Once your life values are stated as objectives, you should review each item on your list to ascertain whether it is really one of your life objectives. You may recognize that some items on the list should be modified, expanded, or removed.

A common item on your list that may not be an objective is an alternative. Like objectives, alternatives can be stated with a verb and an object. An individual could have "visit Croatia" on her list of objectives. Whether this is really an objective or an alternative depends on whether the individual has full control over whether she visits Croatia. If she can afford the trip, make the time, and has the health to go, it is an alternative. Her related objectives would be found by answering the question "Why do I want to visit Croatia?." Some of her objectives may be specific to Croatia, such as "learn more about my ancestors," and others more general, such as "expand my knowledge about European history." If she does not have full control over whether she visits Croatia, it is an objective. Limitations may be money, time, or health. If funds were the problem, she could expand her objectives to include "acquire funds for desired travel."

You want each of your objectives to be clearly and unambiguously stated. A good test for this is whether another interested person can understand the meaning of your objective by reading it. For instance, suppose that one of your listed objectives is stated as "be in control of my life." Control may mean that you do not want to act impulsively without thought and/or that you want to make your own choices without any constraints or influence from others. Another interpretation may be that you do not want to lack resources, such as finances, time, or good health, which would limit your choices to pursue your life objectives.

Another objective might initially be stated as "have a stellar professional career." You should clarify what you mean by a "stellar professional career." This may suggest other objectives that you need to add to your list. A stellar career could include "earn a lot of money," "act ethically," "create value for society," "provide many high-quality jobs for employees," "invent enduring new valuable products," "mentor younger colleagues," "be among the very best in my field," "be recognized for my excellence," "become

famous," "have power," "command respect for my ideas and decisions," or "enjoy it all." A stellar career for most people would likely
include some of these objectives and also other objectives not
listed.

As these two examples suggest, it is often worthwhile with
any objective to clarify what you mean, and this requires being
more specific. Sometimes being more specific requires clarifying
the meaning of a term in the objective, as was the situation with
"control." At other times it requires specifying component objectives that, essentially, define the meaning of the originally stated
objective, such as "have a stellar professional career."

Organizing Your Life Objectives

Organizing your strategic objectives involves separating them
into means and strategic life objectives analogous to those
illustrated in Figure 10.1. This is important, since it will clarify
your thinking about significant life-changing decisions because
the roles of means life objectives and strategic life objectives
are different. Your strategic life objectives provide a succinct
summary of what you desire for your life and your means life
objectives are a basis for suggesting numerous alternatives to
fulfill your strategic life objectives. To organize your life objectives, there are basically three steps: cluster similar objectives
on your list, identify means–ends relationships, and select
your strategic life objectives. I will discuss these steps separately, although it is often natural to switch back and forth
between them in practice.

Cluster Objectives. After all of your hard thinking, experience has shown that you might have identified between 20 and 100
objectives for your life. To reduce the number of objectives that you
need to consider to provide a better overview of your life objectives,
it is useful to aggregate related objectives into a higher-level general
objective. Specifically, you can cluster objectives into groups concerned with a similar focus. Note that the objective "have a stellar
professional career" mentioned above is a cluster objective for the
many specific objectives that characterize a stellar career. Clusters
may also concern components of your life, such as continuing to
learn interesting things and having more free time. You want to
name each cluster using a more general objective that describes the
components within the cluster.

One type of cluster that will simplify understanding the relationships between your objectives is that of inclusion. For example, in Figure 10.2, one cluster objective is "minimize constraints on freedom of choice." In considering what constraints, it includes those due to health, financial well-being, and available time. Objectives concerning each of these components are part of the cluster objective. In a life objectives diagram, you may wish to illustrate only the higher-level cluster objectives, or include a cluster objective's components within a box defining the meaning of that higher-level objective in more detail.

Identify Means–Ends Relationships. Once you have specified clusters for many of your life objectives, it is useful to relate the clusters and any objectives not in clusters to each other. The guiding principles are to identify means–ends relationships, analogous to those discussed in Chapter 5 and illustrated in Figures 10.1 and 10.2.

Means–ends relationships indicate how objectives influence each other. Having good health or more financial resources does not cause you to have greater freedom of choice even though there is an influential relationship, as shown in Figure 10.2. One can use those health and financial resources to make decisions that increase freedom of choice. Without health and financial resources, one's freedom of choice is often limited.

Identify Your Strategic Life Objectives. Your strategic life objectives define, ultimately, what you want to achieve in your life. These strategic life objectives are identified by following a series of means–ends relationships to their logical end. For each objective, including cluster objectives, ask yourself why this is important. It may be important because it is a means to other objectives, or clusters, or because better achieving it directly improves your quality of life. Since better achieving any of the objectives in your life objectives diagram can contribute to improving your quality of life, the key issue is whether this achievement is direct.

Some of your clusters may include both means life objectives and strategic life objectives. In such cases, it may be useful to divide the cluster into those that are only means objectives and those that are strategic objectives. As an example, for a cluster to "have a great college experience," the strategic life objectives may concern knowledge you learned and retained and the enjoyment that you had. Objectives to help you get a job after college, meet interesting people, and manage costs, although important, are means life objectives.

It is worth mentioning that a strategic life objective may also be a means objective. This usually occurs when better achieving one strategic life objective today influences achieving other life objectives at a subsequent time. Referring to Figure10.1, for example, part of being intellectually fulfilled involves learning and enhancing knowledge. This will lead to more opportunities for choices in later time periods. And, with greater choices, I can choose better alternatives to subsequently better achieve my strategic life objectives in these later time periods.

Proactively Guiding Your Life with Your Decisions

We all face numerous decisions throughout our lives. Every day we explicitly or implicitly make many decisions about what activities to spend our time on and how much time to spend on each. It may be that few of these basic decisions matter. At the end of the day, you may think: "I did little of what I wanted to do today, and nothing that was either particularly interesting or important." This circumstance, if repeated daily, is the opposite of what you probably want in life. The point is that numerous seemingly insignificant decisions collectively matter.

To understand how to control such situations, it is useful to recall how your decisions arise. Your decisions, basically, arise from three sources: the actions of others, external circumstances, and yourself. When your manager gives you an important assignment or when your young child is doing poorly in school, you have decisions to make as a result of others' intentional or unintentional actions. If severe weather causes major delays on an important trip, your financial investments have lost value, or you have recently experienced severe pains in your hip that limit mobility, you have decisions to make as a result of circumstances. I refer to decisions that arise in either of these ways as decision problems, because their occurrence is not under your control. If you did have control, you probably would not choose to have to face decisions about how to improve your child's poor school performance, how to reroute or reschedule a trip, or what to do about hip pain. These *are* problems!

It is different if you declare a decision opportunity for yourself, as discussed in Chapter 7. These decisions, which occur because of your control, define opportunities where you can enhance your life. You should use your control to create such decision opportunities, which can significantly improve the quality of your life.

Sources for stimulating your thoughts about decision opportunities range from thinking about things you would like to experience to seemingly random sparks of insight, as discussed in Chapter 7. In order to systematically create decision opportunities worthy of your time and effort, you can use the objectives in your life objectives diagram. Consider each objective individually and ask yourself if you are satisfied with your current situation and your future plans regarding this objective. If the answer is "No" or "Not completely," then an obvious decision opportunity is "decide how I can improve my circumstances with respect to this objective." Even if you are currently satisfied, any desire you have to maintain or improve your achievement on this objective in the future suggests a decision opportunity.

> **Being aware of the potential of decision opportunities, you will develop the ability to naturally create them. The basis for systematically creating decision opportunities is the objectives you have written in your life objectives diagram.**

It is useful to discuss three separate categories of decision opportunities: important single decisions, coordinated classes of decisions, and personal policy decisions. Whether to get married, have a child, pursue a postgraduate degree, or take a temporary job are all important single decisions. How to enhance your professional career, raise a child well, or benefit professionally and personally from a two-year assignment in another country each involves a coordinated class of decisions. Decision opportunities about health, the use of time, or the management of finances are often appropriately addressed with personal policy decisions.

Important Single Decisions. Some important individual decisions are life-changing, as they have implications for several of your life objectives. In addition to the family decisions concerning who you marry, if you divorce, or having a child, other life-changing decisions may involve major medical and/or financial decisions, whether to change your career, and permanently moving to another area or country.

The objectives for appraising the alternatives in a life-changing decision are your strategic life objectives. As a life-changing decision has the potential to influence virtually all of your life objectives, it is worthwhile to think through possible implications for achieving each of them.

Life-changing decisions usually have only a few distinct alternatives. You could begin trying to have a first child or not, or decide whether to have one, two, or three children. You could file for divorce or not. And you could remain in your current job or leave and pursue one of a few other options, such as starting your own business or joining a recent startup.

Your life-changing decisions may greatly affect others in your family. To help you understand the possible impacts to each of them from your different alternatives, you may wish to think through their consequences using a framework of the important objectives of their life analogous to your life objectives diagram.

Most of your important single decisions will not be life-changing, but they still can significantly impact your quality of life. Examples include decisions such as whether to pursue a master's degree, live with a roommate or live in a smaller apartment, sell your car and live without owning a vehicle, or go live near your children and grandchildren. To make sound choices on important decisions such as these, dedicated value-focused decision-making to appropriately formulate your decision, specify the objectives you want to achieve, identify creative alternatives better than the obvious ones, and appraise the pros and cons of the contending alternatives is worth the time and effort required. All of these will nudge you to make better choices about these very important decisions.

▶ Marketing Your Professional Services

Rick Isaacson was a professional risk analyst with 11 years of experience working at an electric and gas utility company. He was accomplished and respected for his knowledge and skills about all of the safety and environmental risks facing a utility company, including those due to operating facilities and the transmission of electricity and gas, as well as those in homes and buildings using electricity and gas. He could manage and coordinate projects involving pipeline or electricity grid operations, relevant science (e.g., about earthquakes), and human behavior involving diverse experts who logically analyzed potential risks and evaluated appropriate actions to reduce them.

With this background, Rick left his firm about a year ago and became an independent consultant offering services to any firm concerned about such risks. Unfortunately, Rick found it more difficult to find adequate work than he had expected. He came to realize that, although he was greatly respected inside his previous firm, he was relatively unknown outside that firm. He recognized the decision opportunity that he needed to market his skills effectively.

His first thoughts were about the objectives for his marketing strategy. Those identified were to increase offers for his consulting services, stress his skills as a leader of large projects, keep the economic costs of the marketing strategy low, meet other risk analysts and professionals with similar interests, and enjoy the marketing process. Based on these objectives, he identified and pursued several complementary alternatives. He researched potentially relevant professional societies and joined the main national risk analysis society and a local affiliated group. He recognized the usefulness of writing articles about uses of his skills in the risk management field and about projects he had participated in. He decided to try to publish some of these in both technical and trade journals, to reach the respective audiences, as well as developing a personal website to describe his professional practice. He blogged on his personal website about the characteristics of good practice in analyzing and making decisions about technical risks in utility companies. In addition, he attended public hearings about proposed projects involving technical risks, such as constructing and operating gas pipelines, and offered remarks about proposals when appropriate. Within the year the implications of these marketing efforts began to have significant positive impacts on his consulting practice. ◄

Coordinated Classes of Decisions. You may sometimes think of worthwhile decision opportunities, where a class of several specific decisions will collectively contribute to how well your objectives are met. In fact, all of the decisions in your life could be considered as a coordinated class, where the objectives are your strategic life objectives.

Coordinated classes of decisions typically have a more specific focus than important single decisions, as they usually address a part of the quality of one's life. Such parts may involve specific interests, concerns, relationships, or time periods. Suppose that much of your social and physically active life involves golf and activities at your golf club, but you have just accepted a job promotion requiring that you move across the country. You now recognize decision opportunities to create a similar social and sports quality of life in your new location. Another example is the decision opportunity to develop financial independence, which directly addresses only financial concerns. Collectively, all of the decisions made within a class may be life-changing. Being financially independent compared to financially struggling results in very different life experiences. However, any individual decision in the class of decisions made to pursue financial independence does not usually have this potential range of consequences.

Your life objectives diagram provides the basis for identifying the specific objectives for any coordinated class of decisions. These specific objectives are used to develop potential alternatives to achieve each of the specific objectives. Various combinations of these alternatives should be integrated into compound alternatives, which should then be appraised in terms of achieving the entire set of specific objectives in order to identify the preferred compound alternative.

To best achieve your objectives for a class of decisions, the alternatives that are part of a compound alternative need to be coherent and consistent. The thinking required to make such coordinated decisions is time-consuming, not only because the separate decisions themselves are difficult and important but also because how well you achieve your objectives depends on the collective consequences of the compound alternative chosen, not on the sum of the consequences of the separate alternatives in that compound alternative. Recognizing and understanding the interrelationships between the separate decisions and coordinating them so as to reduce the chances of inconsistent choices that work at cross-purposes is a unique factor of coordinated classes of decisions.

► An International Work Assignment

Suppose that you have just accepted an offer to live and work for two years in Chengdu, China. You of course desire to get the most from your two-year stay. You are confident that the professional work aspects of your assignment will go well. Your decision opportunity is to organize your personal life while living in Chengdu so that it is an enjoyable and worthwhile experience. The key first step is to define what you mean by "enjoyable and worthwhile."

As always, the question to ask yourself is "What are my values?." Your strategic life objectives provide the foundation to answer this question. A first cut of your objectives for your Chengdu stay is just to limit each of your strategic objectives to the two-year period in Chengdu. Then you can become more specific. Suppose that learning more about Chengdu, China, and Asia is one of your objectives. Specifics of this may include wanting to learn another language, presumably Mandarin in this case. Also, you want to learn and understand much more about Chinese history, culture, and geography, as well as understand more about political and governmental operations. A second major objective might be to develop worthwhile relationships that you plan to maintain well after your assignment ends. You want to meet and socialize with local residents and have fun participating in their celebrations and customs. In addition, you may wish to help your friends and co-workers understand a bit about your home country.

Some of your important decisions will likely affect the achievement of both the professional and personal objectives. Examples are decisions about where you choose to live and whether you will own a car. In addition, these two decisions may be inter-related. Since your office is in a large new technology park devel-opment on the outskirts of Chengdu, you may choose to live in the city to better contribute to your personal objectives, but then a commute to work will be necessary. Thus, you may want to live at a convenient location to use public transport to travel to and from your office. Alternatively, if a car is necessary for the com-mute, or if you plan to own a car anyway, you will want convenient parking.

By beginning with your objectives for both the personal and professional aspects of your life for your two years in Chengdu, and then creating alternatives to pursue those objectives and thought-fully selecting compatible alternatives for your decisions, you will be in a position to have a wonderful stay. ◄

In decisions where the consequences accrue over time—over two years, in the case above—it is obvious that there are many uncertainties about the future consequences. Depending on how the future unfolds, you may modify the current alternatives to account for changing circumstances. Thus, your original choices should include the flexibility to adapt alternatives as appropriate.

The objectives that you established for your two-year assignment should remain relevant in order to provide guidance as to when and how to modify or change alternatives.

Personal Policy Decisions. They sound important, but what are personal policy decisions? A personal policy decision is a decision that selects the rule you will use for making specific decisions that regularly occur to achieve a longer-term objective. Typically, it specifies what you will or will not do in these specific decision situations, as well as how you will do it. We all use policy decisions for some situations, but may not consciously recognize it. Deciding to always wear a seatbelt in a vehicle, to floss your teeth every evening, and to avoid purchasing anything that you do not need are common examples.

> A personal policy decision involves selecting a rule for making specific decisions that frequently occur in your life. Following that rule for these decisions provides consistency and saves time.

Policy decisions allow you to thoughtfully make one decision—the policy decision—and then simply follow the policy so as to avoid making numerous lower-level routine decisions. Such a policy is essentially a nudge to consistently make beneficial routine decisions. It also reduces the decision burden, which saves you time and avoids some stress. If you select a personal policy and follow it to make improvements, the result is often that you develop a habit that will maintain that improvement.

Policy decisions have wide applicability. Decision opportunities for which policy decisions would be useful include how best to get physically fit, eat more healthily, manage your time better, excel in an educational program, avoid drinking too much alcohol, and meet someone who you might like as your spouse.

The objectives for personal policy decisions often directly influence only one or two of the means objectives in the life objectives diagram. For instance, for the decision opportunity concerning meeting a potential spouse, your main objective may be to maximize the number of realistic candidates who you meet in a given time period. For the decision to manage your time better, your objectives may be to focus current time on higher-priority tasks, complete these tasks well using less time, and reduce the time allocated to low-priority tasks.

For some policy decisions, several of the numerous alternatives may be implemented in order to achieve your objectives in a coordinated fashion. A key aspect of addressing such a decision opportunity is the framing of the decision. There is a level at which decisions are appropriate to address. Personal policy decisions are at a higher level than making numerous repeated decisions separately. If you have declared the decision opportunity to better control your expenses, you probably should not separately decide whether or not to purchase an expensive cappuccino each day. Rather, set a policy such as "do not purchase individual expensive coffee drinks" or "purchase at most two cappuccinos per week." Another complementary policy you might find appealing is to leave your credit card at home, unless you know that you need to make a planned purchase. If you have it with you, you may make several independent decisions about whether you can afford or should purchase specific items. These may result in some logically inconsistent purchases, where you spend more money on some unnecessary purchase than you save by avoiding a different purchase that would actually be useful.

► Losing Weight and Getting Fit
Participants in my classes on decision-making are required to identify important personal decisions that they want to address. One, a graduate student who I will call Maria, recognized her decision opportunity to lose weight, specifically about 30 pounds. The alternatives that she considered to achieve this included decisions about both eating and exercising.

Regarding eating, she considered decisions about what to eat, when to eat, how much to eat, how often to eat, with whom to eat, what to drink, and even how to eat. Regarding what to eat, Maria considered decisions in terms of items, ingredients, and/or courses to include or exclude. She included alternatives that specified different guidelines for weekends and for dinner parties with guests. Other specific alternatives she created included never having a second helping, always leaving 10 percent of the food on her plate, no desserts except for special occasions, no alcohol on weekdays, no soft drinks, only salads for lunch, three meals per day and no snacks between meals, and only fruit for snacks. To construct a reasonably easy-to-follow yet effective eating plan, she evaluated the alternatives and chose the following policy: eat only three meals per day, no second helpings or desserts, only fruit for a snack at most once a day, no alcohol on weekdays, and a maximum of two glasses of wine on either Friday or Saturday.

Using a similar process for her exercise schedule, Maria established a policy requirement for physical activity, usually jogging or tennis but at least brisk walking, for a minimum of 30 minutes per day and to always walk upstairs when there were fewer than three floors.

Maria reported that she consistently followed her eating and exercise policies in pursuing her decision opportunity to lose weight. Six months later, a few months after the class had ended, she had indeed lost the desired 30 pounds. ◄

A good policy decision should be effective and easy to implement. It should not be too narrow or too broad. For example, it would obviously be unreasonable to have a policy at the level of whether to eat each particular bite of food on your plate. Higher-level rules should guide decisions about what specific bites of food to eat. Also, a policy limiting your diet to 45,000 calories a month or 1,500 calories a day yields the same monthly calories. However, the latter narrower frame would be more meaningful and much easier to follow.

Pursuing a High Quality of Life in Practice

A key to enhancing your quality of life is to always be aware of your life objectives. This requires that you articulate, understand, and organize your life objectives. Awareness of your life objectives will naturally stimulate thoughts of decision opportunities about how you can enhance the quality of your life.

For all individuals, the quality of their personal relationships, the activities they engage in, and the experiences they have directly contribute to the quality of their life. When you recognize a decision opportunity that might establish a worthwhile relationship, be an interesting activity to pursue, and/or lead to a wonderful experience, consider those opportunities thoughtfully. Suppose that you are in a position where you can choose an alternative to pursue a relationship or activity that might lead to a wonderful experience. If that experience will be unique and memories of it will not blend over time with other experiences in your life, then it is probably a good idea to pursue it, assuming, of course, that it will not cause harm to you or others.

Once you have thought of a decision opportunity, you want to create a few potential alternatives for pursuing it. Sometimes there may be just one general alternative, although there may be many specific alternatives that are consistent with this general alternative.

At this stage you have clarified your decision opportunity. You now should appraise both whether it is realistic and if it is worth your effort to pursue it. If, in your assessment, the general alternative and some specific alternatives seem desirable, then pursue one of your viable alternatives. If one of the alternatives is conceptually the best, but has a shortcoming such as the cost, you may be able to create decision opportunities to eliminate or reduce that shortcoming. If not, choose the best of the other specific alternatives.

If your appraisal suggests that it is not worth pursuing this decision opportunity, your effort is not useless. You likely became a bit more attuned to the process of identifying and appraising decision opportunities. If you maintain your interest in decision opportunities, you will certainly generate others that will be pursued to fruition that will positively impact your quality of life.

Additional Thoughts for Decisions in Organizations

All of the ideas and procedures in this chapter are relevant to organizations and organizational decisions. As with individuals, decisions are the only way to purposefully influence how well the organization performs. Thus, it is very important for an organization to understand its organizational objectives to recognize and pursue decision opportunities to enhance the achievement of their strategic objectives, as well as create and evaluate alternatives.

There is a key distinction between creating the life objectives of an individual and the organizational objectives of an organization. The origin of the values that are the basis for the strategic objectives diagram of an organization is the collective thoughts of several executives and leaders of that organization. Thus, the perspectives of different individuals need to be considered in establishing a common set of organizational objectives that should be used by everyone making decisions on behalf of the organization. Otherwise, decisions made by one part of an organization may conflict with and negate the positive consequences of decisions made in another part.

A complete description of an organization's values can be determined in two ways. The main way is to elicit values in discussions with various executives following the same guidelines as discussed in this chapter to obtain an individual's life objectives. These discussions should include executives who have major responsibilities for different aspects of an organization's functions, as they will better understand the relevant objectives concerning those functions. In addition, an organization often has documented information about its operational values and strategic objectives in its mission statement and various reports (e.g., annual reports) and on its website. One can identify an organization's values by carefully examining such documents.

I have worked with numerous organizations, including large and small companies, government agencies, and NGOs, to help them articulate, organize, understand, and use their organizational objectives.[4]

The US Department of Homeland Security (DHS) has an annual budget of around $70 billion to address its major responsibilities for dealing with terrorism, natural disasters, pandemics, illegal trafficking and transnational crime, and major industrial accidents. The purpose of DHS is to make and implement decisions that reduce the negative implications to people in the United States from all of these five types of threats. To guide their decisions, I elicited values from 13 individuals with various senior responsibilities at DHS. These were used to construct a strategic objectives diagram for the DHS.[5]

Chevron, an international energy company, was the initial organization selected by the Society of Decision Professionals to receive the Raiffa–Howard Award to recognize consistent and sustained excellence in decision-making throughout an organization. Chevron has many corporate documents that contain its values, including a mission statement, its vision, and principles for action that provided the main sources for the values in its strategic objectives diagram. Using these documents, I worked with decision professionals at Chevron to construct a strategic objectives diagram for the company. At the highest level of aggregation, the company's strategic objectives were to act consistently with basic Chevron values, make high-quality decisions, operate safely and profitably, and deliver world-class performance for shareholders, customers, the communities where the company works, partners, employees, and humankind.

Constructing the strategic objectives diagram of an organization uses the same guidelines as those for an individual's life objectives diagram. It begins with a list of all of the stated objectives. When the objectives on the list originate from several organizational members, some organizational objectives are stated by almost everyone involved, such as those concerning safety, environmental impacts, and corporate profitability. Other organizational objectives may be stated by only one or two individuals. However, within an organization, there is rarely disagreement about the appropriateness of objectives stated by others. Any disagreements that occur usually concern the relative importance of specific achievements on different objectives.

An organization's strategic objectives diagram provides a common set of appropriate objectives for organizational decisions analogous to those in a personal life objectives diagram. Having strategic objectives clarified and organized in a strategic objectives diagram reduces the chance that significant objectives are overlooked for important decisions.

The strategic objectives of an organization also provide a logically sound basis for consistently making all organizational decisions. Suppose that a large corporation that sells consumer goods has distinct divisions in different parts of the country. Two divisions were, separately, considering a large expansion in their respective areas. The separate analyses indicated that the costs and benefits of expanding, in terms of the corporation's strategic objectives, were essentially the same in both cases. If the corporation had the funds necessary to fund both expansions, it would not be in the corporation's interest to have one division decide to expand and the other not. These decisions should be made using the same objectives, and, given the same information on costs and benefits, they should be made consistently and reach a common decision regarding expansion.

With strategic life decisions, only one decision-maker is involved, even though the impacts of his or her decisions on others may be significant. With an organization, many different individuals and sometimes groups of individuals make decisions. Thus, in addition to the uses of a strategic objectives diagram for an individual, the organizational strategic objectives diagram has two additional important benefits.

An organizational strategic objectives diagram can enable everyone in the organization to get on the same team. Each individual of the organization should know, understand, and agree with the organizational objectives. If there are any disagreements between the individuals who initially provided the lists of values for the organizational strategic objectives diagram, these disagreements need to be recognized and thoroughly discussed, with the purpose of eliminating them in the process of constructing the strategic objectives diagram. Eliminating disagreements on objectives does not mean that all individuals will agree on the best alternatives to pursue them. If individuals disagree on the best alternatives, it must be that the different individuals have different judgments about how well the relevant objectives will be achieved by the alternatives or that they evaluate specific achievements on some objectives differently. In such cases, identifying the basis for disagreements provides the necessary foundation to guide a productive process to reach an agreement about the best alternative to choose.

The organization's strategic objectives, when communicated accurately to all employees, can positively contribute to the organization's spirit and morale. Moreover, numerous important decisions, each of much less significance than any strategic decision, are made by employees who are not executives in the large organization. The strategic objectives diagram provides guidance for the objectives appropriate for those decisions. In addition, those objectives can stimulate the creation of decision opportunities that are advantageous for the organization to address.

11 USEFUL PERSPECTIVES ON DECISION-MAKING

This chapter provides some useful perspectives on decision-making and the role that it should play in your life to be most useful. Specific topics concern the misnomer of "objective decision-making," the inappropriateness of trying to optimize your decisions, the appropriate amount of time you should spend making decisions and how that time should be allocated, the special importance of avoiding poor life-limiting decisions, the implications of your decisions on an untimely death, how being spontaneous and having fun fit in with your decision-making, and your nudges and your life.

To discuss these topics, a simple view that divides your activities in life into two categories is useful. These categories are making decisions and living your life, which means experiencing the collective consequences of all of your decisions. This decide–experience view is a reasonable description for each individual decision, which makes it useful for our discussion. However, at any given time in your life, you are likely in the process of making many decisions. You have been thinking about different decisions beginning at different times and will make these decisions at different times in the future. So, at any given time you are experiencing consequences that are collectively attributable to many of your past decisions.

Decision-Making Is Not, Cannot, and Should Not Be Objective

I have heard numerous individuals state something similar to "Good decision-making must be objective." Whether this makes sense depends on the definition of "objective decision-making." Businessdictionary.com defines "objective" as "a process based only on hard facts and void of any subjective perspectives concerning feelings and opinions." With this definition, objective decision-making is impossible, and would in fact be undesirable.

Since your values are based on your feelings and beliefs, they are naturally grounded in subjectivity. This does not imply that we cannot define the concept of a good decision or of a good decision-making process. Both are based on the notion that a good decision is one that is logically consistent with your values, the alternatives you have identified, and the information that you had at the time you made the decision. For your decisions, you are the world authority on what you consider and feel is most relevant to them.

There is no universally correct alternative for any real decision problem. For your decisions, your values set the standard that matters and there is no reason for your values to be the same as those of other individuals. Imagine if there were such a thing as an objectively correct alternative for decisions you faced. This would mean that your values and information would have no influence on what you should choose in life. It would simply be fortuitous if your values, information, and logic were the same as the values, information, and logic used by the decision gods. Such a life, it seems to me, would be much less appealing than the one we have, replete with the opportunity to use our own values to guide our decisions and improve and enjoy our lives.

It Is Not Optimal to Optimize Most Decisions

Optimizing a decision means choosing the best alternative for that decision, which is the one expected to contribute the most to your quality of life. Descriptively, it is well established that most individuals do not optimize many of their decisions.[1] Prescriptively, I do not think individuals should try to optimize every decision, or even most decisions. In other words, I think it is rational and advisable not to optimize most of your decisions. Let me explain.

The decide–experience sequence allows us to examine whether it is always desirable to try to optimize a particular decision that you face. You can usually increase your chances of choosing the best alternative when more time is allocated to make the decision. Of course, when one more hour is used to make a decision, that hour is not available to experience your life. If you reach the point where you experience less contribution to your quality of life due to that additional hour spent to improve a particular decision than the contribution of each hour of experiencing the benefits of this and other decisions, you would increase your overall quality of life by ending your decision process now and selecting what you now think is the best alternative. The implication is that it is not optimal for your quality of life to try to optimize each of your decisions.

> **It is not worth your time and effort to try to optimize most decisions. It is worth your time and effort to thoughtfully make your important decisions.**

Some may consider this a paradox: that trying to optimize each decision that you make in life and trying to optimize the quality of your life are mutually inconsistent. It may appear to be a paradox, but the resolution is straightforward. Optimizing the quality of your life is your overall strategic life objective, whereas trying to optimize each decision in your life is only a means that affects the degree to which you achieve your overall life objective. At the extreme, pursuing a strategy to optimize each of your decisions would, essentially, require all of your time for decision-making and provide no time for enjoying your life. Thus, trying to optimize each individual decision makes no sense, whereas those decisions that will significantly impact your life merit your time and attention.

How Much Time to Spend Making a Decision

I consider the time to make a decision as the total time spent consciously thinking about that decision and selecting an alternative. This could be much less than the elapsed time from when you first begin thinking about a decision and when you make that decision.

The appropriate amount of time and effort to make a decision is that which results in the greatest contribution to your quality of life from the decide–experience sequence for that decision. This fact provides a basis for how much time you should spend making specific decisions, but, of course, you don't want to consider your quality of life in appraising each of your decisions.

For any decision worthy of thought, you should spend at least enough time to understand the decision that you want to make. This requires you to state the decision that you want to address, specify your values for this decision, and identify a set of distinct alternatives to achieve those values. Once you have some experience with value-focused decision-making, the time necessary to complete these tasks can

> **Spend the time needed to thoroughly understand the decision you want to face. Then you can meaningfully determine the appropriate time for the evaluation of alternatives.**

be as short as a couple of minutes for less complex decisions worthy of thought and as long as hours or even days, spent over a longer time period, when both the complexity and the importance of the decision are great. The results of your thinking provide the framework for making a good decision and considering whether additional thinking about the decision is worthwhile.

Given your understanding of the individual decision that you want to face, you usually have some idea about how good the alternative is that you would choose if you chose now. You also probably have a notion of how good a great alternative would need to be, where a great alternative is one so good that you would stop your decision process and choose it right away. The difference in the overall desirability of this great alternative and your current best alternative indicates the maximum gain in your quality of life that you could expect from additional time spent on the decision process.

Now consider how much time you would be willing to spend if you could experience this maximum gain. Your answer to this question is the maximum time you should additionally spend on the decision given your current knowledge. If the maximum time can be measured in minutes (i.e., less than an hour), it is probably reasonable to spend a bit more time on your decision. You should stop when you feel that any additional time is not worth the effort, which presumably would occur within an hour. If the maximum time is a few hours, it seems reasonable to spend an additional hour or two and then repeat the thought process on how much additional time to spend. If the answer to the original question is in days or weeks, which could be the case for life-changing decisions, certainly more time is justified, and you should periodically reassess your progress on making a high-quality decision. This would allow you to update the maximum amount of additional time that you might find useful to allocate to the present decision given your current information.

For some decisions that are definitely worthy of thought, but not among your more important decisions, there is sometimes an easier way to determine the value of using additional decision time. These are decisions for which you can compare the contribution of time spent making a decision to time wasted as a result of possible undesirable consequences of the decision.

► Selecting a Surgeon

Suppose that you are unfortunate enough to face the decision of selecting a surgeon to repair your broken ankle. You have identified three surgeons who you believe are equally qualified to perform the surgery. However, you know very little about how their respective office staffs communicate with and treat patients after surgery. From your personal knowledge and discussions with others who have had similar surgeries, you realize that not having timely and high-quality responses to any post-surgery issues by a physician's staff could cause you to experience three or more net days of inconvenience, aggravation, and lingering pain. If you believe that spending three or four hours checking on the quality of post-surgery interaction of the staff at three surgeon's offices could eliminate the potential of three miserable days for you, the additional decision time would be well spent. ◄

How Your Decision-Making Time Should Be Allocated

A decision-making process can be categorized into four activities: recognizing and understanding your decision; identifying the values relevant to it; creating alternatives; and evaluating and choosing an alternative. These activities should initially be addressed in order, although it is often useful to revisit previous activities in the light of thoughts generated in subsequent activities.

For any decision worthy of thought, you must thoroughly understand the decision that you face in order to make a good decision. Thus, the time required to complete the first three activities well is time well spent. Chapters 4 through 6, respectively, offer guidance to perform these activities skillfully and thoroughly. Evaluating the alternatives and choosing one, which is discussed in the Appendix, will be less difficult and yield better results if the first three activities are carried out well. Based on your objectives, it may become clear to you that some of the alternatives are inferior to at least one other alternative. Such inferior alternatives can be removed from further consideration. The set of remaining alternatives will be both smaller and of higher quality than the original set.

Of the remaining alternatives, one alternative may clearly be better than the others. In other situations, you might not be sure which is best. So, from your perspective, these alternatives are somewhat close in preference. You will often understand which alternatives are better in terms of specific values, but how much better is not so clear, and that difference matters. Here, you need to recognize another decision. You could gather information on how well the alternatives measure up on one or more objectives. If you do this, the information might allow you to make a clear choice. However, gathering this information takes time and may be costly. You will therefore need to decide whether gathering the additional information is worth it.

To decide how to move forward, think about the following. Consider how likely it is that the gathered information will change your decision from what you would choose now with no additional information. If you feel there is no chance that the gathered information will change your decision, the information that you could collect has no value, so just choose the alternative that you feel is best now. If you believe that collecting additional information has a chance to alter your decision, consider what the chances are and the net value to you of switching your chosen alternative in that case. When the chances of switching alternatives is greater and the value of switching is higher, the value of gathering information increases. If the value of the information is greater than the value to you of the time and cost to gather the information, collecting the information is the better choice. Otherwise, don't gather any additional information and make your decision now.

The Importance of Avoiding Poor Decisions

We often state that the main purpose of making a decision is to choose the best alternative. However, for many important decisions, trying to avoid the selection of a poor alternative may have a much greater overall influence on your resulting quality of life. Reflecting on the life-limiting decisions mentioned below, you will recognize one crucial

> **It is particularly important to avoid making poor decisions, as one poor decision can eliminate the cumulative benefits of numerous good decisions.**

fact. Many very good decisions cannot compensate for or negate the influence of one very poor life-limiting decision on one's quality of life. The good news is that it is usually much easier to identify the poor alternatives than to select the best.

Consider this example of a very poor decision. You are drunk and decide to drive a friend home, so the chances of a serious accident are significantly increased. If you cause an accident and your friend dies, your life will likely never be the same. If you die, it will certainly never be the same. Poor life-limiting decisions are those that greatly increase the chance of substantially degrading your quality of life.

Some classes of poor life-limiting decisions are readily recognized. Examples are the decisions that significantly contribute to having low educational skills, becoming addicted to alcohol or drugs, or participating in criminal activity. Each of these usually has a profound negative influence on one's quality of life, for many years or forever.

Another class of decisions, where poor choices may result in a serious downgrading of one's quality of life, are the significant personal decisions concerning marriage, divorce, and having children. The implications of each of these decisions can vary from very significant positive consequences to very significant negative consequences on an individual's quality of life. Obviously, you do not have total control over the future consequences of such decisions. However, thoughtful decisions can identify and avoid many poor choices, which can significantly lessen the chances of poor consequences.

Some single decisions can result in either a large positive or a large negative impact. Suppose an individual made and saved a lot of money by working and living a financially responsible life. This situation was the result of many good decisions, sustained effort, and perhaps some good fortune. His self-proclaimed quality of life was high. Then he invested almost all of his funds in an investment or a bet that he thought was almost a sure thing to double his money. As he learned, his judgment about the chance that the investment would be successful was unreasonable, and investing most of his funds in a single endeavor was foolhardy. In short, he chose a poor alternative. As a result, he lost most of his funds accumulated by years of good decisions in one very poor decision. And his quality of life dropped substantially.

What can you do to lessen your chances of a significant downgrading of your quality of life due to one choice on a potentially life-limiting decision? In a nutshell, first recognize that every life-limiting decision is worthy of some careful thought before making a choice. Second, try to anticipate any life-limiting decision that you may end up facing sometime in the future. Before that time, assume that you are now facing that decision and follow the ideas in this book to help you understand the possible consequences of the alternatives. Then appraise the alternatives to identify the alternative that you should choose when and if you face that decision. This appraisal should nudge you away from poor alternatives and heighten your awareness of potential steps to avoid them. Third, if and when you actually face one of those life-limiting decisions, do not quickly or thoughtlessly take an action. This is often how many very poor decisions are made. If you have previously anticipated facing this decision, recall the choice that you intended to make, and make it. If you had not previously anticipated the decision, use the time you have to pause and reflect on your life values and the consequences of the available alternatives. Then—and only then—choose the alternative that you believe recognizes and appropriately accounts for the possible consequences that can significantly disrupt your life.

Your Decisions and a Premature Death

Your decisions have a major effect on how long you live, as well as on the quality of your life while alive. Over 40 percent of the fatalities in the United States could have been avoided if readily available alternatives had been chosen by the individuals who subsequently died prematurely. Readily available alternatives are those that require little time, money, or effort to implement and require

> **More than 1 million fatalities each year in the United States could have been avoided if readily available alternatives had been chosen by the individuals who subsequently died prematurely.**

only information and knowledge that is widely available and understood. Choosing such readily available alternatives would avoid over 1 million fatalities annually that occur in the United States. How can this be?

The pathway from personal decisions to becoming a premature fatality is short and direct. Figure 11.1 shows numerous types of personal decisions and relates these to the actual causes of death. Each actual death is then examined to provide a medical cause

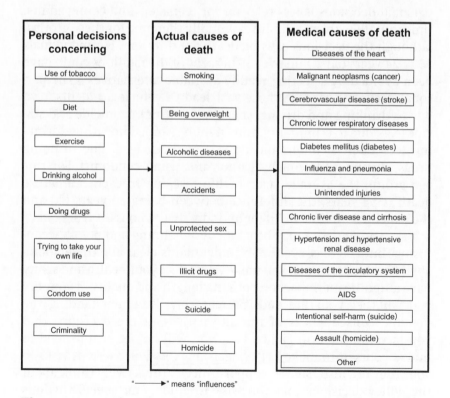

"——▶" means "influences"

Figure 11.1 Influence of Personal Decisions on Premature Fatalities

of death. An analysis of the mortality data relating actual causes of deaths to medical causes indicates that about 55 percent of the fatalities in each ten-year age range from 15 to 64 years old experience a premature death due to personal decisions concerning the topics in Figure 11.1.[2]

The biggest medical causes of death are heart disease and cancer, which collectively account for about a half of all fatalities in the United States each year. Of these fatalities, 46 percent of heart disease fatalities and 66 percent cancer fatalities could have been avoided if individuals had made different choices about smoking (i.e., not to smoke or to quit smoking) or about their weight (e.g., to improve one's diet, avoid excessive drinking of alcohol, and maintain fitness). Since most of the people who suffer a premature death from one of these causes are 50 years old or older, these individuals lose on average 13 years of expected life.

Because most deaths occur to individuals over 50 years old, it might be reasonable to think that the relationship between personal decisions is less relevant for teenagers and young adults. Unfortunately, the results are essentially the same for these groups, although the decisions causing death are different. For individuals 15 to 24 years old, again over 55 percent of the fatalities could have been avoided by selecting readily available alternatives.[3] The personal decisions concern those that lead to vehicle accidents (e.g., due to drinking and driving, speeding, texting), homicide and suicide (e.g., due to criminality, gang membership, doing drugs, drinking too much alcohol), and unprotected sex (e.g., due to doing drugs, drinking too much alcohol, not using condoms). For this age group, the average years of life lost due to each premature death is 58 years, the difference between being 20 years old and the expected lifetime of 78 for an individual who is 20 years old.

The statistics may be a bit overwhelming and possibly confusing, but the message for an individual is clear and understandable. The decisions that you make that affect your health and safety have a significant impact on both the length and quality of your life and whether your life ends prematurely. By understanding the possible consequences of the alternatives in the decisions that you face indicated in Figure 11.1, you will be better informed to nudge yourself to make better decisions involving serious risks to your life. You also have the opportunity to proactively think about the policy decisions that you wish to guide your specific actions concerning the categories of personal decisions in Figure 11.1.

Hence, when decisions arise that involve greatly elevated risks to your life, you will have a basis to clearly and confidently choose alternatives consistent with your values.

Spontaneity, Fun, and Decisions

In a presentation on value-focused decision-making to students in an MBA program several years ago, a young lady stated the following: "This is very interesting and it seems to be useful, but I sure would not want to go grocery shopping with you." Everyone laughed, including me. But she had raised a very important point. It sounded as if all of my decisions are planned and calculated and that there was no role for spontaneity and fun. Who would want to limit their life by using such a controlled scheme? I wouldn't, and don't. Let me explain.

Enjoying life is one of my strategic life objectives, as indicated in Figure 10.1. This includes the enjoyment of having fun. If having fun is one of your fundamental life objectives, your quality of life obviously depends on how much fun you are having. Every decision that you make can influence the fun you have in your life

> **Your decision-making should contribute to the fun and enjoyment in your life, as your decision-making is the only purposeful way to influence anything in your life.**

and should be considered in deciding which alternative to choose.

Spontaneity is also important to me. Being spontaneous is a means objective for enjoying life. With people or with ideas, it is sometimes fun and exciting not knowing what will happen next. Actually, you can never be sure what will happen next in life. It's just the degree of uncertainty that varies, and, depending on the circumstances, more uncertainty often leads to more enjoyment. Most individuals would find it less enjoyable to attend a big sporting event if, miraculously, they knew what the outcome of that event was going to be.

It may seem somewhat counterintuitive but some proactive decisions to create interesting and enjoyable opportunities greatly enhance spontaneity in life rather than reduce it. Suppose that you find that there is not enough fun and/or spontaneity in your life; you can mope about it and hope it gets better. If you just sit at home and follow your best "mope and hope" strategy, probably not much will happen that leads to any fun. But, using one of the main nudging concepts in this book, you can clearly do something about it. Declare a decision opportunity, namely "how do I introduce more fun and spontaneity in my life?." Then pursue that decision opportunity. You will be able to identify numerous alternatives that should contribute to your desires.

You may be considering what to do next Saturday. You could stay home, which is not a good alternative for having fun, or go to a movie or an outdoor concert. One plus of the concert is the likelihood of more interaction with others, some of whom you currently do not know, and more spontaneity. If you are planning to attend an activity such as a party or networking event, you could go alone or with someone. Going alone may lead to more spontaneity, as you will likely interact with more people who you do not currently know or know well. On a trip, you may plan where to go, and consciously not plan what to do. Once you are on your trip, you will follow your heart and do what you feel like doing once you are there.

If you are using value-focused decision-making, you will nudge yourself by identifying decision opportunities of various sorts, which should result in improvements to your quality of life. You should also be making more informed decisions, so, in general, the consequences should be better. As a result, you should have fewer decision problems that appear as the result of circumstances beyond your control. This should lessen the time required to identify and implement alternatives to address those decision problems. With your additional free time, you can do anything you like, including just doing what you feel like without much thinking. You can use this additional time to enjoy your life, which I hope you do.

You, Your Nudges, and Your Life

This book is my nudge to help you to improve your decision-making. If you use the ideas in this book, you will be nudging yourself to improve your decisions and your decision-making skill. The result will be better decisions and less stressful decision-making.

There are numerous nudges for both your decisions and your decision-making. Table 11.1 is a summary of the main nudges for each of the five key decision-making components necessary to construct a decision frame that includes all of the relevant factors of any decision that you face. Your decision frame provides you with a much better understanding of what is relevant, and of what is not relevant that you may have thought was, which helps you to clearly understand your decision and what you need to consider in order to evaluate alternatives. This knowledge provides a few nudges to help you evaluate the alternatives for your decision, which are included as the last item in Table 11.1.

Using the ideas in this book to nudge yourself to make better decisions will also nudge you to become a better decision-maker. Several nudges to help you become a better decision-maker are listed in Table 11.2. As with any skill, when you use it as intended, you will improve your skill level. In addition, your rate of improvement is much greater during the earlier uses. Yet you can keep improving with more use, even though the rate of improvement may be slower. I use tennis to illustrate this, but you can visualize the ideas with any other sport, or any other skill, that you have developed.

Suppose that you occasionally played tennis over the past several years, but had never bothered to take lessons. Recently you became more interested and took a series of tennis lessons. Now you are beginning to play tennis games using what you have just learned. The specific techniques that you learned for each aspect of your tennis game are, essentially, nudges to improve your play. Maybe a couple of these seemed to work immediately, but others were somewhat awkward and did not seem to help much at all. This is natural; you are improving, but real progress with any skill is slow and not easy. However, with each game you soon tend to feel more comfortable with the new techniques, and they become easier to use. As a result, you are playing better tennis. After additional use, these new techniques become a habit. By then your tennis game will have noticeably improved, and this will continue for quite a while.

This simple story is analogous to what will happen with your decision-making and the quality of your decisions. This book presents methods for practicing and becoming skilled in using the concepts of value-focused decision-making and their uses, so that you can nudge yourself in ways that will improve your decisions. Certainly, you can become more effective at nudging yourself by focusing upon your values. The important implication

Table 11.1 Summary of Nudges to Help You Make Better Decisions

1. Concerning your decision statement

- Spend time to define the decision statement
- Begin decision statement with 'decide'
- Consider different decision statements
- Avoid expressing a decision statement as an objective or an alternative
- Require clarity about the decision you face
- Avoid a narrow limiting scope

2. Concerning your values

- Spend time to identify your values
- Use numerous stimulation techniques (see Table 5.2)
- State values as objectives
- Recognize means–ends relationships of objectives
- Identify fundamental objectives
- Consider learning and flexibility objectives
- Believe there are unrecognized values
- Ask others for suggestions of values

3. Concerning your alternatives

- Spend time to create alternatives
- Identify additional alternatives after the first one is identified

4. Concerning your decision opportunities

- Spend time to create decision opportunities
- Use your life objectives
- Think about your desired future

- Use individual values to create alternatives
- Use sets of values to create alternatives
- Set a goal for the number of new alternatives to create
- Search throughout the "alternatives box"
- Modify a good alternative with add-on benefits
- Believe that better alternatives exist
- Have others create alternatives for you

5. Concerning authorizing a desired alternative

- Identify the authorized decision-maker
- Identify the values of the authorized decision-maker
- Modify the desired alternative so it is preferred to the status quo by the authorized decision-maker

- Pursue out-of-the-blue dreams
- Convert decision problems into decision opportunities
- Expand decision opportunities with add-on benefits
- Add learning objectives to a decision problem

6. Concerning the evaluation of alternatives

- Use the decision frame
- Recognize the relevant information necessary to describe consequences
- Recognize the value tradeoffs necessary to compare consequences

Table 11.2 Summary of Nudges to Make You a Better Decision-Maker

---

Concerning your decision-making skills

- Understand the components of making a good decision (Chapter 3)
- Understand the importance and role of key decision-making skills (Chapters 4 to 8)
- Practice using these skills on basic decisions
- Use these skills on your decisions worthy of thought
- Review past decisions and identify what you did well, and how you did it
- Review past decisions and identify what you would like to have done better, and how you could have done it
- Visualize and construct your life objectives
- Keep learning to improve your decision-making skills

---

of developing your new decision skills to nudge yourself is that you will make better decisions, which will cause you to be more satisfied with your decision-making, and your quality of life will improve.

Additional Thoughts for Decisions in Organizations

The perspectives about decision-making discussed above are relevant to any company or organization. They apply directly to each individual who makes decisions within the organization. The personal decisions of an individual should be to enhance his or her quality of life, whereas the decisions made on behalf of an organization should be to enhance the well-being of the organization.

The suggestion to avoid making poor life-limiting decisions for an individual is analogous to suggesting the importance of foresight in organizations so as to avoid being in situations where the only viable alternatives may all have serious risks to the organization's products, financial well-being, reputation, or even existence.

Spontaneity and fun may be strategic life objectives for any individual, but their role in an organization is as a means objective, as an organization per se does not have fun. Yet, when the individuals in an organization are enjoying their work and workplace, they are likely to contribute more to the organization's well-being. Having fun at work is also, therefore, an important consideration.

As is the case with individuals, if you are a manager in a company or organization and improve your decision-making skills, this will enhance your work and your contributions to the company. By identifying all of the relevant values for an important decision being faced in your work and creating alternatives to address it, the organization will have a solid basis for making a better decision. Using the concepts of value-focused decision-making, you and your team can nudge yourselves to make better work decisions, which will result in significant positive contributions for your organization or company. The important implication of using nudges for decisions within an organization is that the management and employees will make better decisions, which improves the organization's achievements in terms of its strategic objectives. Skilled decision-makers make great leaders for companies and organizations, and everybody can benefit.

APPENDIX

Evaluating Alternatives and Making a Decision

From the time that you recognize that you need or want to make a decision, anything that enhances your understanding of the substance of your decision can nudge you to make a better choice. The foundation for creating useful nudges for your decision is the value-focused decision-making process that is outlined in Chapter 3. The six steps of this process identified in Chapter 3 are repeated in Table A.1 for convenience.

Not all nudges are created equal. If you identify one additional objective of your decision that exposes a fatal flaw of the alternative that you had previously thought was the best one, that nudge is very important. If you do an evaluation of two competing alternatives and find out that one has a 60 percent chance of being better than the other, but their consequences would not be much different, that informational nudge helps you only a little.

The first three steps, referred to as the front end of the process, provide a thorough and unambiguous definition and structure for the decision you want to face. The decision frame for your decision, constructed from these three steps, includes all of the objectives relevant to evaluate alternatives and all of the alternatives that you are considering for your decision. When the three front-end steps are carried out well, you will have nudged yourself a great deal toward making a good decision. The back-end steps of value-focused decision-making can provide additional nudges for your decision, but there is usually not as much potential improvement left to be had.

A simple example illustrates this important point. Suppose that you are the manager of a small group in a large international company. Yesterday you received your annual review, as did all other managers, and it was not good. The summary was that your annual performance was 25 on a 0 to 100 satisfaction scale, where 0 is unacceptable and 100 is excellent. Your current level, 25, means

Table A.1 The Steps of a Value-Focused Decision-Making Process

---

Front end: define and structure the decision that you face

1. State the decision problem or decision opportunity that you face
2. Identify your values, and state them as objectives, for the decision in order to clarify what you want to achieve
3. Create alternatives that contribute to achieving your objectives

Back end: evaluate your alternatives and make your decision

4. Describe the possible consequences of each alternative to indicate how well it achieves your objectives
5. Identify the pros and cons of each alternative and weigh their importance
6. Select an alternative using information and insight from your evaluation

---

poor performance. You now have a decision problem to improve matters.

The first step is to state your decision problem. Intuitively, you feel that your decision statement should be "decide how to improve my annual review." Thinking more deeply, you realize that this is the effect of not performing your job as well as you would like. Recognizing that this decision statement addresses the effect and not the cause, you change your decision statement to "decide how to better lead the employees in my group and contribute more to the company." Then you proceed to the other two front-end steps, to clarify your objectives for this decision and identify alternatives. With the better statement of your decision, it is probably the case that any alternatives that you pursue to achieve your objectives will result in at least a satisfaction score of 40 next year.

By structuring your decision thoroughly, suppose that you have identified several alternatives. They likely range in effectiveness and you feel that a randomly chosen alternative would provide you anywhere between a satisfaction level of 40 and a level 85. By appraising these alternatives on one key objective, you should be able to eliminate some inferior alternatives that were easy to identify, namely those that would not possibly lead to level of satisfaction above 70. Next, using various objectives, you might nudge yourself to create an alternative that you feel would provide you at least a level 80 and probably higher. Using this new alternative as a standard, you can eliminate any alternatives that you think are inferior to a level 80. As a result, you may have four contending alternatives that you think are all between level 80 and level 90.

Note the following. Your front-end decision structuring efforts nudged you along on your decision so you will surely improve from the satisfaction level 25 to at least level 80. Your back-end evaluation can at most improve your satisfaction level from 80 to level 90. This illustrates the point that a high-quality front-end structuring of a decision can have a much greater impact than a high-quality back-end evaluation of the alternatives of a decision.

At this stage it may be useful to proceed with a back-end evaluation of the alternatives. The appropriate level of back-end effort depends on the significance to you of the difference between levels 80 and 90 and the importance of using your time on other matters. It may be worth your time and effort to use pairwise comparisons of the four contending alternatives. Examine two alternatives in terms of how well they achieve each of your objectives, and it may be clear that one alternative is inferior, so it can be eliminated. Repeating this process with remaining alternatives may identify the best one, or at least reduce the viable contending alternatives to two or three alternatives, none of which are obviously inferior to another. For the same decision, you may feel that it is not worth your time and effort to proceed with a more systematic back-end appraisal of alternatives.

The Back End of a Value-Focused Decision-Making Process

The three back-end steps in Table A.1 describe the steps and thinking necessary to carry out a systematic evaluation of the alternatives. This material is not covered in depth in this book. However, since evaluating alternatives, either intuitively or formally, is necessary to make a decision, a summary of these steps is presented here, for three reasons.

1. To clarify and stress the critical role that structuring your decisions has in any process to make high-quality decisions.
2. To provide conceptual guidelines for the systematic thought process necessary to evaluate alternatives after clearly structuring any decision.
3. To illustrate a coherent framework for evaluating the competing alternatives using knowledge, information, and data with or without analysis.

The back-end descriptions of each of the alternatives and their evaluation can be clearly illustrated and managed for any decision by using a consequences table, which is a decision frame, as illustrated in Figure 3.1, filled in to describe all of the relevant consequences of each alternative for a specific decision.

To illustrate the main ideas, I will use the following decision. The Lees, a couple each about 30 years old, have been married for three years. They both have very good jobs and live in a metropolitan area about 120 miles from the ocean and 250 miles from an area with mountains and lakes. They have decided to purchase a vacation home to use for themselves and as an investment. Subsequently they carefully completed the front end of the value-focused decision-making process for their decision, which is summarized here.[1]

Their decision statement is "decide which vacation home to purchase." For this important decision, they have carefully identified the following values: "visit the property often," "enjoy each visit," "ease of visiting the vacation home," "its purchase price," "its annual price appreciation," "annual expenses for taxes and maintenance," and the "usefulness of the home for potential children and adult friends for visiting." They have visited several possible areas to identify the possible vacation homes to purchase and, based on their values, identified four viable alternatives. These vacation homes are, respectively, on a large pond in a rural region, in a small seaside town, on lakeside property in foothills to the mountains, and on a lake in the mountains near a ski resort.

With their values and alternatives identified, the decision frame for their decision is shown in Table A.2. The decision frame provides an organized and understandable way to

Table A.2 Decision Frame for a Vacation Home Decision

Values: objectives concerning \ Alternatives	A: inland home on pond	B: seaside home	C: foothills home on lake	D: mountain home on lake in ski area
Ease of visiting		X		
Annual amount of visiting				
Enjoyment at vacation home				Y
Purchase price				
Annual expenses				
Annual price appreciation				
Usefulness for friends				
Usefulness for children				

display and discuss the results of the back end of the value-focused decision-making process to evaluate alternatives.

The first back-end step involves describing the relevant consequences of each of the competing alternatives in the consequences table. The description in each cell of the decision frame indicates how well the corresponding alternative achieves the corresponding objective. For example, in the cell marked with an "X" in Table A.2, the Lees believe that the travel time from their home to the seaside property will take about four hours, which will be the consequence placed in the cell. For the cell marked "Y," this description could be an entire paragraph or a summary, such as "water sports, fishing, hiking, skiing in winter." Reviewing all of the descriptions in any column will provide a reasonable understanding of the consequences of the alternative in that column.

Describing the Possible Consequences of the Alternatives

The appropriate information that you should collect for making a decision is only the information that will help you make a better decision. Two examples are illustrated using the cases below.

Case 1. For most personal decisions and many business decisions, a completely filled-in consequences table is not necessary to make an informed choice. Reasonable descriptions about some of the consequences may be sufficient.

For the vacation home decision, it is useful and fairly simple to fill in the cells that have readily available information. As shown in Table A.3, this includes the costs of the alternatives in thousands of dollars and the expected travel time from home to the vacation property as an indicator of the ease to visit. In addition, the Lees can include estimates for the range of annual appreciation for each vacation home. Also, they can develop a brief description of the relative enjoyment they would expect at each property using a few words, as shown in the table. These words are shorthand for describing the much broader experience that the couple think they will have at each property.

Using this information, the Lees may feel comfortable making a decision. Viewing Table A.3, they may conclude that visiting each of the properties would be enjoyable. However, spending time at the inland property would be a little less enjoyable than the others, and the property where skiing is possible would be most enjoyable. On the other hand, the inland property is the easiest to visit and the ski property is the most difficult to visit. Based on this, they may reason that all four vacation homes are about equivalent in terms of the combination of ease of visiting and the enjoyment each year, because the additional advantage of more enjoyment (i.e., a pro) is roughly canceled out by the additional travel time of visiting (i.e., a con), and vice versa. In addition, the Lees may feel that the total amount of visiting would be about the same for all of the properties. Hence, the couple may conclude that the choice of the best alternative would not depend on these two objectives.

Regarding the purchase cost, the relative costs of the alternatives are clear, with the inland property on the pond being much less expensive. However, the Lees have the assets to purchase any of

Table A.3 Consequences Table Partially Filled In for a Vacation Home Decision

Values: objectives concerning	A: inland home on pond	B: seaside home	C: foothills home on lake	D: mountain home on lake in ski area
Ease of visiting: travel time from home	1.5 hours	4 hours	3 hours	5.5 hours
Annual amount of visiting				
Enjoyment at vacation home	Pleasant getaway	Beach and seashore life	Water sports, fishing, hiking	Water sports, fishing, hiking, skiing in winter
Purchase price	$175,000	$420,000	$280,000	$350,000
Annual expenses				
Annual price appreciation	1–4%	3–5%	2–4.5%	4–5.5%
Usefulness for friends				
Usefulness for children				

the properties, and part of the intent is to own it as a financial investment. Any funds not used to purchase a property can be invested in stocks. They believe that the return over the next five years from stock market investments will be a couple of percentage points higher than the appreciation on the vacation homes. Thus, although the costs of the homes and their appreciation potentials are significantly different, the combined implication of these two factors on their financial well-being differs much less. However, the inland property still has a better financial impact on the Lees than the other alternatives.

At the current time the Lees have no children, so this is not too relevant for the decision. Adult friends could readily be guests at all of the properties, although the inland property is a bit smaller. Hence, accounting for all of their objectives, they feel that the best alternative for them is the inland property.

In discussing the possible consequences of the alternatives, the Lees recognize that they have a lot of uncertainty about how they will actually use any of the properties. They have never owned a vacation home and are unsure how much they will use one and how much they will enjoy it. They realize that owning the inland home, which is the easiest to visit, will allow them to learn about some things that they particularly like and dislike concerning a vacation home. There is a lot of value from this learning. If they find out that a vacation home definitely improves the quality of their lives, compared to learning that it is barely worth the effort given their lifestyle, they can make a decision to upgrade to another vacation home in a few years. Now the choice is very clear, they will make an offer on the inland alternative.

Case 2. Suppose that the information in the partially filled-in consequences Table A.3, along with systematic thinking about the full set of consequences of each alternative, did not lead to a clear preference for the choice of an alternative. Then it would be useful to completely fill in a consequences table, as shown in Table A.4. Note that this consequences table has been expanded to include the objective of learning more about the advantages and disadvantages of vacation homeownership and how much they would use and enjoy a vacation home.

There is significant flexibility about what the decision-maker wishes to include in the cells of a consequences table. For a personal decision, one wants sufficient description for the decision-

Table A.4 Consequences Table Completely Filled In for a Vacation Home Decision

Values: objectives concerning	A: inland home on pond	B: seaside home	C: foothills home on lake	D: mountain home on lake in ski area
Ease of visiting: travel time from home	1.25–2 hours	3–5 hours	2.5–5 hours	4.5–7 hours
Annual amount of visiting	20 one-day trips, 8 two-day trips	8 two-day trips, 4 summer weeks	8 two-day trips, 4 weeks spring and summer	4 two-day trips, 2 weeks in summer, 2 two-week periods in winter
Enjoyment at vacation home	Pleasant getaway	Beach and seashore life	Water sports, fishing, hiking	Water sports, fishing, hiking, skiing in winter
Purchase price	$175,000	$420,000	$280,000	$350,000
Annual expenses	$5,000 (60%) $7,000 (40%)	$10,000 (50%) $13,000 (30%) $15,000 (20%)	$6,000 (30%) $9,000 (70%)	$11,000 (20%) $14,000 (70%) $18,000 (10%)
Annual price appreciation	1–4%	3–5%	2–4.5%	4–5.5%
Usefulness for adult friends	Good	Great	Great	Great
Usefulness for children	Okay	Good	Great	Great
Learning about the use and enjoyment of a vacation home	Much about use and enjoyment	Some about enjoyment, little about use	Some about use and enjoyment	Some about enjoyment, less about use

maker to understand what the consequences of each alternative are. A single word or number may accomplish this well, since the word or number can be understood to imply much more. For a business decision, especially when more than one person is working on inputs to the consequences table and when it may be used to communicate to others (e.g., executives) within the organization, the information in each cell should be more detailed and unambiguous.

Table A.4 indicates several ways to describe consequences in a consequences table. The simplest is point estimates on a well-understood measure, such as money or time. The purchase cost of the vacation homes is an example using one measure of the consequences. Sometimes more than one measure will provide a more complete description of the consequences. For use of the vacation home, both the annual number of trips and days spent at the property are useful. This simply recognizes that, in addition to the travel time, which is accounted for with a different objective, a decision-maker may value seven single-day trips differently from one full-week trip. When uncertainties about specific consequences are relevant, one can use a range of possible consequences on a well-understood measure. The range of travel time from home to the vacation properties is an example. If more clarity about the uncertainties is desired, one can logically construct estimates of these. For annual operating expenses in Table A.4, descriptions with possible levels and the probabilities (or percentages) of each are illustrated.

For several important objectives there may not be an established measure to describe possible consequences and compare them. One way to deal with this is to construct a scale that measures those consequences.[2] For each of the two objectives concerning the usefulness of the properties with children and adult friends, one may create a scale from 0 to 10, where 0 is defined as not useful and 10 very useful. One may also define level 3 as okay and level 6 as good and provide a clear verbal description of all of these. In other cases, an entire paragraph could be used to describe the meaning of each level of such a constructed scale.

For personal decisions, the decision-maker creates the scale and therefore should have a clear intuitive understanding of the meanings and implications of each level in terms of the corresponding objective. For business decisions, it is useful to clarify explicitly in writing the meanings of different levels (e.g., describe specific examples of consequences that correspond to different levels of the scale).

Sometimes verbal descriptions are an effective way to describe consequences, as is the case with the objectives of enjoyment and learning in Table A.4. These may just have a few words, as in the table, or entire paragraphs. Always the intent is to have the consequences clearly understood by all those who need to understand them.

Identifying the Pros and Cons of Alternatives and Weighing Their Importance

Once you have a few of the consequences in the consequences table for your decision explicitly described, you can often make an informed decision with systematic reasoning. In other cases, and more frequently for significant organizational decisions, you will want a completely filled-in consequences table. This provides the foundations for a more systematic and detailed evaluation of the alternatives.

To evaluate alternatives, you need to weigh the pros and cons of the possible consequences of each of your alternatives. This is the second step of the back end of the value-focused decision-making process indicated in Table A.1. It involves making value judgments about the relative importance of the pros and cons of the different alternatives. In practice, there are a range of logically sound ways to do this. They vary from simply comparing the pros and cons of pairs of alternatives in the decision frame to using a thorough quantitative analysis.

Consider, for example, a decision involving the purchase of a product for which there are several possible alternatives. Suppose there are only two objectives: "maximize quality" and "minimize cost." If one of the available alternatives is both more expensive and of lower quality than one other alternative, the former alternative can be deleted from consideration. It is "dominated" by the second alternative that remains viable. By comparing pairs of alternatives in this manner, you can eliminate all dominated alternatives from further consideration.

Of the remaining alternatives, you can continue by comparing two alternatives at a time. If the first alternative is more expensive but better on quality than the second alternative, the issue is whether the additional cost (i.e., the con) of the first alternative is worth the improvement in quality (i.e., the pro) of the second objective. The term "not worth it" as used here means "not worth it compared to the second alternative." If it is not worth it, delete the first alternative from further consideration. If it is worth it, delete the second alternative. If you had only these two viable alternatives for your consideration, your decision is now solved. If there are other alternatives, repeat the process again by comparing two remaining alternatives in the same manner. Whenever you delete inferior alternatives, you are both simplifying your decision, as there will be fewer remaining alternatives to consider, and lowering the chance of eventually selecting an inferior alternative. You will make progress more quickly if the pairs of alternatives that you choose to compare are those that you feel would be an easier comparison.

Given an understanding of the consequences as described in a consequences table such as Table A.4, the decision-maker can readily identify the pros and cons of one alternative versus another. The terms in such a table may not be useful to communicate clearly to others, but they are meaningful to the decision-maker, who created them and uses them as a summary description of the more detailed reality.

Interestingly, almost 250 years ago Benjamin Franklin suggested a straightforward and logical approach to compare pairs of alternatives to his colleague Joseph Priestley, who had asked for advice about making an important decision. Franklin's response, on September 19, 1772, was as follows.[3]

Dear Sir,

In the affair of so much importance to you, wherein you ask my advice, I cannot, for want of sufficient premises advise you what to determine, but if you please I will tell you how.

When those difficult cases occur, they are difficult chiefly because while we have them under consideration, all of the reasons pro and con are not present to the mind at the same time; but sometimes some set present themselves, and at other times another, the first being out of sight. Hence the various purposes or inclinations that alternately prevail, and the uncertainty that perplexes us.

To get over this, my way is to divide half a sheet of paper by a line into two columns; writing over the one pro, and over the other con. Then during three or four days consideration, I put down under the different heads short hints of the different motives, that at different times occur to me, for or against the measure.

When I have thus got them all together in one view, I endeavor to estimate their respective weights; and where I find two, one on each side, that seem equal, I strike them both out. If I find a reason pro equal to two reasons con, I strike out the three. If I judge some two reasons con, equal to some three reasons pro, I strike out the five; and thus proceeding I find at length where the balance lies; and if, after a day or two of further consideration, nothing new that is of importance occurs on either side, I come to a determination accordingly.

And, though the weight of reasons cannot be taken with the precision of algebraic quantities, yet when each is thus considered, separately and comparatively, and the whole lies before me, I think they can judge better, and am less liable to make a rash step, and in fact I have found great advantage from this kind of equation, in what may be called moral or prudential algebra.

Wishing sincerely that you may determine for the best, I am ever, my dear friend, yours most affectionately.

B. Franklin

As Franklin made clear, the major impediment to making a good decision, in the terminology of this book, is your not being aware of your own values (i.e., the reasons pro and con are not present in the mind at the same time). He recommends a few days to write them down. As our decision frame lists all the values, a filled-in consequences table readily provides the information necessary to describe all pros and cons. In Table A.4, alternative C costs $280,000 and alternative D costs $350,000, so alternative C has a $70,000 "pro" relative to alternative D. Regarding the objective of enjoyment, one difference is that alternative D includes skiing in addition to the water sports, fishing, and hiking of alternative C. Hence, alternative C has a "con" relative to alternative D, namely no useful access to skiing. In addition, it is useful to consider whether the water sports, fishing, and hiking options of the two alternatives are equivalent or if one site has much better options. If this were the case, there would be an additional pro and con for eventually comparing the alternatives. With a consequences table, one can directly proceed to Franklin's systematic process to evaluate the pros and cons of pairs of alternatives and eventually identify the best.

A decision-maker who wishes to be a bit more systematic in his or her thinking can use the consequences table as follows. Create a hypothetical alternative that is equivalently valued to one of the real alternatives. To do this, modify one alternative by improving achievement on one objective and reducing achievement on a second objective, where the amount of improvement on the first objective (i.e., an added positive effect) is equivalently valued by the decision-maker as the amount of downgrading on the second objective (i.e., an added negative effect). This modification is called an "even swap," and is done so that the modified hypothetical alternative will have the same achievement on one objective as that for a second alternative, which makes it easier to compare the desirability of those two alternatives.[4]

Let me illustrate this process using the Lees' vacation home example. Suppose that the Lees assess the value of access to skiing as being worth $30,000; the couple should evaluate a hypothetical alternative, C', that is identical to C except that it has access to skiing and cost $30,000 more as equivalent in value to the real alternative C. Now, if the modified alternative C' is preferred to alternative D, then the original alternative C should also be preferred to alternative D. Using an even swap makes the comparison of two alternatives easier, as an objective with the same level of achievement for both alternatives is irrelevant in evaluating which one is preferred. In this case, after the even swap, the enjoyment factor is irrelevant for comparing alternatives C' and D. Multiple even swaps can be used until it is clear which alternative is preferred.

A quantitative analysis is useful for some particularly complex decisions, especially organizational decisions when information and value judgments relevant to the decision come from multiple individuals. Such an analysis would separately describe the consequences of each alternative in terms of each of the objectives, including the uncertainties about those consequences when they are significant. Then, a quantitative representation of the decision-maker's values would be constructed on the basis of the value judgments of the decision-maker. With separate quantitative models that describe the consequences and evaluate each of the possible consequences of the alternatives, the desirability of the various alternatives can be calculated and sensitivity analyses can examine which factors have a significant influence on the desirability of those alternatives.[5] Unless an organization has experience using this quantitative approach, the help of an analyst with such knowledge would likely be necessary. For personal decisions, a quantitative analysis is too complex and time consuming for most people to use, especially because proceeding with the less formal evaluation, as described above, can provide the necessary information to make a sound decision.

Select an Alternative Using Information and Insight from Your Evaluation.

Selecting an alternative is not the same as evaluating alternatives. You should treat the consequence descriptions and the evaluation of the alternatives as useful information for making your decision, the third step of the back end of a value-focused decision-making process. This information much better informs you about all of the pros and cons of each alternative, so it naturally nudges you to make a better decision.

You also need to consider what you learned from this process and what insights this suggests for your decision. Accounting for this new understanding, you might not want to choose the alternative that was appraised as the best. How can this be the case?

The descriptions and appraisal discussed in this Appendix constitute a model of your decision; they are not your decision. The logic is analogous to the famous painting of a pipe by Magritte, with the words underneath saying "This is not a pipe."[6] Quite simply, a painting of a pipe is not a pipe. The model of your decision provides a wealth of information, but it cannot, nor should it, include everything that is relevant to that decision. Selecting an alternative involves using the information you created using your model and anything relevant that you did not include in your model or the appraisal based on it to evaluate alternatives. One example of this was illustrated in the decision about vacation homes, when the appraisal of the alternatives produced the insight that learning about how the family would use a vacation home and how much they would enjoy it would be very useful, which helped lead to a clear choice of the closer inland alternative. The following example further illustrates the logic and the process.

Suppose that you are in the process of evaluating three interesting job offers in three different cities. None of these is where you currently live, so you will have to move regardless of your job choice. You define your decision to decide which job is preferred. You intentionally omit your personal life in each city from your defined decision, as the job decision is difficult enough. After you understand your preferences for the jobs, you will then add consideration of your personal life. Your thorough appraisal of the job alternatives is done by filling out your consequences table and weighing the pros and cons of each alternative. Your even swaps appraisal developed hypothetical alternatives A', B', and C', respectively, for the jobs in cities A, B, and C, which are identical in terms of all objectives other than annual salary. The resulting annual salary of hypothetical alternative A' was $15,000 greater than that of B' and $20,000 greater than that of C'. It directly follows that your preference for the job in city A over the jobs in cities B and C is equivalent to the respective values of $15,000 and $20,000 additional pay annually.

Your actual decision is to choose the combination of a job and a city. You may readily know that you prefer living in city B to city A, which is preferred to city C. Knowing this, selecting the job in city C can be eliminated from consideration, as it is inferior to city A in terms of both the job and living. To compare cities A and B, you will need to think about what the annual dollar equivalent difference is to you of living in these two cities. If you prefer living in city B to city A by an equivalent of $25,000 annually, the job in city B should be chosen, as living and working there is preferred by you by an equivalent of $10,000 annually (i.e., $25,000 – $15,000). However, if you prefer living in city B to city A by an equivalent of only $8,000 annually, then you should choose the job in city A.

NOTES

Preface

1. The original printing is Thaler, R. H., and Sunstein, C. R. (2008). *Nudge: Improving Decisions about Health, Wealth, and Happiness.* New Haven, CT: Yale University Press. It is more readily available as Thaler, R. H., and Sunstein, C. R. (2009). *Nudge: Improving Decisions about Health, Wealth, and Happiness.* New York: Penguin Books.
2. See Halpern, D. (2015). *Inside the Nudge Unit: How Small Changes Can Make a Big Difference.* London: W. H. Allen; and Naru, F. Behavioural insights and public policy. https://twitter.com/faisal_naru/status/978359326845947905. The latter indicates that there are about 200 institutions around the world using nudges concerning public policy.
3. Thaler and Sunstein (2009), page 255.

Chapter 1: Nudge Yourself to Make Better Decisions

1. Edwards, W. (1954). The theory of decision making. *Psychological Bulletin,* **51**(4), 380–417.
2. Simon, H. (1955). A behavioral model of rational choice. *Quarterly Journal of Economics,* **69**(1), 99–118.
3. Tversky, A., and Kahneman, D. (1974). Judgment under uncertainty: heuristics and biases. *Science,* **185**, 1124–31; Kahneman, D., Slovic, P., and Tversky, A. (1982). *Judgment under Uncertainty: Heuristics and Biases.* Cambridge: Cambridge University Press; Gilovich, T., Griffin, D., and Kahneman, D. (2002). *Heuristics and Biases: The Psychology of Intuitive Judgment.* Cambridge: Cambridge University Press.
4. Inventories of decision traps, pitfalls, and biases can be found in Hammond, J. S., Keeney, R. L., and Raiffa, H. (1999). *Smart Choices: A Practical Guide to Making Better Decisions.* Boston: Harvard Business School Press; Baron, J. (2008). *Thinking and Deciding,* 4th ed. New York: Cambridge University Press; Hastie, R., and Dawes, R. (2010). *Rational Choice in an Uncertain World: The Psychology of Judgment and Decision Making,* 2nd ed. Thousand Oaks, CA: Sage; Montibeller, G., and von Winterfeldt, D. (2015). Cognitive and

motivational biases in decision and risk analysis. *Risk Analysis*, **35** (7), 1230–51; and Spetzler, C., Meyer, J., and Winter, H. (2016). *Decision Quality: Value Creation from Better Business Decisions*. Hoboken, NJ: Wiley.

5. Ariely, D. (2008). *Predictably Irrational: The Hidden Forces that Shape Our Decisions*. New York: HarperCollins; Ariely, D. (2010). *The Upside of Irrationality: The Unexpected Benefits of Defying Logic at Work and at Home*. New York: HarperCollins; and Ariely, D. (2012). *The Honest Truth about Dishonesty*. New York: HarperCollins. Also see copies of his long-running column providing insight and advice about decision-making published in *The Wall Street Journal*.

6. See, for example, Pratt, J. W., Raiffa, H., and Schlaifer, R. (1964). The foundations of decision under uncertainty: an elementary exposition. *American Statistical Association Journal*, **59**, 353–75; Raiffa, H. (1968). *Decision Analysis*, Reading, MA: Addison-Wesley; and Raiffa, H. (1969). Preferences for multi-attributed alternatives, Memorandum RM-5868-DOT/RC. Santa Monica, CA: RAND Corporation.

7. The practical use of these steps for personal and business decisions is presented in Hammond, Keeney, and Raiffa (1999).

8. Samson, A. (ed.) (2018). *The Behavioral Economics Guide 2018*. Behavioral Economics. www.behavioraleconomics.com /BEGuide2018.pdf.

9. Prospect theory has had a profound influence for the past 40 years on descriptive models of choice. One of the critical features of prospect theory is an initial editing stage to frame the decision. For more detail, see Kahneman, D., and Tversky, A. (1979). Prospect theory: an analysis of decision under risk. *Econometrica*, **47**(2): 263–91; Tversky, A., and Kahneman, D. (1981). The framing of decisions and the psychology of choice. *Science*, **211**, 453–8; and Kahneman, D., and Tversky, A. (2000). *Choices, Values, and Frames*. Cambridge: Cambridge University Press.

10. For a detailed explanation of the concept of a nudge, see Thaler and Sunstein (2009). One recent meta-analysis of 42 different experiments concluded that nudges resulted in an average 15.3 percent increase in healthier dietary or nutritional choices: Arno, A., and Thomas, S. (2016). The efficacy of nudge theory strategies in influencing adult dietary behaviour: a systematic review and meta-analysis. *BMC Public Health*, **16**: 676.

11. There appears to be no definitive documentation that this statement was made by Albert Einstein. Relevant information

about this issue is found on the following website: https://quotein
vestigator.com/2014/05/22/solve/#content.

Chapter 2: Your Decisions and Your Life

1. The Adult Decision Making Competence (A-DMC) scale provides
   a reliable and valid measure of individual differences in decision-
   making skill. For information about the A-DMC and the Decision
   Outcome Inventory (DOI) and correlates (demographic, cognitive, and
   personality) of both, see Parker, A., Bruine de Bruin, W., and
   Fischhoff, B. (2007a). Individual differences in adult decision-making
   competence. *Journal of Personality and Social Psychology*, **92**(5), 938–56.
   Parker, A., Bruine de Bruin, W., and Fischhoff, B. (2007b); Maximizers
   vs. satisficers: decision-making styles, competence, and outcomes.
   Judgement and Decision Making, **2**(6), 342–50; and Parker, A., Bruine de
   Bruin, W., and Fischhoff, B. (2015). Negative decision outcomes are
   more common among people with lower decision-making
   competence: an item-level analysis of the Decision Outcome
   Inventory (DOI). *Frontiers in Psychology*, **6**: 363.
2. Prior to presenting a seminar to an entire MBA class of 295 students,
   with an average age of 27, I asked two questions in a questionnaire
   about their decision-making abilities. The first asked if they
   considered themselves to be a good decision-maker, and 94 percent
   responded "Yes." The second asked if they were a better decision-
   maker than the average in the class, and 84 percent responded
   "Yes." The latter response indicates a significant overestimation of
   decision-making abilities relative to others, as a reasonable number
   of "Yes" responses for this case would be near 50 percent.
3. Keeney, R. L. (1980). *Siting Energy Facilities*. New York: Academic Press.

Chapter 3: Making Value-Focused Decisions

1. As a practical matter, when you have produced a high-quality front
   end for your decision, clear thinking about the pros and cons of the
   alternatives using that frame will usually allow you to make a very
   reasonable choice. There will not be any back-end analysis of
   alternatives for a large majority of decisions. In fact, for most
   decisions, such an evaluation would not even be possible, because
   there is no explicit structure of the front end that clearly defines all
   of the values that the decision-maker wishes to achieve.

2. For complex decisions, a complete evaluation of alternatives using a mathematical model often provides insight and is useful for explicitly addressing uncertainty, risk tolerance, multiple and conflicting objectives, time discounting, and multiple stakeholders. For excellent introductions, see Hammond, Keeney, and Raiffa (1999); Edwards, W., Miles, R., and von Winterfeldt, D. (2007). *Advances in Decision Analysis: From Foundations to Applications*. New York: Cambridge University Press; Eisenfuhr, F., Weber, M., and Langer, T. (2010). *Rational Decision Making*. Heidelberg: Springer-Verlag; Clemen, R. T., and Reilly, T. (2014). *Making Hard Decisions with DecisionTools*, 3rd ed. Mason, OH: South-Western/Cengage Learning; Goodwin, P., and Wright, G. (2014). *Decision Analysis for Management Judgment*, 5th ed. New York: Wiley; and Spetzler, Meyer, and Winter (2016).

Chapter 4: Defining Your Decision

1. Samuelson, W., and Zeckhauser, R. (1988). Status quo bias in decision making. *Journal of Risk and Uncertainty*, **1**(1), 7–59.

Chapter 5: Identifying Your Values

1. Bond, S. T., Carlson, K. A., and Keeney, R. L. (2008). Generating objectives: can decision makers articulate what they want? *Management Science*, **54**(1), 56–70.
2. Bond, S. T., Carlson, K. A., and Keeney, R. L. (2010). Improving the generation of decision objectives. *Decision Analysis*, **7**(3), 238–55.
3. This is part of a statement in a letter from Benjamin Franklin to his friend Joseph Priestley in 1772 about whether or not to accept an employment offer. The complete letter is included in the Appendix of this book and is reprinted in many places, including Isaacson, W., ed. (2005). *A Benjamin Franklin Reader*. New York: Simon & Schuster.
4. Nietzsche, F. (1879). *The Wanderer and His Shadow*. Reprinted in G. Colli and M. Montinari, eds. (1980). *Friedrich Nietzsche, Sämtliche Werke: Kritische Studienausgabe*. Berlin: De Gruyter. The quote is on page 642.

Chapter 6: Creating Alternatives

1. See, for example, Jungermann, H., von Ulardt, I., and Hausmann, L. (1983). The role of the goal for generating actions. In P. Humphreys, O. Svenson, and A. Vári, eds., *Analyzing and Aiding Decision Processes*. Amsterdam: North-Holland, 223–36; Gettys, C. F., Pliske, R. M., Manning, C., and Casey, J. T. (1987). An evaluation of human act generation performance. *Organizational Behavior and Human Decision Processes*, **39**(1), 23–51; and Butler, A. B., and Scherer, L. L. (1997). The effects of elicitation aids, knowledge, and problem content on option quantity and quality. *Organizational Behavior and Human Decision Processes*, **72**(2), 184–202.
2. Pitz, G. F., Sachs, N. T, and Heerboth, T. (1980). Procedures for eliciting choices in the analysis of individual decisions. *Organizational Behavior and Human Performance*, **26**(3), 396–408.
3. Siebert, J. U., and Keeney, R. L. (2015). Creating more and better alternatives for decisions using objectives. *Operations Research*, **63**(5), 1144–58.
4. Tversky and Kahneman (1974); see also chapter 4 of Hastie, R., and Dawes, R. (2010). *Rational Choice in an Uncertain World: The Psychology of Judgment and Decision Making*, 2nd ed. Thousand Oaks, CA: Sage.
5. This experiment is described in detail in Siebert and Keeney (2015).
6. Bond, Carlson, and Keeney (2010).
7. Siebert, J. U. (2016) Can novices create alternatives of the same quality as experts? *Decision Analysis*, **13**(4), 278–91.
8. Brainstorming was introduced originally by Alex Osborn in a 1953 book, now available as Osborn, A. F. (1963). *Applied Imagination: Principles and Procedures of Creative Problem-Solving*, 3rd ed. New York: Charles Scribner's Sons.
9. Keeney, R. L. (2012). Value-focused brainstorming. *Decision Analysis*, **9** (4), 303–13.

Chapter 7: Identifying Decision Opportunities

1. A decision framework, similar to those in this book, was developed to help a professional woman decide whether and when she should begin trying to have her first child. It is found in Keeney, R. L., and Vernik, D. A. (2007). Analysis of the biological clock problem. *Decision Analysis*, **4**(3), 114–35. The model includes separate

objectives for a woman's professional, social, and family aspects of life and integrates them into a quality-of-life evaluation function that includes the changing relative importance of these aspects with age over a woman's life. For a woman of any age, the alternatives considered are to try to get pregnant now, one year from now, two years from now, and so forth.

2. Frank, S. E. (1997). American Express credit card share increased to 18.9% in first half a year. *Wall Street Journal*, September 22.
3. The Nilson Report is a subscription-only newsletter, now in its 50th year of publication, that covers news and analysis of the global card and mobile payment industry.

Chapter 8: Obtaining Authorization to Select Alternatives Controlled by Others

1. The original edition was Keeney, R. L., and Raiffa, H. (1976). *Decisions with Multiple Objectives: Preferences and Value Tradeoffs*. New York: Wiley. Since 1993 it has been published by Cambridge University Press.
2. Two classic books on negotiation are Raiffa, H. (1982). *The Art and Science of Negotiation*. Cambridge, MA: Harvard University Press; and Fisher, R., Uri, W., and Patton, B. (1991) *Getting to Yes: Negotiating Agreement without Giving In*, 2nd ed. New York: Penguin Books.

Chapter 9: Becoming a Value-Focused Decision-Maker

1. See Siebert, J. U., and Kunz, R. (2016). Developing and validating the multidimensional proactive decision-making scale. *European Journal of Operational Research*, 249(3), 864–77; and Siebert, J. U., Kunz, R., and Rolf, P. (forthcoming). Effects of proactive decision making on life satisfaction. *European Journal of Operational Research*.

Chapter 10: Enhancing the Quality of Your Life

1. See www.goodreads.com/quotes/73656.
2. See www.goodreads.com/quotes/766869.
3. See www.goodreads.com/quotes/7614663.
4. These organizations include British Columbia Hydro and Power Authority (see Keeney, R. L. (1992). *Value-Focused Thinking: A Path to*

Create Decision-Making, Cambridge, MA: Harvard University Press, pages 342–71); BC Gas, now Fortis BC Energy Inc. (see Keeney, R. L., and McDaniels, T. L. (1999). Identifying and structuring values to guide integrated resource planning at BC Gas. *Operations Research*, **47** (5), 651–62); California Seismic Safety Commission; Chevron; Conflict Management Inc.; Energie Baden-Württemberg AG; Kaiser Permanente Northwest; SYKE (a Finnish environmental organization); the US Army Corps of Engineers; and the US Department of Homeland Security (see Keeney, R. L., and von Winterfeldt, D. (2011). A value model for evaluating homeland security decisions. *Risk Analysis*, **31**(9), 1470–87).
5. Keeney and von Winterfeldt (2011).

Chapter 11: Useful Perspectives on Decision-Making

1. Parker, Bruine de Bruin, and Fischhoff (2007b); Spetzler, Meyer, and Winter (2016).
2. Keeney, R. L. (2008). Personal decisions are the leading cause of death. *Operations Research*, **56**(6), 1335–47.
3. Keeney, R. L., and Palley, A. B. (2013). Decision strategies to reduce teenage and young adult deaths in the United States. *Risk Analysis*, **33** (9), 1661–76.

Appendix: Evaluating Alternatives and Making a Decision

1. Other decisions that illustrate the use of value-focused decision-making are found in Hammond, Keeney, and Raiffa (1999). Specific applications are illustrated in Morais, D. C., Alencar, L. H, Costa, A. P. C. S., and Keeney, R. L. (2013). Using value-focused thinking in Brazil. *Pesquisa Operacional*, **33**(1), 73–88; Keeney, R. L., McDaniels, T. L., and Swoveland, C. (1995). Evaluating improvements in electric utility reliability at British Columbia Hydro. *Operations Research*, **43**(6), 933–47; and Merkhofer, M. W., and Keeney, R. L. (1987). A multiattribute utility analysis of alternative sites for the disposal of nuclear waste. *Risk Analysis*, **7**(2), 173–94. Recently, at RWTH Aachen University in Aachen, Germany, the Entscheidungsnavi (decision tool) project directed by Professor Rüdiger von Nitzsch, and with the cooperation of Professor Johannes Siebert, has created a computer program to help individuals follow all of the steps of value-focused decision-making

to define and structure their decision, organize their information to describe consequences, evaluate alternatives, and conduct sensitivity analyses to gain insights about the relative pros and cons of alternatives and their overall desirability. It is available at https:// entscheidungsnavi.de, in German and English.

2. Keeney, R. L. (1981). Measurement scales for quantifying attributes. *Behavioral Science*, 26(1) 29–36.

3. This is a letter from Benjamin Franklin to his friend Joseph Priestley in 1772 about whether or not to accept an employment offer. It is reprinted in many places, including Isaacson, W., ed. (2005). *A Benjamin Franklin Reader*. New York: Simon & Schuster.

4. The even swaps procedure to help evaluate alternatives with consequences involving multiple objectives is discussed in chapter 6 of Hammond, Keeney, and Raiffa (1999).

5. The construction of a value model to combine multiple objectives and its uses to evaluate alternatives are discussed in the following three books: Keeney, R. L., and Raiffa, H. (1993). *Decisions with Multiple Objectives: Preferences and Value Tradeoffs*. Cambridge: Cambridge University Press; Kirkwood, C. W. (1997). *Strategic Decision Making: Multiobjective Decision Analysis with Spreadsheets*. Belmont, CA: Brooks/ Cole; and Clemen and Reilly (2014).

6. René Magritte produced the original painting *Ceci n'est pas une pipe* ("This is not a pipe") on canvas in 1929. His point was that a painting of a pipe should not be confused with the real pipe. Analogously, a model of a decision should not be confused with the real decision.

INDEX